Maximum Joy

1 John—Relationship or Fellowship?

NEW STUDY EDITION

Maximum Joy

1 John—Relationship or Fellowship?

NEW STUDY EDITION

David R. Anderson

GRACE THEOLOGY PRESS

To my beloved wife, Betty,
whose faithfulness to our *relationship*
has allowed me the enjoyment
of many years of wonderful *fellowship*.

— Table of Contents —

PREFACE

This small work did not germinate in the classroom, but in the church. It is not a scholarly treatment of 1 John, but is for any who need rest for their souls. It is for those who labor and are heavy laden. It is for those who are burdened by guilt. This book is for believers in Jesus Christ, who, after releasing their burden of guilt at Calvary's cross, continue to struggle with sin and guilt.

There are many Christians who initially find peace and rest, but because of frequent sin, their peace is short lived. They sin again, and again, and again. The guilt returns. The load increases. They try harder, but the more they try, the more they fail. Fear follows. Will God cast them away? Can He forgive the same sin again and again? If the sin persists, does it mean they never knew Him in the first place?

Though most Christians do not realize it, they are not alone in such fear. Many Christians struggle with these burdens. Over the centuries, pastors and theologians have tried to provide help. Ever since the foundation of the church they have wrestled with the significance and treatment of the sins we commit after our justification. The early church fathers taught that water baptism was the "laver of regeneration," which offered the sinner forgiveness of all his sins up to the point of water baptism. But post-baptismal sins were another matter. They required penance, contrition, and confession in order to be restored to right relationship with God. Some sins were more serious than others (mortal versus venial). Some sins required more penance than others.

As the church became more corrupt through the centuries, some church leaders saw the opportunity for a fundraiser through the sale of indulgences (forgiveness). It was this abuse to which Martin Luther reacted when he tacked his ninety-five theses to the church door at Wittenburg, thus sparking off the Reformation. Luther had been taught that his justification was a life-long process. He was told that he had been infused with some of the character of Christ at his infant baptismal service, but further increases in Christ's character must be forged into him throughout his life in order for him to be blameless at the day of Christ. If he were not blameless at that time, he would go into Purgatory where the excess dross in his life would be burned away so he could enter heaven in a sinless state.

However, Luther's reading of Romans 4 told him he could be declared righteous (justified) by God because of his faith at a moment in time—no works involved. Convinced of what Scripture taught, this became his new belief. Luther was born again. But as Luther continued in his study of Romans, he came to Rom 7:25 where Paul declares that he is a wretched man, still full of sin even after his justification before God by faith. In his commentary on this passage Luther wrote what Melanchthon (his friend and tutor) called the great paradox: *simul iustus et peccator*—justified and a sinner at the same time. Luther hit upon twin truths which appeared to be contradictory: 1) I have been declared completely righteous by God (justified); but, 2) I am still sinful. The first truth deals with our position or standing before God—completely justified. The second truth deals with our condition or situation on earth—still sinful. How can these twin truths live in the same house? How can they be harmonized?

Some pastors and theologians say that the harmonization rests in a proper interpretation of the second truth. That is, what do we mean by "still sinful"? They suggest that if one is very, very sinful (meaning he commits really serious sins, whatever those are), he was never justified in the first place. Others teach that to commit such serious sins could lead to loss of justification. Or perhaps it is not the seriousness of the sin which is at issue, but the continuation in any kind of acknowledged sinfulness. Those who hold such views would have us believe that one who has been truly justified cannot continue in sin, though they are hesitant to suggest any length of time which might help us understand just how long we can continue in sin and still be assured of our justification. John Calvin even suggested that a very brief lapse into sin would be enough to prove that one is not justified if that falling away happens to occur at the end of one's life and the sinner dies without repentance.

Many of those holding to such views find in the little letter of 1 John a chart to help us navigate the sea of salvation. In 1 John, they tell us, are tests we can use to determine if we will go to heaven when we die. These are tests of whether or not we have a *relationship* with God. By "relationship" they mean something eternal like the relationship between a father and his child. That is a forever relationship. Once I have a son, nothing and no one can ever change that relationship. He will always be my son; I will always be his father.

Others do not believe 1 John is about tests to know whether we will go to heaven when we die. They think, as does this author, the letter is not about our relationship with God, but it is about our *fellowship* with God. We might define "fellowship" as the enjoyment of a relationship. My son and I might have a forever relationship, but if he is a dishonorable son, we will not have much fellowship. We will not enjoy the relationship we do have.

These words—*relationship* and *fellowship*—are simple ways to reflect the twin truths of Luther's paradox. *Iustus* (just or justified) deals with our *relationship* with God. It is permanent. It is forever. It is the everlasting and unbreakable link between a father and child. That is our *position* before God, our standing—perfectly sinless, perfectly forgiven of all our sins (past, present, and future). But *peccator* (a sinner) can be understood as a statement of our *condition* or our situation on earth. Even though Paul was a saint (Eph 3:8), at the end of his life he still considered himself a sinner (1 Tim 1:15). Could it be that on-going sinfulness in the life of a justified person can drastically affect his *fellowship* with God but not his *relationship* with God? Could this be a way to unravel the paradox that in justification we are forgiven of all our sins, even future sins, but we still need to seek His forgiveness when we are aware of any particular sin? Perhaps there is *relationship* forgiveness and *fellowship* forgiveness.

If this is true, then we can explain why the two apparently contradictory truths in Luther's statement are not a contradiction at all. It is because we are dealing with two different plains of truth—our *relationship* and our *fellowship*, or our *position* and our *condition*. Of course, without a relationship with God there will be no fellowship with God. The latter is conditioned on the former. But, it would be very possible to lack fellowship with God while still having a relationship with Him. In other words, my sinfulness in my present condition can keep me from enjoying my forever relationship with my heavenly Father—this is loss of fellowship (neither I nor my Father are enjoying our eternal relationship). But loss of fellowship does not mean loss of relationship or that there never was a relationship. Understanding these twin truths is imperative for having the fullness of joy John writes about in his introduction to 1 John. It is the goal of this study to unravel the strand of these two intertwined truths so that we will be relieved of our burden of guilt and fear, and live with *Maximum Joy*.

THOUGHTS FOR SMALL GROUP LEADERS:

1. Think of yourself as a facilitator rather than a teacher. Your task is to engage everyone in the discussions and to encourage participation in a safe environment.

2. It is more important to have members involved in the group sessions than to cover a certain amount of the lesson.

3. Lessons are divided in a rational way, however, do not hesitate to do two lessons in one session or to take two or more sessions to cover one lesson if the interest and participation from the group seem to warrant such a time investment.

4. If some members seem to dominate discussions (need lots of "air time"), it is your job to address questions to members who are more hesitant to participate.

5. Practice asking open-ended questions rather than "yes" or "no" questions. For example, "What is your thought about . . . ", "How has this lesson impacted you?", "How might you use what we have talked about this week?"

6. Try to avoid "guess what I'm thinking" questions. One idea is to try to ask questions whose answers are already known to you (try to elicit ideas from the group). Redirect questions that are addressed to you back to the group when appropriate.

7. Of course, there may be times when you will share your opinion. Don't ever shy away from positions that are clearly scriptural in their base. However, there will be many times when you will want to hear opinions with which you do not agree. Listen carefully, acknowledge and value the person speaking, invite others to respond and try to tie the discussion back to what the Bible says.

8. Many groups like to share prayer requests. If you do this, consider starting with the prayer time and then move to the lesson. If the lesson goes first, the prayer time may be shortened and not be given enough attention due to time constraints.

9. It may be helpful to establish some "norms" before you begin your study.

    a. It is wise to agree on the time you start and stop (people are busy and you honor them by keeping time commitments).

b.   Ask people to agree to confidentiality within the group. Sometimes, people share very personal information and it would be hurtful if they assumed the group was a "safe" place and it became the source of gossip or discussion in a broader arena.

c.   Decide how often you will meet, where you will meet, and who will lead the discussion. Don't be a slave to a schedule. Allow time off for holidays, vacations, and other needs. Some groups rotate the meeting place among group members while others always meet at the same home. Whatever works for your group.

d.   Will you have "goodies"? Some very successful groups never have desserts or snacks while other groups see this as a way to foster increased "fellowship."

e.   Groups generally grow closer when they eat together. An occasional "potluck" or dinner at a restaurant might be a positive activity. Every month that has a fifth Wednesday (or whatever day you meet) could be a time for a session that is more geared to fellowship and less to a lesson.

f.   When new members join the group take time to acquaint them with your group norms. Some groups compile an information sheet for each couple or individual in the group (name, address, telephone, email and brief biographical data such as employment, family information, where they grew up, etc.). These sheets can then be shared with new group members as they join and this can aid their learning about the other members without taking time to go through all this information again.

There is no one right way to conduct small groups. Periodically, assess the effectiveness of the group by talking about what is working and what could be changed or improved. If your group grows to the point that participation is limited for everyone it may be time to reproduce!

– 1 –

HEART TO HEART

1 JOHN 1:1

According to Larry Crabb, a man's greatest need is to be admired, while a woman's greatest need is to feel secure.[1] I remember the night I was in need of a little admiration from my beautiful wife. She was sitting in our bathroom putting on her make-up while I was getting dressed for an evening out. I was standing in front of the mirror hoping she would notice that after thirty years of marriage my physique really hadn't changed all that much (just kidding). She was preoccupied with her task of beautifying the beautiful. Not even a glance my way. So I decided to encourage her to admire me.

I began flexing in the mirror. With each flex I gave a little grunt with a comment. It went something like this: "How is it...(flex, grunt) that after thirty years of marriage...(flex, grunt)...I still look the same as on our wedding night...(flex, grunt)?" Now, my wonderful wife Betty usually thinks carefully before she speaks. This was an exception. Without any hesitation at all, which might have led me to believe that she was truly mulling over my question, she placidly said, "Because your eyes are getting bad." Talk about deflation. My ego shrunk up like a popped balloon. This was not the admiration I was hoping for.

Women are similar. They need to feel secure. They need to feel loved.[2] It reminds me of the couple who were celebrating their sixtieth anniversary. They were sitting in their living room enjoying the afterglow of an evening on the town. With a content but longing sigh the wife said to her husband, "Honey, why don't you come over here and sit on the couch next to me like we used to do when we were first married?" He didn't need much encouragement, so he slid next to her on the couch. "Well, why don't you put your arm around me and kiss me like you used to do when we were first married?" He willingly obliged. "Now, why don't you just nibble on my ear like you used to do when we were first married?" The old man jumped up with a look of horror on his face and promptly left the room. "Where are you going?" pined his wife with a note of disappointment in her voice. "I'm going to get my teeth," replied her mate resolutely.

Teeth or no teeth, I don't think it mattered to her. She just wanted to be cherished and loved. According to the Bible, the security of being loved leads to a recognition of our significance. When we are loved unconditionally, it helps us know that we matter to someone. That's why Romans spends its first eleven chapters trying to meet our need for security (nothing can separate us from the love of God in Christ Jesus) before moving on to our need for significance (the unique giftedness of each person and his place of service in the Body of Christ) in the last four chapters. Security … significance; love … admiration; acceptance … approval.

First John is a book about love. Another word for love is the word intimacy. If you have a growing relationship with someone, you are becoming more and more intimate with them. You are becoming closer and closer. Someone might say, "But that is why God provided husbands and wives. Adam was alone, which God said was not good. So He made Eve to take away Adam's loneliness through intimacy—body, soul, and spirit." I agree. Adam and Eve probably had perfect intimacy before the fall. They felt no loneliness before the fall. But our sin nature, which came through the fall, is so evil and horrid, it creates huge blocks to love and intimacy.

One of those blocks to intimacy lies at the very core of the sin nature. It is selfishness. Selfishness focuses on getting, not giving. Love, by definition, is giving, but the sin nature grabs and gets. People often confuse love and lust, but the main difference between the two is selfishness. Love asks, "How can I meet your needs?" whereas lust asks, "How can you meet mine?" So the sin nature works against intimacy because it is selfish.

But there is something else contained in the sin nature which is a block to intimacy, and that's fear. Fear is one of the greatest stumbling blocks to opening up. You can't be intimate with someone if you don't open up. You can't be close to someone if you don't share the things which are close to you. But we are afraid to do that. We are afraid to let the other person see what is deep down inside. We are afraid they won't like what they see. We are afraid they will simply reject us.

This fear of rejection keeps us from opening up and getting close. But there is good news. God has given us 1 John to show how to have intimacy after the fall, to show how we can have our most fundamental need for love met even though there is sin in the world, in the universe, and resident within us. That's why 1 John was written.

Not everyone agrees with this suggested understanding of the purpose of 1 John. In fact, it may be the most controversial book in the New Testament.

Many wonderful and popular teachers of Scripture think 1 John is a book which helps us determine whether we can know that we will go to heaven when we die. This is called the "tests of life" or "tests of relationship" view. This view did not develop out of thin air. It would be unfair to say it has been imported into the text. For in 1 John 5:13 we read, "These things I have written to you who believe in the name of the Son of God that you may know that you have eternal life and that you may continue to believe in the name of the Son of God." Most would say that John gave this verse as the purpose of 1 John, placing it at the end of the book, just as, they would argue, he gave the purpose of his Gospel of John at the end of that book (John 20:31).

One popular preacher/teacher wrote a book called *Saved without a Doubt*.[3] It is a book about how to be sure of one's salvation. Here are eleven tests he drew from the little book of 1 John by which you can determine if you are a Christian:

1. Have you enjoyed fellowship with Christ and with the Father?
2. Are you sensitive to sin?
3. Do you obey God's Word?
4. Do you reject this evil world?
5. Do you eagerly await Christ's return?
6. Do you see a decreasing pattern of sin in your life?
7. Do you love other Christians?
8. Do you experience answered prayer?
9. Do you experience the ministry of the Holy Spirit?
10. Can you discern between spiritual truth and error?
11. Have you suffered rejection because of your faith?[4]

I don't know about you, but when I read questions like the ones above, more questions pop up in my mind. For example, what if I can just say yes to ten of these questions, or eight, or five? Will a simple majority do? Or let's take one of these and focus on it, say, question number three. Do I obey God's Word? If I must obey God's Word, how much of it must I obey? How consistently must I obey it? Can I obey the big stuff and slide on the little stuff? Is there a curve out there somewhere? Since no one can say, "Yes, I absolutely obey God's Word," the answer must be relative, and if it's relative, then there must be a curve. And if there's a curve, who makes the cut?

Suppose I became a Christian when I was young, but when I was seventeen I wandered off the path of righteous living and stayed off for ten years. During those ten years, I couldn't say yes to any of these questions. What does that mean? Did I lose the salvation I received when I was young, as some groups teach? Or as other groups teach, perhaps I was never a genuine believer at all. Do you see where this leads? Instead of helping a person to know that he is saved without a doubt, these kinds of tests only multiply doubts in the minds of introspective, thinking people. They only multiply guilt and fear.

I would like to take a different approach to 1 John. I suggest it is a book about intimacy. But before I establish this thesis from the book itself, it is very helpful to see 1 John from the backdrop of the Gospel of John. And when we look at the Gospel of John, it is very helpful to understand the book's outline as a parallel to the temple or tabernacle. In fact, of the many writers who present 1 John as "tests of relationship," none that I have read mentions the parallels between the Gospel of John and the tabernacle.

The Tabernacle in John

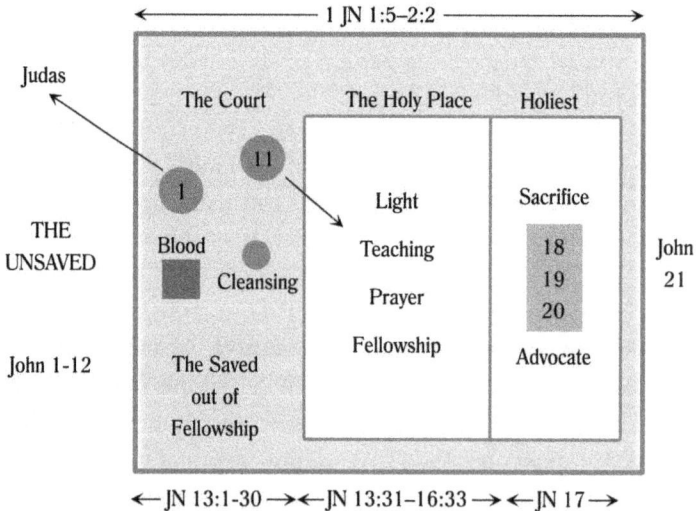

Diagram 1

The first twelve chapters of the Gospel of John are about evangelism. This is where the seven signs are presented in order that men might believe in the name of Jesus (John 20:31). In fact, John's signature phrase for a new believer is the Greek construction *pisteuō eis* (believe in). This phrase is found nowhere in Greek literature outside the New Testament, and of the thirty-four uses in John, thirty of them occur in the first twelve chapters.

Thus when we come to the Upper Room Discourse (John 13–16), there is a shift in John's presentation. Here the focus is not evangelism. If the sole purpose of John were evangelism, chapters thirteen through sixteen could have been completely omitted. This truth is not for unbelievers, but for believers. That is why in John 13:1-30 Judas must be sent out of the room as one of the two steps to prepare Jesus' disciples for the intimate truth He wishes to share. The first step of preparation was to wash the feet of the disciples (Judas was included in this washing so as to not reveal that he was the betrayer). Then Judas was sent out. Judas had no place in this setting because he was not a believer. Unbelievers had to come into the temple/ tabernacle through the blood, but believers could only go into the Holy Place through the laver of cleansing. The truth Jesus wished to share in the Upper Room was for the ears of believers only. But even these believers needed to be cleansed of their daily sins in order to be in fellowship with the Lord. If they were not in fellowship with Him, they would not be able to comprehend the truth He wished to share.

This truth comes in two levels in John 13: Relationship Truth and Fellowship Truth. Jesus presents this in a symbolic way: taking a bath (Relationship Truth) and foot washing (Fellowship Truth). When Jesus stooped down to wash the feet of Peter, Peter pulled back. When Peter yields, he asks facetiously for an entire bath. The Lord explains that Peter has already had a complete bath; now he simply needs his feet washed. Jesus says Peter is "completely clean," but if Peter does not allow the Lord to wash his feet, Peter can have no part with Him. That this is all symbolic truth is obvious from Christ's statement that His disciples will not understand what He is doing at that moment, but they will understand later on.

How could Peter be completely clean, yet still dirty? Here we see the Lord's truth expressed by Luther's statement: *simul iustus et peccator* (simultaneously justified and a sinner). At the same time a believer can be justified (declared righteous, completely clean—his position in Christ) but also be sinful (in need of foot washing—his condition on earth). On the relationship level the believer is seen as completely clean (all sins cleansed once and for all time—past, present, and yet future sins); but on the fellowship (intimacy) level the believer needs daily foot washing (daily cleansing from sins in his walk on earth).

If Peter was not willing to have his feet washed (cleansed in his condition from his daily sins), he could have "no part" with Jesus, that is, no intimacy, no fellowship, and no significant role in His mission. Jesus was about to leave this world. In less than twenty-four hours He would be on the cross. He was about to entrust His entire mission, or at least His Great Commission, to these eleven men. But they had dirty feet which needed washing.

Peter and John were the servants of the day who should have washed the feet of their brethren in the Upper Room. But there was an on-going debate among the disciples as to which of them would be the greatest in the future kingdom which Christ would establish. They already knew they would be rulers in that kingdom (Matthew 19:28), but now they wanted to know who would be the greatest among them. With greatness on their minds Peter and John were not willing to stoop down to wash dirty feet, especially the feet of their brothers with whom they were competing. The result was dirty feet, a full basin of water, and a clean towel. Dirty feet meant dirty hearts. Unless their hearts were cleansed the gospel mission would die. Dirty feet do not spread the gospel.

So Jesus is not trying to establish a new relationship with these eleven men. He has already done that. They believe in Him. They have received Him (John 1:12). They have been completely cleansed. They do not need a bath. But they do need clean feet, that is, clean hearts. In order to have intimacy and fellowship with Him, the disciples needed to have their hearts cleansed of the ugly spot of pride. Once Jesus had done this and demonstrated to them what true greatness really was, He was ready to unveil the most intimate truths He had ever shared with human beings. No longer would He call these men servants; now they were being called His friends. He wanted to share with them truth about love between Him and them (John 14:21), how to stay close to Him so He could produce fruit through them (John 15), and how to have a vital prayer life. He wanted to prepare them for future suffering (John 16:1-4), but also for the coming of the Comforter. These are truths for those "in fellowship" with Him.

Again, the tabernacle may well have been in John's mind when he structured his gospel. It is in the Holy Place that we find the table of shew-bread and the candelabra of light. Here is food and light for the believer who has been cleansed by the blood (relationship) and the water (fellowship). So, if we have Preparation in John 13:1-30 (the unbeliever is sent out and the believers are cleansed with water), then we have Preaching in John

13:31–16:33. It is no coincidence that we find Prayer in John 17. Here the High Priest intercedes for those who are His own, His disciples and all who would believe through their ministry. The High Priest has entered the Holy of Holies to intercede for His people. But this High Priest does more than just intercede in prayer. He actually becomes our mercy seat (Romans 3:25) as He loved His own to the uttermost (John 13:1). Thus in the Passion and Resurrection narrative of John 18–20, Jesus has become the Lamb of God who takes away the sin of the world. His sacrifice was accepted by the Father as fully sufficient, as proved by His resurrection. Now Jesus leads His own out of the tabernacle and into the world (John 21). They have a mission to complete.

The importance of seeing the parallels between the structure of John and the tabernacle cannot be overstated. With this visual aid we can see that a major portion of John does not focus on evangelism or relationship. The focus of Jesus' words in the upper room is on intimacy or fellowship. As we look at 1 John we will see that it is this theme of the Upper Room Discourse that is repeated over and over in this short letter. In fact, as noted in the diagram above, all the major elements of the tabernacle (blood, fellowship, confession, light, intercession of the High Priest) are also found in 1 John 1:5–2:2.

When coupled with the purpose statement of 1 John 1:3-4, the evidence mounts that the thrust of 1 John is not *relationship*, but rather *fellowship*. If this is true, then it would be highly unlikely that 1 John would give us a list of tests of relationship. Quite the contrary, if we wanted to describe the flow of 1 John as a series of tests (which I am not persuaded to do), these would be tests of fellowship. The major thrust of the Gospel of John is relationship (John 1–12 and 18–21); but a secondary theme is fellowship (John 13–17). In 1 John the major thrust is fellowship, although there are secondary issues which deal with relationship (1 John 5:5-13). Here is a suggested outline for 1 John:

1 John
"The Fruit of Fellowship"

I. Introduction: "The Joy of Fellowship" 1:1-4
II. Body: "The Principles of Fellowship" 1:5–5:17
    A. Principles of Fellowship Introduced 1:5–2:27
        1. Right Living—Dealing with our Sins 1:5–2:2
        2. Right Loving—Dealing with our Brothers 2:3-11

Fellowship or intimacy is John's primary concern. In this letter, it is transparent from the first verse:

> That which was from the beginning, which we have heard, which we have seen with our eyes, which we have looked upon, and our hands have handled, concerning the Word of life (1:1).

"That which was from the beginning" is John's abstract way of referring to Jesus, just as in his gospel John begins with "In the beginning was the Word, … and the Word was God." No one disputes that John's reference in 1 John 1:1 is Jesus. But notice the progression in sensory perception: heard ⟹ seen ⟹ looked upon (a word which goes even deeper than mere ocular perception) ⟹ handled.

The impression we have is John's apostolic experience of growing closer to Jesus. He was probably first introduced to a voice in the distance speaking to a large crowd. As John got closer, he could see where the voice was coming from, that is, a man preaching. As he got even closer, John looked more deeply into this person of Jesus and realized there was something special about Him. Finally, we know that it was John the apostle who laid his head on the chest of Jesus in the upper room. Of course, John may be portraying Jesus in this very physical way because His opponents may have taught that Jesus did not have a body of flesh and blood. But the obvious progression of getting closer and closer to Jesus physically contains significant spiritual truth and a hint as to the theme of this letter: intimacy with Jesus. This is what I call our Magnetic Messiah, as depicted by this diagram:

Our Magnetic Messiah

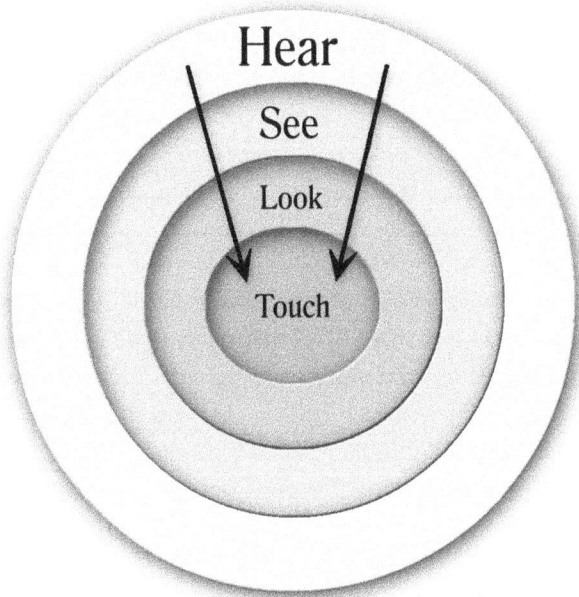

Diagram 2

In this diagram we see the centripetal force of Jesus, that is, our Messiah is Magnetic. He draws us closer and closer to Himself. This is the experience John had with Jesus, as did the rest of the disciples, except Judas, of course. This is the apostolic experience John wants to share (fellowship = *koinōnia* = sharing—v. 3) with his readers. He wants them to enjoy an increasing intimacy with their Savior.

What I am suggesting is a clear distinction between relationship and fellowship. Many pastors and theologians make no such distinction. I once had a three hour conversation with Robert Shank, a writer and spokesman for the Churches of Christ.[5] When we discussed 1 John he told me he had never considered a distinction between having a permanent relationship with God and having intimate fellowship with Him. He interpreted 1 John as tests of relationship. One either had a relationship with God or he did not. Of course, in his way of thinking, one could have a relationship with God one moment and lose that relationship the next. Grievous sin could destroy that relationship and send the sinner down the road to hell. According to Shank, the relationship could be restored through confession (1 John 1:9) and the sinner turned saint was then back on the road to heaven. Thus, the relationship with God could be won and lost many times throughout the course of one's life.

But the approach espoused by Shank does not jive with the New Testament portrayal of a heavenly Father and His children. When a child is born into a family, he has a permanent, eternal relationship with his father. Nothing can change that relationship. It will last forever. But to enjoy that relationship the child must stay close to his father, not bring disgrace to his father, and not be disobedient to his father. Rebellion cannot destroy their relationship, but it can devastate their fellowship. And the estrangement of family members who have an eternal relationship can be miserable.

Hollywood recently produced a G-rated movie which was nominated for an Academy Award as best picture. It was called *The Straight Story*, and was a movie about family values. It is the true story of a man who was about seventy years old and was estranged from his elder brother. The two had not talked for ten years. The younger brother got word that his older brother had suffered a mild stroke. Although these two brothers had an eternal relationship (they will always be brothers even if one goes to heaven and the other to hell—see Luke 16), they were not enjoying their relationship (= fellowship) at all. The younger brother did not want his older brother to die before they could reconcile. The estrangement between the two was causing the younger brother misery.

So the younger brother decided to pursue his older brother. But there was a problem. His older brother lived several states away in Wisconsin, while the younger brother lived in Iowa. That would not seem like much of a problem, except the younger brother's poor eyesight prevented him from getting a driver's license. But his desire to reconcile with his older brother was so strong, he hitched a small trailer to his John Deere riding lawnmower and rode his lawnmower all the way from Iowa to Wisconsin. Along the way he passed on his concern for family values with many others who were estranged from their own family members.

The Straight brothers had a relationship—they were brothers—but no fellowship. A relationship brings with it certain rights and privileges, but not necessarily peace, joy, love, and happiness. These internal riches are the "Fruit of Fellowship," my suggested theme for 1 John. If you are a believer in Jesus Christ, you have been born into God's family. He is your heavenly Father. That is a permanent, eternal relationship. But to enjoy that relationship you need His fellowship. The beautiful thing about fellowship with our heavenly Father is that it is available to anyone who believes in His Son.

Whether you are a man, woman, boy or girl, married or single, widow, widower, or divorced person—if you have believed in Jesus for everlasting life, you are a permanent child of God. You have an everlasting relationship with Him. But God not only wants you to have a relationship with Him, He wants you to enjoy that relationship through fellowship.

And our Father has made a way for us to have this fellowship with Him in the midst of a sin-saturated world. He does not excuse our sin, but He has made a provision for it. This provision is not only that we might have a permanent relationship with Him but also temporal fellowship. This intimate fellowship is what we were created for and what all Christians long for. In their book *The Sacred Romance* Curtis and Eldridge write:

> We come into this world longing to be special to someone and from the start we are disappointed; it is the rare soul indeed who has been sought after for who she is, not because of what she can do or what others can gain from her, but simply for herself. Can you recall the time when someone in your life sat you down with the sole purpose of wanting to know your heart more deeply, fully expecting to enjoy what they found there? ...
>
> "In fact," we continue, "if I am not pursued, it must be because there is something wrong with me, something dark and twisted inside." We long to be known and fear it like nothing else. Most people live with the sudden dread that one day they will be discovered for who they really are, and the world will be appalled.[6]

Yes, that might be true in the world of human beings. If someone knew everything that goes on inside of you, he or she might be appalled. But God isn't. He knows every single thing inside of you. He knows every thought, good or bad. And He still pursues you, still loves you, still was willing to creep into this world *incognito* and make a dramatic raid on a world that was at enmity with Him.

Oh, the wonder of it all! George Herbert put it this way: "My God, what is a heart that Thou shouldst it eye and woo so, pondering upon it with all Thine art, as if Thou hast nothing else to do?" The marvel is that He could actually know what is inside of me and still want to pursue me and use His magnetic power to draw me closer and love me for who I am, not because of what I can do or have done, but love all of me simply for my essence and my being.

There is only one source of that kind of love, and He is drawing you to Himself.

---

[1] Larry J. Crabb, Jr., *Effective Biblical Counseling* (Grand Rapids: Zondervan Publishing House, 1977), 59-74.

[2] Eggerichs Emerson, *Love and Respect: The Love She Most Desires; The Respect He Desperately Needs* (Brentwood, TN: Integrity, 2004). This book goes into great detail on Eph 5:22-33 showing that a woman needs love and a man needs respect. When these are received unconditionally, security, significance, and intimacy flourish.

[3] John MacArthur, Jr., *Saved without a Doubt* (Colorado Springs: Cook Communications, 1992).

[4] Ibid., 67-91.

[5] Robert Shank, *Life in the Son: A Study of the Doctrine of Perseverance* (Springfield, MO: Westcott, 1961).

[6] Brent Curtis and John Eldredge, *The Sacred Romance* (Nashville: Thomas Nelson Publishers, 1997), 83-84.

LESSON 1A "HEART TO HEART"

Read the Preface, I John 1:1, John 1:1 and "Heart to Heart" for Lessons 1 and 2.

1. In the Preface, Dave sets forth the reason for writing this book. How would you explain his purpose to someone?

2. The title of the book is "Maximum Joy." Have you used, or have you heard someone else use the word "joy" in conversation recently?

3. How is "joy" different from "happy"?

4. Do you think of "joy" as a term that applies only to one's relationship with God? Read Galatians 5:22-23. What significance do you attach to "joy" being in this list?

5. What is the significance of John's use of the term "fullness of joy" rather than just "joy"?

6. Consider the following. How can joy and via cruces (way of the cross) coexist?

"Joy is the serious business of Heaven" by C.S. Lewis,

"I do not think that the life of Heaven bears any analogy to play or dance in respect of frivolity. I do think that while we are in this 'valley of tears,' cursed with labour, hemmed round with necessities, tripped up with frustrations, doomed to perpetual plannings, puzzlings, and anxieties, certain qualities that must belong to the celestial condition have no chance to get through, can project no image of themselves, except in activities which, for us here and now, are frivolous . . . How can you find any image of this in the 'serious' activities either of our natural or of our (present) spiritual life? Either in our precarious and heartbroken affections or in the Way which is always, in some degree, a via crucis?

No, Malcolm. It is only in our 'hours-off,' only in our moments of permitted festivity, that we find an analogy. Dance and game are frivolous, unimportant down here; for 'down here' is not their natural place. Here, they are a moment's rest from the life we were placed here to live. But in this world everything is upside down. That which, if it could be prolonged here, would be a truancy, is likest that which in a better country is the End of ends. Joy is the serious business of Heaven."

Letters to Malcolm: Chiefly on Prayer—C.S. Lewis, (San Diego: Harvest, 1964),92.93

7. Maximum Joy deals with "love." How has our culture cheapened "love"? What are some things that people say they love?

8. Many of us have heard this epistle used to explain our relationship to God. What are some of the barriers that make it difficult for some to understand that the book is about fellowship rather than relationship? (Early learning, past classes or sermons, previous experiences, etc.) Explore the idea that previous learning may interfere with new learning.

9. What is the relationship between fellowship with God and Maximum Joy?

10. What do we know about the author of I John?

11. Compare the beginning of John's Gospel with the beginning of I John. What do you find that is similar and what is the significance of that similarity?

Prayer Reminders: Use the space at the end of each lesson or the back of the page to note prayer requests from the group. This will serve as a reminder during the week and also help to see how God is answering prayer.

LESSON 1B Continuing "Heart to Heart" I John 1:1

1. Love and intimacy go together, but do you think our world has succeeded in separating the two?

2. Excluding the sexual aspect of intimacy, what are some characteristics of an intimate relationship?

3. Would these same characteristics apply to an intimate relationship with God?

4. Dave identifies "selfishness" and "fear" as two blocks to intimacy. How have you experienced either of these in relationships with other people? How do these two blocks impact our relationship with God?

5. The paragraph that follows the list of questions on page 17 leads one to see the mistake of trying to use some sort of formula for determining if one is a Christian. What thoughts do you have when you read that paragraph?

6. Read John 13:1-17. How does Dave make a point about Relationship Truth and Fellowship Truth by using the foot-washing scene?

7. What parallels to the tabernacle are noted in this chapter?

8. What is the connection between the sensory perceptions in I John1:1 (heard, seen, looked, handled) and intimacy?

9. What do you think about the Herbert quote on page 25?

– 2 –

HOW'S YOUR LOVE LIFE?

1 JOHN 1:2-4

In Edmund Rostand's comic play *Cyrano de Bergerac,* there is a French soldier who loves a beautiful young woman named Roxanne. But, alas, Cyrano has such a big nose that, by his own description, you could launch a ship from the peninsula jutting out from the front of his face. Because of this ugly nose Cyrano doesn't have the courage to declare his love to Roxanne in person. Too bad, for this man has the gift of eloquence, and he can express his heart better than any Frenchman has ever done.

But Cyrano is not the only man with a problem. Roxanne is actually in love with a very handsome young man named Christian. In the French army Christian actually is under the command of Cyrano. Yes, Christian is handsome, all right, but clumsy of speech. He loves Roxanne but can't express himself. *His tange gets tongled.* But he teams up with Cyrano to win Roxanne's heart. As he stands under the window of Roxanne, Christian repeats the words of love that Cyrano has conceived. Even the love letters which come to Roxanne from the battlefront are written by Cyrano. Roxanne is swept away by the expressions of love she reads in the letters and hears below her window. She can't wait to spend the rest of her life with the man who spoke or wrote them. If only this war with Spain would end.

But both men are miserable. Neither is able to share his love with Roxanne. Christian, because he cannot speak for himself, and Cyrano because he is afraid he is too ugly for Roxanne to return his love. Both of these men suffer from the same problem which keeps them from enjoying the love they have in their hearts for Roxanne. Neither is able to openly declare his love for her in her presence. And the comic tragedy is that poor Roxanne never gets to share the love of either man throughout her life.

This play teaches a simple truth. *Love needs expression for fulfillment.* Love needs to be declared in order to be fulfilled. It was John Donne who said, "Love's not love, tis not equally mixed." Of course, he was referring to love between two humans, but a more accurate statement of human love might be, "Love among men is not all it can be, tis not equally mixed." One of life's greatest joys is for a heart full of love to open up to the beloved.

OUR FERVENCY FOR JESUS

Our love for God can never equal His infinite love for us. He loved us when we were His enemies (Rom 5:5-10). But if our love for Him is to grow and be maximized, then it needs expression. Love longs for expression. Many are the people who have lots of love bottled up within but nowhere to express it. But there is good news. 1 John pops the cork on the bottle. It's a book about intimacy and love between the believer and God and between believer and believer. In his introduction to the letter (1 John 1:1-4), John speaks of two forces which increase our experience of God's love. First is the "Centripetal Force" of our Magnetic Messiah—He keeps drawing us closer to Himself if we let Him (v. 1). Second is the "Centrifugal Force" of Jesus— He sends us out (v. 2) to share His love with others.

> The life was manifested, and we have seen and bear witness, and declare to you that eternal life which was with the Father and was manifested to us—(1:2).

In verse one Jesus draws us closer. In verse two we are compelled to go out. Again, we find a progression in John's words: the life was manifested, and we have seen, and bear witness, and declare to you this eternal life. Just as the Magnetic Messiah drew us in through concentric circles, the ripples of our love relationship with Him go out. The concentric circles are expanding as we move from *seeing* to *witnessing* to *proclaiming*.

If a crime takes place but I don't see it, I can't talk about it. On the other hand, I might *see* it but decide not to tell anyone. If, however, the police suspect that I have seen the crime, I might receive a subpoena to *bear witness* in the courtroom as to what I have seen. I'll talk if you force it out of me. But to openly proclaim (*apanggellō*, which is translated "declare" in the NKJV) is a very proactive declaration. There is no subpoena behind this word. It is used of Mary Magdalene and the other Mary when they heard the good news that Jesus had risen from the dead and ran to *report* these things to the disciples (Matt 28:8). Our Magnetic Messiah becomes our Motivating Messiah. It looks like this:

Our Motivating Messiah
1 John 1:2

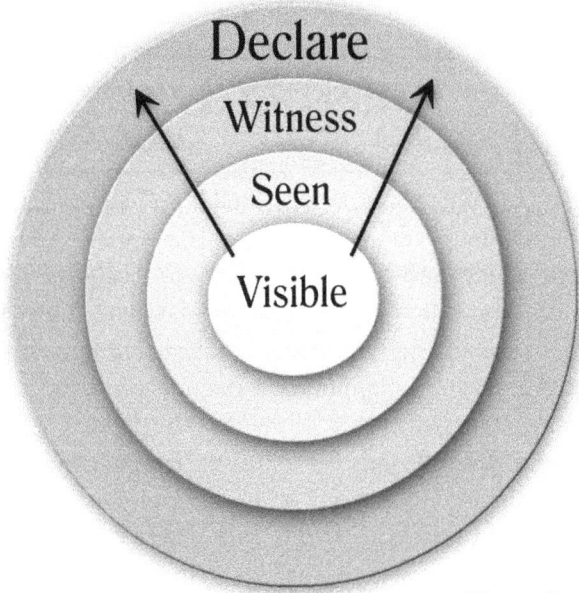

Diagram 3

The principle is that the closer we get to Jesus, the greater our desire to witness becomes! Lovers know about this principle. As I write these words, I am studying at a seminary in Germany. During chapel yesterday a young couple announced their engagement. They kept it a secret until just the right moment. They wanted the whole student body to celebrate in their joy. Everyone stood and clapped as they proclaimed their love for each other. Have you ever seen a newly engaged damsel with a sparkler on her finger? Does she walk around with her hand behind her back so no one can see her engagement ring? No, she flashes it everywhere she goes.

The truth is that we talk about what we love the most. Most folks love their kids more than anything on earth, so they brag about their children every chance they get. Some people love possessions more than anything else, so you will hear them talking about money, or their new boat or new vacation home. Some guys love sports, so they talk about historic plays and record batting averages. Then there are some people who talk about Jesus more than anything else. Why? Because they love Jesus more than anything or anyone else in the world. Consequently, they can't help themselves. They just can't keep from talking about Jesus for very long.

Such open proclamation of our love for Christ actually intensifies that love. As we talk about Jesus, we find ourselves even more in love with Him. The Communists discovered this principle and utilized it in building the strength of their party. Douglas Hyde, who was the head of the Communist Party in London for twenty years before he became Christian and renounced his party membership, describes this dynamic in his book *Dedication and Leadership*.[1] He said the first assignment given to a new member of their party was to go out onto the streets of London to pass out tracts promoting the Communist cause. If the new convert to Communism successfully carried out his mission, the effect within him was always the same: he came back with an increased fervency and love for the cause. Why? Because people either ignored him, ridiculed him, or asked him questions. By openly proclaiming the virtues of Communism the new convert's positive feelings about the cause increased. Hyde wondered why modern Christians don't give their new converts the same assignment. That's what Jesus did with His disciples. According to Hyde, many of the principles for reaching the world used by the Communists came straight from Jesus.

But if the first two verses of this letter describe our fervency for Jesus, then the next two (vv. 3-4) describe our fellowship in Jesus.

OUR FELLOWSHIP IN JESUS (1:3-4)

> That which we have seen and heard we declare to you, that you also may have fellowship with us; and truly our fellowship is with the Father and with His Son Jesus Christ. And these things we write to you that your joy may be full (1:3-4).

This is the purpose statement for the book. It is typical for a good writer to put his purpose statement at the beginning of his communication, as John does here.[2]

John tells his readers that he wants to share the apostolic experience of Jesus with them so their joy can be full. "To share" is the basic meaning of the word translated "fellowship" (*koinōnia*). The "we" and the "us" in these verses refer to John and the rest of the eleven. The "you" refers to his readers.

When John says "that you also may have fellowship with us," he speaks of horizontal fellowship, that is, believers sharing with believers. But he goes further in his concept of Christian fellowship to qualify it as fellowship "with the Father and with His Son Jesus Christ." There are all types of fellowship, but the basic idea is to share what you have in common. There is a joy which comes from shared experience.

One of the strangest types of fellowship I have entered into recently is what I will call "motorcycle fellowship." I am not referring to a Christian motorcycle club. I am talking about the universal sign of motorcycle fellowship we experience as we ride down the road. Whenever one motorcycle rider encounters another coming the opposite direction, the left arm is lowered and extended to the left as the two pass each other. This is their way of saying, "Yo, we are cool dudes. We are among the select and unique group on the planet who know the thrill and freedom of bustin' bugs and eating air." We don't know each other. We have never met. Nevertheless, there is this unspoken bond when two riders pass each other.

That's not the type of fellowship John wants to share. It is much deeper. He wants to share what the apostles experienced with their heavenly Father and His Son Jesus Christ. Small groups are a big ministry in churches today, and well they should be. Jesus was a small group leader. And when these groups get together, the members often talk about things they have in common—their children, golf, business, Rotary, political views. But even though these are Christians sharing with each other, this is not what John means by Christian fellowship. It is much deeper than even this.

In 1 John Christian fellowship does not truly begin until Christians share with each other their experiences with Jesus and their heavenly Father. Only this kind of fellowship feeds the need of the regenerated human spirit. Not that there is anything wrong with sharing other things we have in common, but until we share on the deepest level our spiritual experiences, we will often leave the group that night with the sense that we really haven't connected, that something is missing.

When John said "our" fellowship, he meant the shared experience that he and the other disciples had with Jesus. That's what he wants to pass on. That's what will meet our need for intimacy at the deepest level. And that intimacy will bring joy. Verse four tells us John's ultimate purpose in writing this letter. He wants his readers to share his experience of Jesus so they can have the joy of fellowship with Jesus that John does. He does not write this so they can be born again and go to heaven when they die. He is not dealing with their position in Christ. He is dealing with their present condition and experience on earth.

He is not talking about relationship, but fellowship. Perhaps this chart will help high-light the contrasts between relationship and fellowship:

RELATIONSHIP	FELLOWSHIP
Position	Condition
Eternal Life	Abundant Life
Eternally Secure	Temporally Challenged
Indwelt by the Holy Spirit	Led by the Holy Spirit
Sealed by the Holy Spirit	Fruit of the Holy Spirit
Substitutionary Death of Christ	Substitutionary Life of Christ
Provided by the Blood of Christ	Sustained by the Blood of Christ

Although it is fair to say that the emphasis of this book is the present "Fruit of Fellowship," this kind of fellowship is not without its eternal consequences. In fact, John hints elsewhere in his writings that the degree of intimacy we enjoy with Jesus on earth may be directly proportional to the degree of intimacy we enjoy with Him forever.

Take Revelation 2:17, for example: "He who has an ear, let him hear what the Spirit says to the churches. 'To him who overcomes I will give some of the hidden manna to eat. And I will give him a white stone, and on the stone a new name written which no one knows except him who receives it.'" John motivates his readers in Revelation with the promise of a special intimacy with Christ in eternity. Just as God in the Old Testament and Jesus in the New Testament often give new names to those who are closest to Them, so Jesus will give a special nickname or term of endearment to certain believers in heaven. This is a practice often adopted between husbands and wives, or parents with their children. Such giving of new names reveals great love and deep intimacy.

But John's primary concern in 1 John is the joy his readers can have before eternity. When he says "full" in verse four, he writes in such a way that he means a state of fullness. He says this is specifically one of his reasons for putting all this on parchment. Of course, since John was writing the inspired Word of God, in a manner of speaking, these letters are love letters from God to His children. And love letters have a special way of bringing us into a state of joy.

When I was a freshman in college, I came to Texas from Tennessee, leaving behind a girlfriend I thought might become my life partner. Like a lot of college freshmen I thought I would marry the "girl back home." So we wrote to each other every day. Those daily love letters were my life-line. I was a brand new Christian and had not yet learned that human love is not the greatest love in the universe. To me it was. So I would wake up and read one of her letters before I headed off to class. It might start like this: "My dearest, darling, adorable Dave..." Those words were heaven sent, the elixir of life.

Then as I sat through my first soporific lecture of the day, I would often day dream of her terms of endearment: "My dearest, darling, adorable Dave." Those words would get me through my eight o'clock class. Then off to the next lecture. But as the professor droned on about quantum theory, I might forget just how my girlfriend phrased that opening. Was it, "My dearest, adorable, darling Dave," or was it, "My darling, dearest, adorable Dave"? Her words were getting fuzzy in my mind, and with the fuzziness came frustration. I had to know just how she put it. So I might skip the next class, run back to my dorm, bound up three flights, rush into my room, snatch her letter from my desk drawer, open it, and there is was: "My dearest, darling, adorable Dave." Yes. That's how she put it. What discernment she had! And my joy was restored as I basked in the light of her love for me.

That's one of the reasons God gave us His Word. These "love letters" are there to refresh our forgetful hearts. Much of what He has inspired deals with His love for us. John knows this. So he has been a willing participant in communicating God's love for His children in this letter and his other writings. One could even call John, the disciple "whom Jesus loved," the "Apostle of Love" because he has written so much about the subject. When the fires of our devotion to Christ are burning low, or we begin to forget just how much He really loves us, we can come running back to His inspired Word, His "love letters," and experience a fresh state of joy as we read again the old, old story of His love for you and me.

One of my favorite stories of Christ's love for us deals with a little girl and her love for dolls. A man once came to her house to visit her mother and father. Her dad was not home from work yet, but her mother went into the kitchen to put together some refreshments while they waited for her husband to arrive. The little girl saw her chance. She coyly came up to the stranger as he waited in the living room and asked him if he liked dollies. Wanting to be polite, he assured her he did. "Would you like to see my dollies?" the little girl asked. Not wanting to discourage her, the stranger said, "Of course."

So the little girl began bringing out her collection of dolls. It was quite large and surrounded the coffee table. "Now, which of these is your favorite?" asked the visitor. "Are you sure you like dollies?" queried the little girl. "Oh, yes," he confirmed. So the little girl rushed back to her room and returned clutching an old Raggedy Ann dolly. She held it close and patted its head. The visitor was nonplused. This doll wasn't nearly as impressive as the others. It had lost one leg; half its hair had fallen out; its belly button was missing, as well as part of an arm below the elbow. With astonishment in his face he asked, "But why is this your favorite dolly?"

The little girl looked at him shyly and then back at Raggedy Ann. Then, holding the tattered doll very close, she said, "This is my favorite dolly ... because if I didn't love her ... nobody would." I like that. Sin ravaged the early years of my life. But my Savior proved His love for me in that while I was still ugly (no belly button, one arm missing, hair torn out), He died for me. Now that's true love.

Francis Xavier (1506–1552) apparently understood this kind of symbiotic love between the Savior and himself:

> My God, I love You; not because
> I hope for heaven thereby,
> Nor yet because who love You not
> Are lost eternally.
> You, O my Jesus, You did me
> Upon the cross embrace;
> And manifold disgrace,
> And griefs and torments numberless,
> And seat of agony;
> Yea, death itself; and all for me
> Who was your enemy.
> Then why, O blessed Jesus Christ,
> Should I not love You well?
> Not for the sake of winning heaven,
> Nor of escaping hell;
> Not from the hope of gaining aught,
> Not seeking a reward;
> But as Yourself has loved me,
> O ever-loving Lord.

So would I love You, dearest Lord,
And in Your praise will sing;
Solely because You are my God,
And my most loving King.

To summarize John's introduction (1 John 1:1-4) to his first letter, he speaks of our fervency for Christ (vv. 1-2) and our fellowship with Christ (vv. 3-4). It's all about love. As our Magnetic Messiah draws us closer (v. 1), we have an increasing desire to tell others about Him (v. 2). And, as we proclaim Him, we are drawn even closer to Him. His centripetal force works together with His centrifugal force to increase our fervency for Christ. And John's purpose in writing this letter is that his readers might also share in this fervent intimacy with Jesus. This is true Christian fellowship. And this kind of fellowship brings the fruit of joy. Once again, this is not a letter about how to receive eternal life, or how to know we have it; it is a letter about how to experience the everlasting life we do have. It is about living an abundant life. John specifically wrote it so that we might experience an abundance of joy as we enter into the deep, intimate fellowship that he and the other apostles had with Jesus.

---

[1] Douglas Hyde, *Dedication and Leadership* (Notre Dame, IN: University of Notre Dame Press, 1966), 42-43.

[2] John 20:31 is the purpose statement for the Gospel of John. Since it is found near the end of John's Gospel, many have assumed 1 John 5:13 to be the purpose statement of John's first epistle. This issue will be discussed in chapter 20.

LESSON 2 "HOW'S YOUR LOVE LIFE?" I JOHN 1:2-4

1. Dave cites a simple truth (page 31), "Love needs expression for fulfillment." How is this true in the human context? And how is it true for the believer?

2. Read Romans 5:5-10.

3. How might Romans 5:8 relate to the quote in the previous question?

4. In what sense were you ever God's enemy? Before or after "reconciliation"?

5. Who can explain the physics lesson of Centripetal and Centrifugal Force? How do these have anything to do with God's love?

6. "We talk about what we love the most" (p. 33). Do we also talk about what we hate the most? What do you think your talk reveals? Consider "what you say" as well as "how you say it." Is "the truth" always appropriate?

7. What can Christians learn from Douglas Hyde's experiences in Communism?

8. Consider the pronouns in verses 3 and 4: "we," "you," "us." To whom are they referring?

9. What are some examples of "motorcycle fellowship" that you have noticed?

10. So, what is this "fellowship" that John wants his readers to have?

11. Review the chart on page 36. What questions or comments do you have related to that chart?

12. The summary of I John 1-4 speaks to our (1) fervency for Christ and (2) our fellowship with Christ and states, "It's all about love." How would you demonstrate this love? Do you have certain people or venues in mind?

– 3 –

DEALING WITH DARKNESS: PART I

1 JOHN 1:5-7

In the summer of 2000 I taught a course in theology at Jordan Evangelical Theological Seminary in Amman. While I was there the president of the seminary, Imad Shahadah, was invited to Jordan University to lecture to theological students of Islam on what the Bible teaches about going to heaven. Since that was the same course I was teaching to Christian Arabs who came from Iraq, Israel, Egypt, Syria, Lebanon, and the Sudan, I was interested in the reaction of the Islamic students at the university to the Christian message.

Imad said in his initial lectures there was some heckling from the students. But the professor who had invited him asked for respect, since Imad was their invited guest. So Imad was able to finish his teaching without interruption. When his lectures were finished, the professor of Islam (a mufti) made this conclusive observation: "Well, Dr. Shahadah, we have many areas of agreement and disagreement, but there is one huge difference in our approaches to heaven: you Christians have a way to deal with sin, while we Muslims do not."

In Islam there is no assurance of salvation for the average Muslim. A Muslim will never tell you, "Yes, I know for sure that I will go to paradise when I die." However, they will often say, "I think, or I hope, that I will go to paradise after I burn in hell awhile to pay for my sins, but only God knows if I will make it."[1]

Because they do not believe that Jesus is God's Son who died on the cross in their place to pay for their sins, the Muslims must pay for their own sins. The only exception to their general lack of assurance is to be killed in holy war (jihad). Such martyrs have paid for paradise by dying for the cause (Surah 47:4). Ayatollah Khomeini once said, "The purest joy in Islam is to kill and be killed for Allah."

Of course, what Islam lacks, among other things, is the blood of Christ. This is God's provision to deal with man's sin. And deal with it we must, if we want to have intimacy with God. I do not refer to the intimacy of going to heaven when we die only, but also to that portion of heaven we can have on earth through intimate fellowship with Him today. Both are available through the blood of Christ, the work of another.

We are now ready to enter the body of this letter on "The Fruit of Fellowship." The wonderful joy of intimate fellowship with God can be blocked by the barrier of sin in our lives. Because sin at its core is anything contrary to God's character, it stands to reason that without dealing with the sin in our lives, we cannot be close to the One in whom there is no sin. A rabbit does not hop around with a rattlesnake, nor does a sea lion swim around with a killer whale. Without Christ we are "at enmity" with God. Our character and His character clash. Someone must solve the sin problem if we are to be close to Him.

But the problem of sin extends beyond the moment of justification for a believer. Augustine and subsequently the Catholic Church taught that justification (the act of declaring something or someone righteous) was a life-long process of building Christ's character into a believer and you could never know if you were going to heaven until you died. Luther said a new believer in Christ is declared righteous (justified) by God in the courtroom of heaven the moment he believes. That was radical; so radical it became the doctrinal cornerstone of the Reformation.

What was so radical about "courtroom" justification? It introduced the concepts of position and condition into the doctrines of the church for the first time since the first century. Luther said "*simul iustus et peccator*," which meant you could be justified by God in your *position* in the heavenly places while you were still sinful in your *condition* on earth. The Protestants were teaching that the justification which opens the doors of heaven for a believer after his death is a justification which gives the believer a new standing, a new position before God. "In Christ" this newly justified believer is declared righteous. The gavel in heaven's court room comes down and the former sinner is declared innocent. No charges will be against him, even though he might still be sinful in his actual condition on earth.

Even more radical was the idea that this declaration of righteousness was not only effective for sins in our past but also for sins in our future. Sins we would commit after we became believers in Jesus were covered in this heavenly transaction. This concept was so radical the Roman Catholic Church convened for almost twenty years (Council of Trent, 1545–63) in an effort to dissuade the reformers. They believed such an approach to future sins would take away the believer's motivation for holiness.

Some of the reformers were persuaded to modify their views. John Calvin's first edition of his *Institutes* was completed in 1536 and had six chapters with a clear delineation between the believer's position in heaven (justification) and his condition on earth (sanctification). But under pressure from the Council of Trent and the accusation of promoting license, the final edition of Calvin's *Institutes* contained eighty chapters and no clear distinction between position and condition. Under pressure from Rome, he remarried justification and sanctification, saying in effect that if one is truly justified (Position), he will inevitably be sanctified (made holy in his Condition).

Yet Calvin did not have the final say on this issue. Throughout the centuries of Christianity, theologians have constantly wrestled with the question of what to do with ongoing sin in the life of a professing believer. There are typically four different approaches:

1) The first is to say that baptism washes away all sins up to that point, but post-baptismal sins are a threat to our going to heaven. Post-baptismal sins can be cleansed through repentance, confession, and acts of penance (anything from a day of sackcloth and ashes to ten years of servitude to the father-confessor). This was the approach of the church for centuries and in some cases still is. Obviously, this approach views our present sinfulness as a threat to our *relationship* with God. In other words, we have a *relationship* with God after water baptism, but we lose it if we sin long enough or seriously enough after baptism without the proper response of repentance, confession, or act of penance.

2) Another approach to the present sinfulness of professing believers is to claim that they never had a *relationship* with God in the first place. In other words, a genuine Christian will not continue in sinfulness if he truly has a *relationship* with God. This is where Calvin wound up due to pressure from the Council of Trent. This is also the approach taken by those who think 1 John gives us eleven tests to determine if we truly are Christians. They teach that if a person continues in sin, such a person never had an initial *relationship* with God.

3) A third approach is simply to deny our sinfulness; not to admit that we are sinful in our *condition* on earth after we have established a *relationship* with Christ. These are the people who fool themselves through rationalization to make wrong right. They explain away the evil they are doing as OK. John addresses such people in 1 John 1:5–2:2 by saying their *relationship* with God is not threatened, but their *fellowship* is. They need to stop rationalizing their sin and deal with it realistically.

4) The approach defended in this work is that our present sinfulness is not a barrier to heaven once we have established an eternal *relationship* with God through Christ, but it is a barrier to our *fellowship* with Him while we are on earth. Our present sinfulness in our *condition* on earth does not threaten our *position* before God in heaven (our eternal *relationship*), but it most certainly is a threat to our *fellowship* with God on earth.

If we are to enjoy fellowship with our heavenly Father and His Son Jesus Christ, then there are three principles John wants to teach us: the principles of right living, right loving, and right learning. Each principle deals with a potential barrier to close fellowship with God. Right living deals with our potential problem with sin; right loving deals with our potential problem with our Christian brothers; and right learning deals with our potential problem with the enemies of Christianity. So, in the first section of the body (1:5–2:28) these three principles are introduced: right living (1:5–2:2); right loving (2:3-11); and right learning (2:12-28).

Now we want to begin John's introduction to right living. The structure of the passage is simple, because John loves to present things in triads. Notice the "if we say that we" phrase, which occurs three times (vv. 6, 8, 10). These "if" clauses give us three hypothetical responses to the message that God is light and in Him is no darkness at all. Each of these responses is an improper response, which John quickly corrects with the related truth. So the passage looks like this:

Premise: God is light, and in Him is no darkness at all (v. 5).
> Error #1 "If we say that we have ...." (v. 6)
>> Correction (v. 7)
> Error #2 "If we say that we have ...." (v. 8)
>> Correction (v. 9)
> Error #3 "If we say that we have ...." (v. 10)
>> Correction (vv. 2:1-2).

Let's look at the initial error.

DARKNESS IS DEATH (1:5-6)

> This is the message which we have heard from Him and declare to you, that God is light and in Him is no darkness at all. If we say that we have fellowship with Him, and walk in darkness, we lie and do not practice the truth.

John begins the body of his letter with a basic concept about the character of God. He expresses this insight into God's character as one would look at two sides of the same coin. On one side of this coin it says, "All Light." This picture pours all of God's attributes together like the colors of the spectrum to come up with pure, white light. On the other side of the coin we get the same truth stated negatively: "No Darkness." Darkness represents sin and anything contrary to God's character. John's basic starting premise is that there is nothing about God's character or actions to impugn Him of evil.

Not all agree with this basic message. Some are so determined to defend the sovereignty of God that they accuse Him of being the efficient moral cause of all the evil and sin in the universe. One such writer said:

> Foreordination means God's sovereign plan, whereby He decides all that is to happen in the entire universe ... He decides and causes all things to happen that do happen ... He has foreordained everything ...: the moving of a finger, the beating of a heart, the laughter of a girl, the mistake of a typist—even sin.[2]

Some who believe similarly have tried to escape such conclusions by retreating to contrived distinctions in God's will. They say that God has a perfect will and a permissive will that are, at times, at odds with one another. Wherever one lands in this theological conundrum, we must be careful not to make God responsible for evil and sin in the universe. And in order to emphasize that God is the efficient moral cause of evil and men are only instruments, Calvin says, "Paul has used the word *vessels* in a general sense to mean *instruments* .... for the Lord uses us as instruments ...."[3] He even turns Satan into one of God's servants doing the will of God: "*Satan himself*, who works inwardly with compelling power, *is God's minister* in such a way that *he acts only by His command* ...."[4]

There are two huge problems with this kind of thinking. On the one hand, it absolves fallen creatures (men and angels) from any responsibility for their sin. After all, if man is only the agent, the instrument, then how can he be held responsible? When a murder takes place, we do not hold the gun or the knife responsible. We do not put guns and knives on trial. No, they are not the efficient moral causes; they are the instrumental moral causes. The guns and knives may have been used to commit evil, but they were only instruments. They had no choice in the matter. It is the human wielding the gun or knife who is responsible. The human is the efficient moral cause.

This leads to the second problem with this approach to sovereignty. If the human is only the instrument in the act of evil, he cannot be held responsible. Therefore, God is responsible. The efficient cause using the instrument is responsible for the evil. If fallen angels and humans are instruments (ministers acting at His command) in God's hand, then the One wielding the instrument is morally responsible. Of course, this is the conclusion of the cynics in this world as they look at the concept of a loving God in a world with too many Hitlers, Stalins, and Mao Zedongs. If such a God is in control, then either He is not loving or His powers are weak. Better to simply say He does not exist. If such a God does exist, we don't want to have anything to do with Him. We concur with Norman Geisler that this kind of defense of God's sovereignty makes God immoral and man amoral.[5] (It's the same defense used at Nuremburg by Nazi war criminals: they were just doing what Hitler told them to do.)

John would say such a view of God is not only morally repugnant, it is also impossible. He will argue in 1 John 3 that God's seed cannot produce sin. It's not in His genes, we might say. That's just another way to say that light cannot produce darkness. There is no darkness in God's character. He cannot produce it. Nor can He use others as instruments to produce it.

But this leaves fallen man, and the born-again Christian who is still a fallen man, with a problem. Psalm 5:4 says that evil cannot dwell with God. This is why Lucifer and company had to leave when they rebelled against the Most High. Evil has no part in heaven and no part of God. If we have a Sin(ful) Nature how can we be close to God? Who does not have a sinful nature? This is precisely what John addresses. How can sinful people be close to a sinless God? More specifically, how can sinful Christians (*simul iustus et peccator*—justified and a sinner simultaneously) get close to a sinless God?

The first error that could be made is simply to say that I am close to God while I am fully aware that I am walking in darkness (the erroneous response to the message of v. 5 given in v. 6). John calls this a lie, pure and simple. It's hypocrisy. It's a heart disease of the first order. This argument comes from a person who has something in the closet, but simply rationalizes it in his mind so that it is OK. An example of this way of thinking is what occurred on 9/11. The people who crashed the four planes had rationalized in their minds that what they did was justified, that is, right. They made wrong right. They did what they did in the name of their god. They fully believe that America is the Great Satan.

Although we would clearly deny such an allegation, we have to admit certain truths about the United States: 1) The citizens of our country consume more illegal drugs than any country in the world [illegal drugs are a capital offense in many Muslim countries]; 2) Our country is the number one producer of hard core pornography in the world; and 3) Our country is the number one producer of vicarious violence in the world. For these and other vices we are condemned by fundamental Muslims.

But wait a minute. Listen to this. Afghanistan is the number one producer of opium in the world, even greater than Burma with over 1700 metric tons produced in 1999. They also are upping their heroin and hashish production. Furthermore, the Taliban government participated in the profits. Is this a case of the pot calling the kettle black?

But what about the United States? Is this the nation that claims to be a Christian nation, but the same nation which has taken the Bible out of schools and won't allow creationism to be taught as a viable option to evolution? My fourth child just finished her first year at a secular college. During the year her English teacher assigned a paper to be written on a controversial topic of the student's choosing. So my daughter picked evolution as her topic and collected some of my books on the subject. A couple weeks later she called to say her teacher wouldn't let her write on evolution because the teacher did not think there was enough evidence to support creationism. So my daughter chose abortion. This was rejected as well because it was too controversial. Wait a minute. I thought this was just an English paper on a controversial subject to see if the writer could present both sides of an issue fairly.

Of course, this is hypocrisy on a grand, national scale. But we do it on a personal scale whenever we choose to persist in darkness. What are some of our favorite rationalizations?

1. "Well, nobody is perfect." Oh, that's a good one. Since none of us can be perfectly sinless, I might as well raise the white flag and succumb to temptation. Hey, this is my sin and that's yours. I won't judge you; you don't judge me.

2. "Everyone else is doing it." This is what we hear from so many young couples who live together before marriage and expect God to bless their union. Of course, if everyone else is doing it, it must be OK. And what about drugs and beer? "All my friends are doing it and they go to church. It must be OK."

3. "It's a new generation." Don't you know the rules change from generation to generation? Really? Does God change from generation to generation? Does His standard of holiness change? I don't think so.

4. "My needs aren't being met though the normal channels. Therefore, it must be OK with God for me to get my needs met outside the normal channels."

5. "The Bible doesn't address this activity, so there must be freedom,"

6. "My dad makes lots of money. He won't miss a couple of twenties from his wallet."

7. "God created us to reproduce in our early teens, but in our culture people are postponing marriage until their mid to late twenties. Surely God doesn't expect us to deny ourselves for ten or fifteen years?"

8. "He started it." Now there's a good one. I can always blame my sin on being provoked by the sin of another. "Ya, I hit her, all right. But she shouldn't have made me mad. It's really her fault."

Folks, we could go on and on. There is no end to our creativity when it comes to making wrong right, that is, if we are the ones doing the wrong. But I assure you, this kind of rationalization will plunge you into darkness. The House of Hypocrisy is built over a Cellar of Darkness. And darkness is death.

In John 8:11 Jesus says, "I am the light of the world. He who follows Me shall not walk in darkness, but have the light of life." Notice how light is connected with life. Just so, darkness is a picture of death. I don't mean physical death, but rather the death of 1 Tim 5:6 and Rom 8:6. First Timothy 5:6—"But she who lives in pleasure is dead while she lives." Romans 8:6—"For to be carnally minded is death ...." By death in these contexts Paul means misery, the torture of claiming to be a Christian while secretly or openly doing that which is evil. He did not question whether the widow living in pleasure was elect or not. A Christian living for carnal desires experiences misery, depression, continual guilt, and fear.

But, "Men loved darkness rather than light because their deeds were evil"—John 3:19. For John, practicing obvious evil plunges one into darkness. And darkness is death. That's why in Rom 8:6 the parallelism within the verse helps us understand the meaning of death: it is the opposite of life and peace. The only way people can walk in darkness and claim to have fellowship with God is to rationalize. This life leads to depression or neurosis. The late O. Hobart Mower, the most prolific writer on psychology in the world in his day (though not a believer) observes: "Everyone in psychiatric hospitals for other than physiogenic reason is there because of unresolved guilt."[6] In other words, unresolved sin and guilt can drive us crazy.

That's the bad news: darkness is death. But there is good news.

LIGHT IS LIFE

[7] But if we walk in the light as He is in the light, we have fellowship with one another, and the blood of Jesus Christ His Son cleanses us from all sin.

The erroneous response to the message of verse five was in verse six. It was hypocrisy, pretending to be a Christian in fellowship (close and intimate) with God while we knowingly walk in darkness. The correction for this error is verse seven, that is, to walk in the light as He is in the light. The only one who can rightfully claim to be close to God (to have fellowship with God) is the one who is walking in the light as He is in the light.

When a believer is willing to come out of darkness and into God's marvelous light, he can have fellowship (be close) with God even though he does not have complete victory over sin in his life. How is it possible for a person who is sinful in his condition to get close to God when God will not allow sin in His presence? Only one answer works. There must be a provision to cleanse the person of his sin.

Voila! The blood of Christ is God's provision. Notice the present tense of "cleanse." We do not need to do acts of penance to make up for our sinfulness after we have become Christians. But we do need to come to the light. When we do that, the blood of Christ will cleanse us and keep cleansing us (as we keep walking in the light).[7] This is God's provision for our sin that the Muslim mufti in Amman noticed. He rightly observed that Islam has no provision for man's sin. Perhaps that is why the young (third year physics major) convert to Islam sat in my office and attacked the blood of Christ. His way of invalidating Christianity was to say the God of the OT (Allah to him) never commanded blood sacrifices. One had to wonder what OT he had been reading. Of course, he probably hadn't been reading the OT at all, but was just repeating propaganda from his Islam Discovery class at the local mosque. The enemies of Christ attack the blood of Christ for good reason. It is God's provision for both our eternal relationship with Him as well as our temporal fellowship. It cleanses us from sin, all sin.

I am persuaded that we don't even know about most of our sins. If God's X-Ray machine (the light of the Holy Spirit) revealed all of our tumors of sin at once, we would probably go into anaphylactic shock. But God's grace is greater than our sin, and by this grace the blood of His Son cleanses us of all these "unknown" sins, thus allowing us to continue our wonderful fellowship with Him. It reminds me of my friend Lanier Burns, head of Systematic Theology at Dallas Theological Seminary. Lanier and I were classmates at Dallas Theological Seminary, and during Senior Preaching Week Lanier stood before the august body of professors and students and shared that his feeling at that moment was a little like teaching his first Sunday School class at Believers' Chapel in Dallas, Texas. Lanier has a wonderful smile which puts his audience at ease, and he was teaching away with his big grin in this Sunday School setting, while a young lady on the front row stared at him with a persistent frown. Lanier couldn't stop grinning, and she couldn't stop frowning. Now all good public speakers know that the audience is just a reflection of the teacher, so Lanier couldn't figure out why this girl was frowning while he was grinning. So finally he stopped the class and politely asked the young lady if something was bothering her. "Well," she said hesitantly, "Mr. Burns, your fly is down."

Can you imagine Lanier's shock and embarrassment? I assure you his grin left quickly until he could remedy the situation. But my point is that all the time he had been teaching with his big grin on his face his fly had been down. If he had known that at the beginning of the class, he either would have fixed it or would not have been teaching with a big grin on his face. But since he did not know, he could teach with impunity—he was carefree and happy, grinning away. So it is with unknown sin. It's not that the sin isn't there. It's there, all right, far more than we would like to know. But it does not affect our Christian happiness or fellowship with the Lord because His blood keeps right on cleansing us as we walk along in the light.

Walking in the light for John is the same as walking according to the Spirit in Paul's writings (Romans 8, Galatians 5). When we walk according to the Spirit, we are spiritually minded, and this brings life, as we have already seen—"To be spiritually minded is life and peace" (Rom 8:6). And when we walk in the light as He is in the light, God's light will dispel our darkness—Eph 5:11-14. When we expose the darkness, His light turns darkness into light.

The highlight of the year for the men in our church is our annual retreat. After challenging messages Friday night, Saturday morning and early Saturday evening, the men are ready for some serious application. So around eight o'clock on Saturday evening we challenge the men to come to the light.

We explain that the power of Satan is in darkness. If he can convince you to keep a little part of your life closed to the Lord, then he has a wedge into your life, and it will be difficult to have victory over the tyranny of sin in your life. But if the men will come to the light by asking the group for prayer, then God's light will dispel the darkness, and they will be on the road to freedom.

But there are certain rules: 1) If you come forward, then two men or more are going to come up, lay hands on you, and pray for your deliverance; 2) Those same men will be your accountability group for the next year to help you walk through and out of your problem; and 3) God willing, you need to come back next year to help us celebrate your first anniversary of freedom. Now, with those kind of stipulations, you would think maybe one or none of the men would come forward. Or, to keep the retreat from looking like a failure to first timers, maybe a few would go up to share some minor peccadilloes. But the outpouring of repentance on those Saturday nights is nothing short of miraculous. Men share their addictions to pornography, struggles with their parenting, difficulties in their marriages, in some cases affairs. I even saw a little group of five men who had been divorced by their wives for various causes come together to try to win their wives back (since none of the women had remarried). Last year this group of about 130 men were still coming forward at midnight when we decided to shut it down because of Sunday morning responsibilities.

Now we are not claiming that coming to the light in this kind of public way is the only way; nor are we saying that coming to the light in this way brought instant victory or deliverance (though in some cases it did). What we are claiming is that coming to the light brought these men back into fellowship with the Lord and gave His light a chance to dispel the darkness.

Light is life.

CONCLUSION

As the writer of Hebrews tells us, without the shedding of blood there is no remission (forgiveness for sin). Israel is the perfect picture of the individual believer. She, as a nation, already had an eternal relationship with God (established by the irrevocable Abrahamic Covenant). But she did not enjoy that relationship when she wandered off into her various sins of idolatry (notice the last verse of 1 John—"My little children, keep yourselves from idols"). She was chastised and felt abandoned by God. When she repented and confessed her sins, fellowship was restored.

God had set up a system to help maintain fellowship between Himself and Israel. This system had nothing to do with His relationship with Israel—that was established, permanent, and eternal (Romans 9–11). But if she wanted to stay in fellowship with Yahweh, Israel had to take advantage of the system God established for her to be cleansed of her sins. That system was the sacrificial system of the Mosaic Law. It was given for fellowship, not relationship. The blood sacrifices were good for one year's forgiveness, not for relationship, but so she could enjoy the blessings of the Lord in the land. Without the shedding of blood there is no remission of sins.

The blood of Jesus is so much better than the blood of bulls and goats. It is God's provision for forgiveness on two levels: position and condition, or relationship and fellowship. Paul speaks of forgiveness for our position when he says, "In Him we have redemption through His blood, the forgiveness of sins, according to the riches of His grace" (Eph 1:7). And John speaks of forgiveness for our condition when he says, "If we walk in the light as He is in the light, the blood of His Son Jesus cleanses us from all sin" (1 John 1:7). This kind of fellowship forgiveness brings us close to the Father and the Son, and their joy is reciprocal.

When I was a young pastor, we lived in a one story, four bed-room house. Since we had only two children at the time, we kept the corner bed-room for a TV/reading room. I liked to lean back on a Hollywood couch on Saturday night meditating and praying for the ministry of the next morning. This was my private time with the Lord. I didn't like to be disturbed. One Saturday evening, while sitting there quietly I heard the door handle turn and saw the door open a few inches. It didn't open all the way, so I wondered what would happen next. Then I saw four little fingers crawl around the edge of the door. Now I knew what was coming. My five year old son was supposed to be asleep in the room across the hall. Obviously, he wasn't. I geared myself to sternly send him back to his room. But as he pushed the door slowly open and treaded lightly into the room, I could tell by the look on his face that he was scared. Something had awakened him. His big blue eyes looked like he had seen the proverbial ghost.

Nevertheless, I asked, "What are you doing, Jimmy? You're supposed to be in bed." You see, this was my time with the Lord. I didn't want to be disturbed. "What do you want?"

"Nothing, Daddy. I don't want anything … I just want to be close to you." Wow. What are you going to do? I opened my arms, he came running over and jumped up on my chest. I put my arms around him and pulled him close. Then I knew what James was trying to say when he wrote, "Draw near to God, and He will draw near to you."

Just as with my son, we often think, "I don't know, Lord. There's really nothing I want right now. It's just kind of dark in my life … And I'm scared … I know you're awfully busy, but it would mean so much to me … could I just be close to you for awhile?" What do you think the Lord is going to do, send you away? There's nothing quite like being close to God. And the blood of His Son makes it all possible.

---

[1] Patrick O. Cate, *Understanding and Responding to ISLAM* (Dallas: DTS, 2001), 15.

[2] Edwin H. Palmer, *The Five Points of Calvinism* (Grand Rapids: Baker Book House, 1972), 25.

[3] Ibid., 211.

[4] Ibid., 207-208, emphasis mine.

[5] Norman Geisler, "God Knows All Things," in *Predestination and Free Will*, eds. D. Basinger and R. Basinger (Downers Grove, IL: InterVarsity Press, 1986), 75.

[6] Orval H. Mowrer, *The Crisis in Psychiatry and Religion* (Princeton: Van Nostrand Company, 1961), 81-102.

[7] The context of progressive action (walking) calls for continuous cleansing (not the present tense itself).

LESSON 3 "Dealing With Darkness: Part 1" I John 1:5-7

1. How are Christian and Islamic views of sin different?

2. According to Dave, what is sin? How does it affect intimacy with God? What is "enmity"?

3. How would you explain the concept that you can be justified by God (position) and still be sinful (condition)?

4. Why is it so important to understand that a new believer is declared "righteous" and that this declaration of righteousness is effective not only for our past sins but also for sins in the future?

5. Dave gives four typical approaches to dealing with sin in the lives of believers. Look at all four and raise any questions you may have about them. What is the main point of the fourth approach?

6. Name the three principles John wants to teach us about fellowship with God.

7. What do you understand about "God is light and in Him is no darkness at all" as it relates to mistaken views of God's sovereignty and "perfect and permissive" will?

8. How have you seen/heard the rationalizations listed on pages 47 and 48 evidenced in our culture?

9. In what sense is verse 7 a remedy for verse 6?

10. What does it mean to "walk in the light"? What is the result of walking in the light?

11. What did you learn from the story of Dave and his son, Jimmy?

– 4 –

DEALING WITH DARKNESS: PART 2

1 JOHN 1:8-9

Charlie Brown was feeling good about himself. He looked at his hands and said to Lucy, "These hands, … these hands could have painted the *Mona Lisa*; these hands, … these hands could have written *War and Peace;* these hands … these hands could have sculpted Michaelangelo's *David.*" Lucy looked at Charlie Brown's hands with wonder and said, "Your hands have jelly on them." Schultz was right. Man's greatest works are tainted with sin. Why? Because within each of us is "the dark side." Even a religious cynic like Mark Twain said that every man is like the moon; he has a dark side that he doesn't want anyone to see.

There was a time in my life when I argued against this point. I was a new Christian, and the campus worker for Campus Crusade for Christ was trying to convince me that everything we do is tainted with sin. I said, "That can't be true. If a mother nurses her baby, how can that be sin? If a person shares the gospel with his neighbor, how can that be sin?" His reply was, "Oh, it's not sinful to nurse a baby or share the gospel as acts in and of themselves, but what none of us is aware of is how much unknown sin there is in our lives every minute of the day. He said you are overlooking the devastating effects of Adam's sin, which left us totally depraved: body, soul, and spirit."

It wasn't until years later when I had learned a little more about the Scriptures and mankind that I realized the CCC staff member was absolutely right. You know, scientists have discovered that the worm does not enter the apple from the outside in, but from the inside out. It's actually planted there by a huge insect, a little egg in the blossom of the apple. And then as the egg hatches, so to speak, the worm eats away at the apple from the inside out. Satan is like a giant insect. He planted an egg in the flower of humanity, way back there in the Garden of Eden. And it hatched, and the worm of sin has eaten all the way through the human race. David said, "In sin did my mother conceive me" (Ps 51:5). That doesn't mean David was born out of wedlock. It meant from the moment of conception, there was sin.

One Sunday morning between services I was walking down the hall and ran into one of our faithful mothers and her little girl. The little girl was holding her mommy's hand; she looked so cute in her Sunday bonnet that I bent down to say hi. "What's your name?" I asked. "My name is Meagan Murray," she said with a big smile. "Well, you sure are cute," I responded, as I looked her in the eye. She and her mother marched a few steps down the hall when this little three year old called for me. I turned around, and she said with all the force and defiance a three year old girl can muster, "I can be mean!" How honest. She wanted me to know she wasn't just cute. She had another side to her moon.

Now, when it comes to dealing with darkness in John, there are three areas of sin which we must deal with in order to be close to God: 1) Our Sin(ful) Nature; 2) The sins we know about; and 3) The sins we don't know about. First John deals with all three.

Let's remember that we have three improper responses to the basic message that God is light and in Him is no darkness at all. These three improper responses are signified in verses six, eight, and ten by the words "if we say that we have." In 1 John 1:6-7 we dealt with the first erroneous response, which was outright hypocrisy, that is, someone who knows he is walking in darkness, but claims to be close to God. He is an outright liar. In 1 John 1:8-9 we will look at the second erroneous response, that is, someone who lies to himself—he says he has no Sin(ful) Nature. Then in 1 John 1:10–2:2 we will examine the third wrongful response to the message of verse five, when a Christian calls God a liar by denying his specific sins. So, we are ready for verses eight and nine where a believer deceives himself into thinking he has no Sin(ful) Nature.

THE ERROR

> If we say that we have no sin, we deceive ourselves, and the truth
> is not in us (1:8).

The error here is to deny that we have a Sin(ful) Nature after we become Christians. It is usually a claim made from Rom 6:6 where Paul addresses believers and tells them that their "old man" was crucified with Christ when they were born again. They equate old man with sin nature. Or they may say that the old man is all that you were before you were born again, but the old man was crucified "so that the body of sin might be done away with." In this case they equate the "body of sin" with the sin nature.

The problem with understanding Rom 6:6 in this way is Paul's continual reference to the Sin Factory in the rest of Romans 6–7. In Rom 6:12, for example, he says "do not let *sin* reign in your mortal body, that you should obey it in its lusts." If the Sin Factory has been destroyed or done away with back in verse six, what does "sin" refer to in verse 12? And in the next chapter Paul says that "sin" is responsible for the evil he does that he doesn't want to do (vv. 17 and 20). And he says this sin "dwells" in him. There appears to be a possible connection between this "sin" and the "flesh" of verse eighteen. If this is the same "flesh" referenced in passages like Gal 5:16-25, then "the sin" of Romans 6–7 and "the flesh" of Galatians 5 may be the same. Or, *a la* Romans 7:18, it could be that "the sin" dwells in "the flesh." In either case, there is still something dreadfully wrong with us after we become believers. We are still fallen creatures (though something wonderful and new has been added). We still struggle with sin and/or the flesh.

Some want to argue that the born again Christian is no longer a sinner, but a saint. The line of thinking is that the devil wants to convince us of the lie that we have not changed since we became Christians. "You're no different than the scum-sucking sinner you were before trusting Christ," he whispers in our ear. They want us to confront this lie by believing that we no longer have a sin(ful) nature. We are supposed to believe that the NT no longer calls us "sinners" after our conversion, but "saints." Though we agree that we need to resist the devil's lie that we are not fundamentally different after we become believers, we do not agree that we are no longer sinners or that the Bible does not address us as such.

James addresses his Jewish Christian brothers and tells them to draw near to God and God will draw near to them (Jas 4:8). But in the rest of the verse he says, "Cleanse your hands, you sinners; and purify your hearts, you double-minded." He calls at least some of his brothers "sinners." Even Paul, at the end of his life (1 Tim 1:15) says of himself, "Christ Jesus came into the world to save sinners, of whom I am chief." Though some would like to say that Paul's reference to himself points back to a time before he knew Christ, the present tense[2] of the verb will not allow us to go back to Paul's pre-Christian experience. Even after decades of knowing Christ, Paul refers to himself as a "sinner."

What I am calling for is a bit of balance. The believer in Christ is a completely new creature. There are huge, fundamental changes in his make-up after Christ and the Holy Spirit comes to live within him. We will develop this fundamental change in our make-up, which is so important for victorious

Christian living in 1 John 3. We need to be reminded over and over that we are the children of God instead of children of the devil. But to say we no longer have a Sin Factory within us would be a grievous error. Call it "the flesh," if you will; or call it "sin." But whatever you call it, the evil within us will never be destroyed[3] in this life. First John 1:8 says it is a serious error to believe that there is not something very sinful in our make-up, no matter what name you want to use for it. He calls it "sin," as does Paul.

The story is told of two brothers who were rather notoriously immoral. They were synonymous with the vice that had overtaken their city. When one of them very suddenly died, the surviving brother went to the local pastor and requested him to perform the burial service. He offered an enormous sum of money if, in his eulogy, he would refer to his deceased brother as a saint. After much pondering, the pastor agreed. As the funeral service came to an end, the pastor, (in the thick of his description of the departed individual) said, "The man we have come to bury was a thief. In fact, he deserves every vile description the mind can muster. He was depraved, immoral, profligate, lewd, obscene, hateful, vicious, licentious, and the scum of the earth…but compared to his brother, he was a saint."

Our problem is one of comparison. "Why, *compared to* the terrorists who took down the World Trade Center, I am not sinful at all." This kind of comparison is a form of self-deception and self-righteousness. We need to remember the words of G. K. Chesterson when a newspaper editorial asked, "What's wrong with the world." In reply Chesterson wrote, "I am."

I would have to say that one of my deepest longings as I anticipate the return of Christ is to wake up one day and know that my sin is gone forever. This is one reason Paul may have called himself the chief of sinners after so many years of walking with Christ. Some have suggested Paul was being falsely humble. More probably he was more *aware* of his depravity than the rest of us. The comparison has been made to getting closer and closer as we walk along to a high mountain. In the distance the mountain may not look all that big, but as we get closer to it, we cannot but be overwhelmed with its enormous size and just how small we really are. As Paul got closer and closer to Jesus, the holiness of God as seen in the light of the Son must have revealed more and more of his own sinfulness to him until he could actually describe himself as the chief of sinners. As long as we are on this earth in its present state, then there will be a daily struggle with our "dark side," a side which will never improve.

A certain professor understood this well when he asked the members of his class to sit one seat apart during the examination in order to avoid all appearances of evil "as the Good Book says." "What if we don't believe in the Good Book?" asked one student. "Then you put two seats between you!" replied the wise professor.

But, again, this is the bad news (v. 8). There is more good news in verse nine.

THE CORRECTION

> If we confess our sins, He is faithful and just to forgive us *our* sins
> and to cleanse us from all unrighteousness (v. 9).

Now we come to John's corrective theology. What do we do in our present condition if we become aware of some specific sin(s) we have committed? Perhaps just a side note to clarify that we are talking about our condition, not our position. There are those among us who understand 1 John as a book on "tests of relationship," who explain 1 John 1:9 as unbelievers confessing their sins as they come to faith in Christ. One of the main problems with that approach is the use of the word "we" at the beginning of the verse. Who are the "we"?

If we trace the word "we" from the first verse all the way through to verse nine, the identification of the "we" obviously includes the apostles. In the first five verses "we" refers exclusively to the apostles. There is nothing in the text to warrant a sudden removal of the apostles from the meaning of "we" in the rest of the chapter. If this is so, verse nine could not possibly be understood as confession for salvation. I should hope the apostles were saved long before 1 John was written.

So, 1 John 1:9 gives us God's instructions for our fellowship with Him. We are to confess our sins. But what does that mean? The word for "confess" (*homologeō*) is often explained as meaning "to say the same thing, to agree." Rightly so. But with whom do we agree? With God, of course. This means when I confess my sins I agree with His view of my sins. He hates sin (Ps 45:7), and sin grieves Him greatly (Eph 4:30).

I have actually met people who use 1 John 1:9 as some sort of button they push to fill themselves with the Holy Spirit. As they explain it, all they have to do is agree with God that what they are doing or have just done is sinful. Then God is required by His promise in 1 John 1:9 to forgive them and fill them with the Holy Spirit. Well, without dwelling on the fact that the Holy Spirit is nowhere mentioned in this text, let's just say that this type of glib "agreement" with God probably won't even restore these people to fellowship. If we agree with God's view of our sin, there should be some distaste for it in our mouths. I should not be delighting in my sin, that is, if I am confessing it. There should be some degree of regret or remorse that I have offended God, since all sin is against Him (Ps 51:4). There may be pleasure in sin for awhile (Heb 11:25), but the aftertaste should be repulsive.

Now, what are we confessing? The text says "our sins." However, this translation overlooks a very important word that occurs immediately before "sins." It is *tas*, which is simply our word for "the." It is used to specify something. If I ask my daughter to get me an apple from the refrigerator, she would go there and get me one apple from among many. It really doesn't matter which one. But if I ask her to get me *the* apple on the top shelf in the refrigerator, she knows I want a very specific apple. The importance of this distinction for 1 John 1:9 cannot be overemphasized. It is the specific sins I know about which break fellowship between me and God.

Jesus gives a nice parallel to this concept in the Sermon on the Mount (Matt 5:23-24). If a brother is worshipping the Lord and *remembers* (this is the key word) that his brother has something against him, he should stop his worshipping and reconcile with his brother. Then he can come back to continue his worship. Known offenses are a barrier to human fellowship and divine fellowship. In 1 John 1:9 we are dealing on the divine level, but Matthew 5 links the two, as John will do later in this letter. Jesus is saying our worship is worthless if we know that there is unresolved conflict between us and a brother. We need to be right on the horizontal plane in order to be right on the vertical plane. It's our *awareness* of offenses that breaks fellowship.

If we confess these sins which we know about, God is faithful and just to forgive us of these sins. The word *forgive* comes from a word (*aphiēmi*) never used in the Gospel of John when speaking of the relationship between man and God. If the Gospel of John was written to establish an eternal relationship between God and those who believe in His Son (John 20:31), it seems strange that John would not use this word in the sense of God forgiving man in twenty-one chapters … unless, of course, John reserves that word in his own thinking for fellowship instead of relationship.

This is precisely what we are suggesting. For John forgiveness is personal, not judicial. Remember, the reformers established justification to be a courtroom term. It is judicial—declared righteous in the courtroom of heaven for all time. But for John forgiveness deals with fellowship, not relationship. A perfect example from the gospels would be found in the story of the estranged brothers in Luke 17:3. Two brothers (permanent relationship) have a problem with their fellowship because one brother sins against the other. The sin does not destroy their relationship as brothers, but it does destroy their fellowship. This fellowship cannot be restored until the sinning brother comes to the offended brother and seeks his forgiveness. Luke 17:4 tells the offended brother how many times he should forgive the brother who sinned against him: 70x7 (a figure of speech for infinity). We might ask why. Isn't there a limit? No. Why? Because they are brothers. They have an eternal relationship. Thus, our eternal relationship with God (Father/child) is one of the reasons He will always forgive us.

Sometimes we may feel that going to God with the same sin over which we have had no victory presumes upon His grace and mercy. "How can He forgive me over and over for the same sin?" we might ask. The answer is simply that God is *faithful*. He has promised to do so. And His forgiveness for our fellowship is based on His forgiveness for our relationship. It's like the parents who decide to have children. They already know their children will not be perfect. They will not only make mistakes, they will do some things that are sinful. But this does not keep the parents from deciding to have the children. And when the child is first conceived, an eternal relationship begins. And because this relationship is going to last forever, the child, in a sense, has positional forgiveness for all his future sins. And based on that positional forgiveness, the parents are predisposed to fellowship-forgiveness whenever the child sins against them but also decides to come back to them and ask for their forgiveness. God gave us relationship-forgiveness when we became His children. Based on that, He will always be faithful to offer us forgiveness for fellowship whenever we come to him to ask for it.

But this may not seem right. To keep coming over and over asking forgiveness for the same sin the umteenth time—isn't this taking advantage of God's grace? It just doesn't seem right. Oh, but it is right, not because we deserve this forgiveness by having victory over our sins or by doing acts of penance; it is right because the blood of our Savior Jesus Christ (v. 7) is the provision God gave to make sure there is sufficient forgiveness for our sins once and for all time. That's why the verse says God is not only faithful, but also *just* (*dikaios* = just or right). It is right for God to forgive us, even over and over for the same thing, because of the provision of the blood of Christ. This is not to say our repeated sin does not grieve Him. Nor does it mean He does not want us to find the ultimate victory over that sin. That's why in true confession the sinner is looking for a way out of whatever sin has beset him. If not, then it is doubtful if his attitude toward his sin aligns with God's attitude, one of the presuppositions of true confession.

Finally, there is the additional promise that through true confession we get forgiveness from *all unrighteousness*. What is this? Haven't we confessed the specific sins we have seen and recognized? Precisely. "All unrighteousness" refers to all the rest of the sinfulness and/or sins I do not know about, that is, the ones I do not see. Certainly, as already discussed, I have far more sin in my life than I can see. But God sees it all. And for the sake of fellowship, when I confess the sins I see, the blood of Christ cleanses me of these *as well as* all the sins in my life I do not see. This is good news.

CONCLUSION

We have been trying to elucidate from 1 John the truth Martin Luther landed upon when he wrote that he had been justified (*iustus*) as Rom 5:1 concluded, but he was still a sinner (*peccator*) as Romans 7 explained. He had been justified in his position, but not yet sanctified in his condition. His relationship was permanently secure and unalterable, but his fellowship could vacillate according to his walk with the Lord.

John's concern in 1 John 1, and the entire letter for that matter, is our fellowship with the Lord. Fellowship is a word he repeats four times in the first chapter. That should be some kind of clue as to his intent. He sees present, known sin in the life of a believer as a huge barrier to intimate fellowship with God. But he does not paint a picture of God with a big ax in His mighty right hand just waiting for us to mess up so He can chop our heads off. He speaks of God as our Father and us as His children. Accordingly, our heavenly Father wants to help His children when they fall and hurt themselves. He doesn't stomp on them with His foot. He comes along side to pick them up and help them back on the right path.

One of the most moving scenes I have seen in recent years occurred during the 2000 Olympics in Sydney, Australia. The gun went off for the running of the 400 meter final. Not far into the first turn the runner from Great Britain pulled a hamstring muscle and immediately came to a halt, searing pain shooting up and down the back of his leg. Of course, the people watching in the stands felt his pain and expected him to limp dejectedly off the track. To their surprise he did not limp off the track. He had spent years preparing for that race. It was a dream come true to qualify to represent his country in the Olympic Games. He was not prepared to limp off the track.

That wasn't in his mind. That's not how the script was written. So he kept moving forward, limping along, staying in his lane so as not to be disqualified from a race he had no hope of winning.

As he limped/skipped along, the grimace in his face turned to tears. The race had long since finished, but the fans were on their feet cheering, tears streaming down their faces. The other runners, who had finished the race, turned around to see what was happening. The stands were clapping, cheering and crying all at the same time for they could see the determination in this Afro-Englishman to finish the race.

Then there was a disturbance barreling its way through the stands and onto the track. It was a big, burley, Afro-Englishman fighting through the security guards, running toward the Olympic runner. He went up to this limping Olympian and put his arm around him. Suddenly, everyone knew what was happening. This was a loving father coming down to help his son off the track, saying, "Son, son, you don't have to finish this race." His son said, "Dad, I've got to finish this race." So his father responded, "Then, son, I'm going to finish it with you." So together, arm in arm, they went around the track and finished the race with the crowd cheering and stomping their feet.

What a picture of the love of our heavenly Father for His wayward children and how He longs to come down from heavenly heights to pick us up when we stumble, to put His arm around us, to help us finish the race, even if we have to limp all the way home. All He asks is that we don't lie or deny the reality of our pulled hamstrings. Limp if we must, but don't leave the track. Stay in the race. Don't try to hide your failure from Him. He's there to help us home. And someday, after a particularly serious fall, you may look back and realize your most intimate moments with Him were when He was there to pick you up when you turned your face toward Him.

----

[1] The word for "sin" (*hamartia*) lacks any word like "the" in front of it which would point to a specific sin. We get that in verse nine. But here no specific sin has been identified, thus pointing toward the generic sinfulness within each of us.

[2] The grammar here will not allow for the "historical" present because the "historical" present is never used with the verb "to be." See Daniel B. Wallace, *Greek Grammar Beyond the Basics* (Grand Rapids: Zondervan Publishing House, 1996), 529.

[3] We would understand the word translated "done away with" (*katargeō*) in Rom 6:6 as "put out of business" or "deposed." The idea is that the body of sin no longer has any jurisdiction or legitimate authority over the new believer.

LESSON 4 "Dealing with Darkness: Part 2" I John 1:8-9

1. Considering Psalm 51:5 and the concept of sin being innate in everyone, is it really true that a sweet cuddly little new born baby is sinful? Why is it important to answer this question?

2. How is the person's response in verses 6 and 7 different from the response in verses 8 and 9?

3. What pronouns are used in verse 8? What does this imply? Is John speaking to Christians or non-Christians? How does James 4:8 figure into your thinking? What does Paul say about himself in I Timothy 1:15?

4. Why is it important for believers to understand that we still have a "sin nature"?

5. As our walk with the Lord becomes closer and closer, would you say that our sense of our own sinfulness increases?

6. What argument does Dave set forth for concluding that "confess our sins" is not a condition for salvation?

7. How would you explain what it means to confess one's sins?

8. What hope can you give to the person who says, "How can God forgive me over and over for the same sin?"

9. Explain "all unrighteousness" in verse 9.

10. How many times does the word, "fellowship" appear in chapter 1? What implications can you draw from this?

11. Do I have a "pulled hamstring"? How does Dave encourage me to deal with my limp?

– 5 –

DEALING WITH DARKNESS: PART 3

1 JOHN 1:10–2:2

A little Jewish boy was growing up in a country where the *Juden* (Jews) were despised and often persecuted. When he was about twelve years old, that impressionable young boy watched as Gentiles beat his father up and rubbed his face in the mud and snow. The little boy couldn't fight back. He was too small; the attackers too many and too strong. Nor did his father fight back. But the little Jewish boy vowed he would get even one day.

The little Jewish boy grew up and possessed a strange brilliance which helped him sail through his studies in medical school. But his Jewishness and his involvement in the Jewish secret society of the Cabala with its Satanic rituals and magic kept him from acceptance in what we might call the GMA, the German Medical Association. Facing failure in his chosen profession and deep depression, this Jewish medical doctor decided to make a pact with the devil. He sold his soul to the devil for the price of success. Both success and fame came to the depressed Jewish doctor. In fact, he is known as one of the seven men who rule the world from his grave.

Sigmund Freud found success on the devil's silver platter, a platter which offered the succulent dish of pyschoanalysis to the world. As he delved into the meaning of dreams and the subconscious mind, Freud distilled the cauldron of the human psyche down to three basic elements—the superego, the ego, and the id (the conscience, the rational mind, and the subconscious). Many modern psychologists, even Christians, have unknowingly, or knowingly, eaten at the table of Freud's Faustian feast by popularizing these elements as the parent, the adult, and the child. These Satanic doctrines have succeeded in sucking sin right out of the vocabulary of modern medicine, society, and even the church. Rare is the church you can walk into today and even hear the word "sin" mentioned.

But as I will try to show, when we stop acknowledging sin, depression comes in. Our spiritual health, and consequently our joy and intimacy with God, are directly dependent on our willingness to be honest about the sin in our lives and our personal responsibility connected with it. For with sin comes guilt, and with guilt comes darkness, and when we walk in darkness, we cannot fellowship with God. We cannot be close to him.

As Minirth and Meier point out in their book *Ask the Doctors*, the three greatest causes of emotional pain are: 1) Lack of self worth—a low self-concept; 2) Lack of intimacy with others—or loneliness; and 3) Lack of intimacy with God. Although the three are interrelated, it's the latter we are discussing—how to be close or intimate with God. According to these doctors, "At the heart of these problems is an awareness of sinfulness and a need for cleansing." In other words, guilt keeps us from being close to God.

So let's look at 1 John 1:10–2:2 so we can learn another lesson in "Dealing with Darkness" and how to stay spiritually healthy. We have said that it is God's desire that we live a life of sustained joy. By sustained we don't mean there aren't times of genuine sadness and grief in the lives of victorious Christians. But the joy of the Lord is our strength. And this joy comes from being close to Him. He is light, and in Him is no darkness at all. And if I walk with Him in the light as He is in the light, then the blood of Jesus Christ cleanses me from all the sin in my life I don't know about. But if (v. 8) I am foolish enough to say there is no sin in my life just because I am not aware of any, then I am deceiving myself and the truth is not in me. When God puts His spotlight on one of my sins, then I need to confess that sin. If I do so, then He is faithful and just to forgive me of that sin and to cleanse me of all the sins in my life I don't even know about (v. 9). But what if God puts His spotlight on one of my sins, but I disagree with Him that this is indeed sin? What then?

The Error

> If we say that we have not sinned, we make Him a liar, and His word is not in us (v. 10).

"If we say we have not sinned"—this is to look at the specific sin God's light has revealed and to disagree with Him. This is the opposite of confessing the specific sins we recognized in verse nine. Remember, to confess is to agree. In verse nine we agreed (confessed) with God about *the* sin(s) we knew about, and He forgave us. But here in verse ten we err if we disagree with Him. We "make Him a liar."

One tool God uses to convict us of specific sin is His Word, for His Word is the sword of the Spirit, the spotlight the Holy Spirit uses to convict us of sin. If we deny the sin, we deny His Word and make Him a liar. It is this denial of sin which loads us up with guilt. Guilt is like the red warning light on the dashboard of a car. You can either stop and deal with the trouble, or you can decide the light is giving a false signal. The latter decision can be big trouble.

I was recently driving back to Houston from a seminary meeting in Dallas. I like to drive old cars because old cars carry a special meaning for me. Old Car = Paid For. I like cars that are paid for. But old cars also have some built-in liabilities. I got about half way home when a warning light came on, which said "Check Engine." I had another old car with the same problem, only in that car the "Check Engine" light never went off. So I decided to just ignore the light and view it as a false warning. Bad decision. The engine froze up. I wound up hitching a ride with a couple of truck drivers back to Houston.

Many a Christian has been stuck on the side of the road with engine failure because of ignoring the warning signal of guilt. Much of the influence of Sigmund Freud has trickled down into even Christian psychology as a way to label genuine guilt as false, a carry-over from bad programming from our parents, schools, or church. When Hymenaeus and Alexander (1 Tim 1:19-20) ignored their consciences, they made a shipwreck of their faiths. It was Leo Tolstoy who said, "The antagonism between life and conscience may be removed in two ways: By a change of life or a by a change of conscience."

WHAT EVER HAPPENED TO SIN?

Approach	Problem	Source	Solution
Freud	False Guilt	Authority Figures	Resocialization
Skinner	False Guilt	Environment	Reconditioning
Rogers	False Guilt	Negative Thinking	Self-Help
Mower	Real Guilt	Hurting Others	Group Therapy
Christ	Real Guilt	Sin	Confession

This past week I underwent the most humiliating medical test of my life. Our family doctor suggested at my age I needed to have my colon tested for cancer. I will not bless you with the description of this test and the preparation for the same. Suffice it to say, I trust my doctor. There is no history of cancer in my immediate family, but you never know. So I humbled myself on the examination table as they x-rayed thirty times from every angle

I could imagine. The test was somewhat painful. But it was also purifying. And, glad to say there is no sign of cancer. Now why would I go through such a humbling process? For my physical health, obviously.

If we need to humble ourselves for the sake of our physical health, much more so do we need to do so for the sake of our spiritual health. But if I see a particular sin and don't agree with God that it is sin, then I am calling Him a liar, and His Word is not in me. That would be like having the doctor look at his x-rays and notice cancer, point it out to me, and I tell him he doesn't know what he's talking about. I am sure he is mistaken. There is no history of cancer in my family. My denial would not be good for my health. The cancer would continue to grow. When the x-ray machine of God's Word points its light at one of my sins and I tell Him He's wrong, I leave the light and enter darkness. I have insulted Him. Not a good way to stay close. Guilt begins to seep into my soul and cloud my vision of God. My conscience is pricked. And with the guilt comes self-deception, depression, and defeat. I lose my intimacy with God. Emotional pain spreads. Psychologists have long recognized the problem of guilt when it comes to mental health. They just don't know how to get rid of it.

Through his analysis of the human psyche Freud thought he had found a way of getting rid of guilt. In his view men and women are not responsible for their guilt. They are victims of the authority figures in their lives: their parents, church, grandparents, and others. These people have programmed our consciences as to what is right and wrong. Of course, this is false programming. Our authority figures were probably too strict. And when our subconscious mind gives us the urge to gratify some natural desire, our conscience comes along to beat us up and tell us these desires are wrong. Guilt follows, but this is false guilt. Nothing wrong has been desired or acted upon. The cure here is for Freudian psychoanalysts to resocialize the poor victim. In therapy the analyst will take the part of the strict parent and become accepting and understanding. The harsh rules will be taken away. The adult mind will be set free to determine what really is truth. The conscience is chopped down to size. The value system is restructured. Sin is tossed into the garbage can of Victorian values. Anna Russell put Freud's philosophy into a poem:

> I went to my psychiatrist to be psychoanalyzed
> To find out why I killed the cat and blacked my husband's eyes.
> He laid me on a downy couch to see what he could find,

And here is what he dredged up from my subconscious mind:
When I was one, my mommie hid my dolly in a trunk,
And so it follows naturally that I am always drunk.
When I was two, I saw my father kiss the maid one day,
And that is why I suffer now from kleptomania.
At three, I had the feeling of ambivalence toward my brothers,
And so it follows naturally I poison all my lovers.
But I am happy; now I've learned the lesson this has taught;
That everything I do that's wrong is someone else's fault.

Along comes B. F. Skinner. He is not an armchair therapist sitting with his feet propped up while he analyzes dreams. He goes into the laboratory and experiments with pigeons and mice. He believes science can produce a problem-free society. Man is simply an animal, albeit the highest in existence, the top of the evolutionary ladder. He is a product of his environment. And his behavior can be conditioned by changing his environment. Again, as with Freud, man is not responsible for his problems. The culprit is his environment. The behavior of the subject can be modified by a series of rewards and punishments. Personal responsibility is nonsense to Skinner. Change the environment and you will change the behavior. Of course, who is to say what kind of behavior is appropriate? There is no right and wrong for Skinner except that which advances society. Sin does not enter his vocabulary.

Next we look at Carl Rogers. He believes man is good at the core level. He has the power within himself to pull himself up by his moral bootstraps. Within man is the answer to all of his problems. He needs a counselor only to help him discover the answer to his own dilemmas. The therapist helps the client help himself. No authoritative standard from the outside can be imposed upon the Rogerian client. God is an intruder. He is unnecessary and only complicates the situation. Man is autonomous. Needless to say, sin is never discussed because there is no standard by which sin can be defined.

For these three men, Freud, Skinner, and Rogers, all guilt is false guilt, the result of standards falsely imposed upon us from the outside. When outside authorities with their rigid standards are discarded, the guilt will go away. But one modern psychologist has challenged these approaches. He believed in real guilt, although he did not believe in God. This was O. Hobard Mower. He believed bad behavior is the root of man's problems. By bad behavior he means behavior that hurts other people. This produces real guilt because man is not behaving up to his own standards. He shouldn't hurt other people. He believed people are in psychiatric wards because of unresolved guilt. But his answer to guilt was to confess to the person you hurt and make restitution. He knew nothing of violating God's standards. He would never confess to God because he did not believe in God. He used group therapy, sensitivity groups, *et cetera*, to bring people to confess on a horizontal level.

But because Mower did not offer his clients a personal Savior, he was like the high priest of Judaism who stands daily, offering the same sacrifices over and over. Final atonement for sin is never made. His counselees had to spend their lives looking for those they have hurt so they can confess and make restitution. But they never look up. Everything is horizontal. Whereas Rogers saw the potential for salvation in the individual, Mower saw the potential for salvation in the group. But the graduates of the groups become groupees. That is, they just sort of hang around the group hoping for something more. They have had a taste of change, but they want lasting change. They still feel hollow on the inside because they have never been to the only One who can permanently take away the stain of sin.

Only God's Word tells us that all sin is ultimately against God because God set the standard. The Greek word *hamartia* means to miss the mark. The mark is God's perfect holiness. When we fall short of that mark, we have sinned. I recently listened to the testimony of a former Muslim who came to Christ. She was raised in Kenya as a devout, practicing Muslim. She told me she prayed five times a day. Then her family moved here to Texas. She always felt empty inside, but did not know why. Then she came to church and heard that we all sin and fall short of the perfect holiness of God. For the first time she realized her problem. Sin. She was sinful. She had never been told she was sinful. All she knew was that she was to pray to Allah five times a day. But now she understood the reason she felt so far from God no matter how much she prayed. It was because her sin kept her from being close to Him. Fortunately she also heard the good news. Christ died for her sins. And He would only die once. No further atonement was necessary. She trusted Him and discovered a new relationship and new fellowship with God she had never known.

THE CORRECTION

> My little children, these things I write to you, so that you may not sin. And if anyone sins, we have an Advocate with the Father, Jesus Christ the righteous. And He Himself is the propitiation for our sins, and not for ours only but also for the whole world (2:1-2).

Prevention of Sin (1a)

The privilege of confession can be abused: "If God promises to forgive me every time I sin even the same sin over and over, I might as well sin as much as I want." This is false confession. Remember, to agree with Him about my sin is to agree with His attitude toward my sin. I should be seeking victory over my sin.

I remember a fellow who told me the key to the Christian life was 1 John 1:9. He called it spiritual breathing. When he sinned, he entered darkness, but when he confessed, he was filled with the Holy Spirit and entered the light. He said he does this spiritual breathing at least *forty times a day*. "Forty times a day?" I asked. "How long have you been doing this?" "Fifteen years. Ever since I realized that smoking is a sin."

Now, my intent here is not to rail against smoking. But this man was convicted it was wrong. Nevertheless, for fifteen years after he was convinced it was wrong for him to smoke, he continued smoking two packs a day. Apparently, he confessed his sin after each cigarette. In his mind he was then filled by the Holy Spirit until he smoked another cigarette. So, get the picture here. He's filled with the Spirit, smokes a cigarette, the Spirit leaves him, he confesses, the Spirit fills him, he smokes a cigarette, the Spirit leaves him, he confesses, and on and on through forty cycles each day. Does something seem missing here to you? Yes, it's called true confession. I'm not saying a Christian cannot wrestle with on-going sin. But in true confession he at least wants and prays for the victory.

God doesn't give us the wonderful promise of restored fellowship through confession with the idea that we will knowingly abuse the privilege. The idea is that there will be victory over the activity or attitude we now recognize as sin. God wants us to know that we can still fellowship with Him while we are looking for that victory, but His intent in assuring us of His forgiving love is not to encourage us to keep on blithely sinning. Nevertheless, though John's intent in writing is that we sin less instead of more, he does want us to know that we have someone on our side to intercede for us no matter how far we have strayed from the straight and narrow.

Paraclete for Sin (1b)

The word used here that is translated "Advocate" (*paraklētos*) is used only by John in the NT (John 14:16, 26; 15:26; 16:7; and here). Notice all these uses are from the Upper Room Discourse (fellowship, not relationship). So much of the wording of 1 John comes straight out of the Upper Room

Discourse, further underscoring the point we are suggesting over and over—that this letter is intimate truth, fellowship truth.

Now this use of *parakletos* in 1 John 2:1 is the only time the word is used of Christ. The other times it is the Holy Spirit. The use of the word for a "lawyer" is possible, but "mediator" is more likely. When we sin, we don't need a lawyer (see Rom 8:33-34), because no one can lay any charge against God's elect, but we do need an intercessor, a mediator, a High Priest.

For example, Luke 22:31-33 gives us a good illustration of what Jesus is doing on our behalf right now as He sits beside His Father. This is where Christ predicts the great failure of Peter. He says Peter will deny Him three times. But look at what Christ does before making that prediction. The Lord tells Peter that Satan has asked for him that he might sift Peter like wheat. Satan is out searching for people he can sift like wheat, especially if you have crossed the line into Christian service. It doesn't matter if it is teaching Sunday school, working in the nursery, or going to the mission field—if you have consciously entered His army, then Satan is looking for you to sift you like wheat.

But there is encouragement. Christ tells Peter that He has prayed for him. Christ prays three things. First, that Peter's faith would not fail. Christ already knows that Peter will fumble the ball. But after the fumbling, Christ prays that Peter would not be so completely shattered that he would quit the game, that he leaves Christian service. Secondly, Christ prays that Peter will come back to Him after he has fumbled the ball. He prays for Peter's return to fellowship and Christian service. Finally, Christ prays that Peter would be restored to his place on the team and that he could be there to strengthen his other teammates because Satan would be out there like a mad middle linebacker trying to knock them out of the game.

I want to encourage those of you who feel like your performance in the Christian life has been so bad that He has cut you from the first team. I want to remind you that Peter was one of the starting eleven. Twelve came to try-outs, but one was cut from the team. There were eleven left—Christ's Eleven going up against Ocean's Eleven. And Peter was their quarterback. He always had his mouth open calling the plays. Then he fumbled the ball, not once, but three times in the same quarter. He was so discouraged and embarrassed he took himself out of the game. For awhile he sat on the bench wondering if he would ever play again. But His backfield coach interceded on his behalf with the Head Coach, and in the final quarter they put Peter back in the game. He was restored to the starting line-up. When he got back in, he was so thankful for the grace extended to him by his Coaches that he played as he had never played before. Someone in the huddle heard him say the other team would have to kill him before he would take himself out of the game again.

If you have fumbled the ball like Peter, or if you ever do, you have some-one sitting right beside the Head Coach in heaven to intercede on your behalf. It's the Coach's Son, who never fumbled the ball. And he is saying, "Put him back in the game, Father. Give him another chance. I don't think he will let you down this time. You're gonna be proud of him, I just know it, because I'm going to be right by his side to help him throw the ball and run to the goal line."

This is encouraging. But what assurance do we have that the Father will listen to the Son? It's because the Father is completely satisfied by the Son.

Propitiation for Sin (2:2)

Here's a hundred dollar word: "Propitiation" (*hilasmos*). It means "satis-faction." Christ takes away God's displeasure at our sin; as The Father looks at the nail-pierced hands of the Righteous One, He is fully satisfied. A vari-ation of this word was *hilastērion* (propitiatory sacrifice), which was used of the Mercy Seat (Heb 9:5 and Ex 25:17-20) and Rom 3:25-26. Do you see how the tabernacle is in the back of John's mind as he writes these words, just as it was when he was writing his gospel?

Because guilt feelings often persist even after our confession, we desper-ately need to *believe* that God is fully satisfied. Our interceding High Priest seated at His right hand points to His hands and to the mercy seat as He prays for us. It is especially crucial for us to know that the Father is complete-ly satisfied after we have committed some egregious error like fumbling the ball as Peter did. Even fumbling the ball more than once, as Peter did.

That's why John lets us know in no uncertain terms that the death of Christ not only satisfied God's anger against my sins and the sins of other believers, but also for the sins of the entire world (verses like John 14:19, 27, 30; 15:18; 16:33; and 17:6-26 should make it apparent that the world includes all unbelievers). That means the work of Christ was so great that it not only was sufficient to satisfy God's anger against the sins of the believ-ers, but also men like Nero, Hitler, Stalin, and Osama bin Laden. If His sacrifice was enough to satisfy God's justice with regard to their sins,[1] it is certainly enough to take care of mine and yours.

CONCLUSION

Our accuser (Satan) can use unresolved guilt as a whip to keep us enslaved to our sin(ful) natures. We can resolve that guilt with the promises of verses 1:7, 9, and 2:1-2.

A little boy was visiting his grandparents and given his first slingshot. He practiced in the woods, but he could never hit his target. As he came back to Grandma's backyard, he spied her pet duck. On an impulse he took aim and let fly. The stone hit, and the duck fell dead. The boy panicked. Desperate, he hid the dead duck in the wood pile, only to look up and see his big sister watching. Sally had seen it all, but she said nothing.

After lunch that day, Grandma said, "Sally, let's wash the dishes." But Sally said, "Johnny told me he wanted to help in the kitchen today, didn't you, Johnny?" And she whispered to him, "Remember the duck!" So Johnny did the dishes.

Later Grandpa asked if the children wanted to go fishing. Grandma said, "I'm sorry, but I need Sally to help make supper." Sally smiled and said, "That's all taken care of. Johnny wants to do it." Again she whispered, "Remember the duck." Johnny stayed while Sally went fishing.

After several days of Johnny doing both his chores and Sally's, finally he couldn't stand it. He confessed to Grandma that he'd killed the duck. "I know, Johnny," she said, giving him a big hug. "I was standing at the window and saw the whole thing. Because I love you, I forgave you before you even confessed. I was just wondering how long you would let Sally make a slave of you."

When you trusted Christ, God looked down from His heavenly window and gave you advanced forgiveness for any sin you would ever commit. That's positional forgiveness. It gives you a right standing before God. But until you come to Him with subsequent sins *after* trusting Christ as your Savior, you will not enjoy the sufficient price paid for all the sins you ever have or will commit. And Satan has free reign to keep you as his slave by whispering in your ear, "Remember the duck!"

Don't let him do that.

---

[1] Theologians usually distinguish between *sufficient* and *efficient*. The death of Christ was *sufficient* penalty to pay for the sins of the entire world, but only *efficient* for those who believe in Him. It's like being given a gift certificate to Baskin Robbins. The gift has been paid for. That which was paid was sufficient to cover

whatever the certificate says. But that certificate has no real meaning in your life until you go to Baskin Robbins and appropriate what was paid for you. Only then will you enjoy the gift. Before going to the store, the gift certificate was *sufficient*, but not *efficient*.

LESSON 5 "Dealing With Darkness: Part 3" I John 1:10–2:2

1. Why do you think there seems to be such an aversion to acknowledging "sin"?

2. Dave suggests that the three greatest causes of emotional pain are interrelated, although he chooses to deal only with the third one. How are the three related?

3. How can we make "God a liar"?

4. Review the various psychological approaches to sin in the chart on page 67. What is the common element in each?

5. What is the only standard for identifying sin? Who is the object of all sin?

6. How can "confession" be abused?

7. Read Luke 22:31-33. How does this scripture relate to I John 2:1?

8. How can we be assured that the Father will listen to the Son's mediation?

9. What is your reaction to knowing that Jesus is praying for you? (Read John 17:20.)

10. Discuss "sins of the whole world" in verse 2.

11. Review the footnote on page 74–75 to understand "sufficient" and "efficient."

12. How can we deal with Satan's "remember the duck" whispers?

– 6 –

GOD'S LOVE LANGUAGE

1 JOHN 2:3-5

Author and marriage counselor Gary Chapman has suggested that husbands and wives have five general ways in which they perceive love from their partner: 1) Words of Affection; 2) Quality Time; 3) Receiving Gifts; 4) Acts of Service; and 5) Physical Touch.[1] Usually one of these "love languages" is primary for a husband or wife. Unfortunately, mates usually don't have the same "love language." Like a Russian who speaks only Russian being married to a Chinese person who speaks only Chinese, a husband might be saying "I love you" in his language, but his wife does not get the message because she has a different love language. According to Chapman, marital intimacy is difficult to achieve unless each partner learns to speak the "love language" of his/her mate.

It took me about seven years of marriage before I learned my wife's love language, but I'll never forget it. We had seen and become enamored by the "Muppet Movie." Betty especially identified with Miss Piggy. She had never seen herself so perfectly portrayed in books or on the screen. Now I didn't exactly identify with Kermit the Frog, but if I'm married to Miss Piggy, we can all guess who I am. Well, this is all well and was good for fun and games, but one night we were lying about a foot apart in our king size bed, lights out, almost asleep, when I hear this strange, squeaky little voice saying, "Kermie, … whisper sweet nothings in my ear." Well, how can a real man respond to that? So I just laid there pretending to be asleep. Now, I'm sure some of you are aware that Miss Piggy has a variety of voices. Suddenly, out of the darkness came a guttural command which said, "Noowww!" Well, a real man knows when he's being manipulated, so I began some soft snoring. But Miss Piggy also has a variety of talents. For example, she knows karate. The next thing I felt was a huge karate chop to the ribs attended by the karate call of "Haaayyahh!!!"

Guess which love language belongs to Betty. You're right—Words of Affection. That's her primary love language—Sweet Nothings. And if I don't know that, I might assume that I am doing the things which display true love, when in her eyes I am missing the boat completely. Could it be that

God has a primary "love language"? Surely there are many ways to show God we love Him, but what if He has a primary love language and I miss it? Could it be that intimacy with Him will be difficult to achieve if I don't learn to speak His love language?

Not long after he had become a Christian, Chuck Colson wrote a book on how we can love God.[2] He says he interviewed scores of people but could not come up with a consensus on how to love God. So he decided to make a study on this in the Bible. He wound up his study in the passage we want to focus on at this point in 1 John 2 as well as a significant cross-reference from the upper room (surprise, surprise). It was his conclusion that God's primary love language is: Keeping His Commandments. Let's see this in 1 John 2:3-5.

THE MAIN MESSAGE:
LOVE = KEEPING HIS COMMANDMENTS

> Now by this we know that we know Him, if we keep His commandments (2:3).

We have already mentioned that 1 John is the most controversial book in the NT. Some see the book as "tests of life" (relationship), while others see it as "tests of intimacy" (fellowship). The passage before us heats up the controversy. It would certainly appear that verse three tells us that the way we can tell that we know Christ as our Savior is if we keep His commandments. In other words, the way to get assurance of one's salvation is to look at the fruit of one's life. If you keep His commandments, you are a Christian and will go to heaven when you die; if you don't keep His commandments, you are not a genuine Christian and will go to hell when you die. This all seems pretty plain and obvious, plus the fact that we don't see the word "love" in this verse, a fact which would naturally lead us to think this verse isn't teaching us anything about love.

Well, let's back up and set up the structure of the passage and the context of the verse. Here again is the outline we are using for 1 John:

1 John
"The Fruit of Fellowship"

I. Introduction: "The Joy of Fellowship" 1:1-4
II. Body: "The Principles of Fellowship" 1:5–5:17
    A. Principles of Fellowship Introduced 1:5–2:27

1. Right Living—Dealing with our Sins 1:5–2:2
2. Right Loving—Dealing with our Brothers 2:3-11
3. Right Learning—Dealing with our Enemies 2:12-27
B. Principles of Fellowship Developed 2:28–4:6
1. Right Living—Dealing with our Sins 2:28–3:10a
2. Right Loving—Dealing with our Brothers 3:10b-23
3. Right Learning—Dealing with our Enemies 3:24–4:6
C. Principles of Fellowship Climaxed 4:7–5:21
1. Right Loving—Dealing with our Brothers 4:7–5:5
2. Right Learning—Dealing with our Enemies 5:6-13
3. Right Living—Dealing with our Sins 5:14-17
III. Conclusion: "Encouragement for Little Children" 5:18-21

From this outline we should be able to see that 2:3 begins a new wave or principle of fellowship, just as 1:5 began our first wave or principle of fellowship. The first principle was what we called "Right Living," in which we were introduced to basic principles on how to deal with our sins in order to have close fellowship with God even though we are not sinless after we are justified. And in that first section, 1:5 gave us a primary message ("God is light"), which was followed by three erroneous responses (1:6, 8, 10) with their corresponding corrections.

Here in 2:3 the new section also begins with a main message or topic sentence. It also is followed by three responses, which are signified with the words "He who says …" in 2:4, 6, and 9. As we mentioned earlier, John loves doing things in threes. This is important. We need to see that 2:3 does not stand alone. It begins a new section. Them's the facts, ma'm, no matter what approach one takes to the book.

But if we follow the responses of 2:4, 6, and 9 through the section which ends in 2:11, it's pretty easy to see that the primary subject of this section is love. John somewhat innocuously begins with a statement about God's commands, but then subtly leads his readers down the commandment trail to the old verses new commandment Jesus talked about in, guess where, the Upper Room: "A new commandment I give to you, that you love one another; as I have loved you, that you also love one another" (John 13:34).

Thus we see that 2:3 is a verse set in the context of love, specifically loving our brothers. As many have observed, "Loving the whole world for me is no chore; my only problem is my neighbor next door." Difficulty with other Christians is one of the big three barriers to fellowship with God in the mind of John. Our personal sin is a huge barrier, for sure (1:5–2:2); but so is not loving our Christian brother, which is, of course, a very specific personal sin. And even though 2:3 does not mention the "love of God," 2:5 does. It says our love for God is perfected when we keep His Word, and John is going to go on to connect our love for God with our love for our brother via God's commandments.

But let's get more specific on 2:3. How do we answer the fact that on the surface this verse appears to teach that you can have assurance of your salvation if you keep God's commandments? This gets a bit technical, but it's helpful. Something we cannot observe from the NKJV is that the verbs for "know" in 2:3 are not the same. The root word is the same, all right, but the tenses are different. We cannot see this from the English translation.

The first use of "know" is in the present tense (*ginōskamen*); but the second use of "know" is in the perfect tense (*egnōkamen*). If we miss this deliberate shift on John's part, we miss his intent for the verse. Others have pointed out that this root word for "know" (*ginōskō*) speaks of "experiential" knowledge as opposed to intuitive knowledge. It is what is called by Greek grammarians a "stative" verb because it describes a state of being as opposed to a verb of action. In other words, to "know" or to "believe" speak of inner truths but not outward actions.

Now a Greek grammarian named McKay has written an excellent article dealing with the perfect tense of stative verbs in which he demonstrates that putting a stative verb into the perfect tense has the effect of intensifying the basic meaning of the verb. It's a deeper state of whatever the meaning of the verb is. In this case, the verb means "to know" in the sense of an experience. So putting it into the perfect tense means "to know intensely," "to experience deeply," or "to know fully." It's much like the OT meaning when it says, "Adam *knew* his wife Eve, and she conceived and bore Cain … " It's an intimate knowledge.

None of the commentators who take the "tests of life" view of 1 John have observed this significant change in tenses here in 2:3. Some of the translations have noticed this change, such as the NASB which says, "And by this we *know* that we *have come to know* Him, if we keep His commandments." But this does not solve the problem, nor does this translation reflect the perfect tense of a *stative* verb. I hate to belabor this point, but it is crucial, since 2:3 is referenced more than any other "test of life" in 1 John by those who believe this book is how to know if you are a Christian or not.

The perfect tense in the Greek language has the basic meaning of "completed action in the past with present results." But, according to its use in context, a typical verb can put its emphasis on the completed action in the past *or* on the present results. When the translator thinks the emphasis is on the completed action in the past, he will translate it with the English word "have" to emphasize the completed action: have heard, have written, have finished, have been sanctified. But when the translator thinks the emphasis is on the present results of the completed action in the past, he translates the verb like an English present tense: It is finished (*tetelestai*—Christ's statement on the cross).

But in a stative verb McKay's point is that it should always be translated with the emphasis on the present results. In other words, "have come to know" does not recognize the significance of a stative verb in the perfect tense. A more accurate reflection of the emphasis on the intensified state of experiential knowledge here would be, "And by this we *know* that we *know* Him *intensely*." And what is intense knowledge if not deep, intimate knowledge? Once again, the emphasis here is on *fellowship*, not relationship. It is not a test of whether a person is born again; it is a test of whether a person is having close fellowship with God.

In 1:5–2:2 we saw the most common denominator for fellowship with Christ: walk in the light and confess the sins we know about. A brand new Christian can walk with the Lord and fellowship with Him on this level. In 2:3-11 we have fellowship at a deeper level. Now the Christian is learning His Word (His commandments). When he chooses to obey these commandments, a deeper fellowship awaits him.

Once again we see the dependency of 1 John on John 13–17. John 14:21-24 tells us in no uncertain terms that keeping His commandments is God's language of love. "If you love Me, keep My commandments" (John 14:15). It doesn't get much more clear than that—God's primary language of love is keeping His commandments. But more than that. When we show Him we love Him, He reciprocates. That's what Jesus is trying to say in John 14:21. If we have Jesus' commandments and keep them, then we show Him we love Him. When we do that, He tells us His Father loves us and He loves us and *He will manifest Himself to us!* The word "manifest" means to "make visible." In other words, He reveals a little more of His love He had hidden in His heart for us.

Isn't this exactly the way it works with deepening love relationships? We don't dump the whole load on the first date. We test the waters. I reveal a little of myself. If she reciprocates by revealing some of her feelings for me, I may reveal a little more of myself. Of course, I am referring to positive feelings. When I was in grammar school, we used to communicate through emissaries and notes. If I saw a girl I liked, I'd write her a note, but I'd have my friend Joe deliver it for me. Then he would bring back a return note. One time I sent a note through Joe to a girl named Cathy. With great anticipation I saw Joe coming back with a return note. If Cathy reciprocated my feelings, we could dispense with the notes and get rid of the middle man. Alas! Cathy's note said, "Sorry, Dave, I don't like you." Well, that kind of response necessitated a return-return note. I sent Joe back with a note which said, "Then I don't like you either."

In love relationships we reveal a little of ourselves at a time. The sting of rejection is too strong to dump all our feelings at once. Besides, those feelings tend to intensify as each reveals or makes manifest a little more of him/herself. The Lord is no different. That's one reason He compares His relationship with the Church to a husband/wife relationship. I actually believe He loves everyone He has ever created the same because He is omnibenevolent, that is, He does not show partiality (Rom 2:11) and He loves the whole world (John 3:16). He causes it to rain on the just and the unjust. But those who see His message of love written on the cross and believe in it experience His love in a deeper way than those who reject this overture of love from the Lord. Yet, even we believers are probably loved by Him more than we will ever know. Nevertheless, as we communicate to Him in His love language (keep His commandments), He reveals more and more of His love for us. It's a growing, dynamic love relationship.

It's probably the same with you and your children. Let's say you have two children. You love them both the same. But your first born is much more compliant than your second born. Your second born can't really compete and outdo his older brother who is bigger, stronger, and knows more than he does. So, instead of getting your attention with his good behavior, he goes the other direction and rebels. Well, even though you love both of them the same, you must display that love in different ways. For the compliant child there are positive rewards. For the rebellious child there is the rod. It grieves you to have to manifest your love for your rebellious son with the rod. You would love to reward him for his good behavior. But you can't; not until he begins to keep your commandments. Then you can manifest your love for him in a positive way.

THE ERROR

> He who says, "I know Him," and does not keep His commandments, is a liar, and the truth is not in him (2:4).

Again, this verse and the prior are among the numerous "tests of life" (relationship) found in this book by those who count themselves among the Fruit Inspectors in the Church. According to them, anyone who claims to be a Christian but does not keep Christ's commandments is simply a liar, a false professor of Christ.

I won't go through the fifty questions this kind of teaching brings to mind concerning how-when-which of the commandments must be kept. Suffice it to say, I do not believe you can know you are a Christian until you die with this understanding of the text. You will always be adrift on a Sea of Subjectivity wondering if you are being faithful enough.

In his early writings John Calvin did not think looking at one's fruit could bring any assurance of salvation. He thought we were doomed if we looked to ourselves, at least as far as assurance is concerned. He said we should look to Christ and that assurance was part of saving faith. But after his death Theodore Beza assumed control of the Geneva Academy, which trained so many pastors for the Continent as well as the British Isles. Beza supported the concept that Christ died only for the elect. If that were so, he reasoned, it would be invalid to look to Christ for one's assurance, since the looker might be among the reprobate (those God predestined for hell, according to Beza) and thus be looking to a Savior who didn't die for him. Well, if we couldn't look to Christ for the assurance of our salvation, we would have to look to ourselves and our own fruit, said Beza. This began what I call the great Fruit Inspecting Industry during the Reformation, practiced to perfection by the English Puritans and brought to America on the Mayflower.

According to William Perkins, one of the leading preachers of Puritanism during the days of Beza, there are nine fruits to look for in your introspective endeavors to determine if you are really among the elect and will go to heaven when you die. Here they are:

1. Feelings of bitterness of heart when we have offended God by sin;
2. Striving against the flesh;
3. Desiring God's grace earnestly;
4. Considering that God's grace is a most precious jewel;
5. Loving the ministers of God's word;
6. Calling upon God earnestly and with tears;
7. Desiring Christ's second coming;
8. Avoiding all occasions of sin;
9. Persevering in the effects to the last gasp of life.[3]

It must be obvious from these fruits that no one could have assurance of his salvation until he died, if, after all, one must persevere in the faith until his last gasp. When would he be assured of his salvation? Obviously, after his last gasp.

Assurance of one's salvation became the preoccupation of the English Puritans who moved to America. Whole volumes of hundreds and hundreds of pages were written just to help people try to figure out whether they would go to heaven when they died or not. The Puritans dedicated entire volumes to the introspection necessary to ascertain whether one's faith was sufficient to save them. In commenting on his 650-page tome called *Discourse concerning the Holy Spirit,* J. Owen (d. 1683) stated that his main purpose was to help professors of Christ to determine whether or not they were possessors of Christ.[4]

Fruit inspectors all. And, as the early writings of John Calvin pointed out, such an approach leaves one in doom and despair. That is why churches that take this approach to the Christian life are so lacking in joy. How can one have any joy as long as he is looking to his own life and fruit as the source of his assurance as to whether or not he is going to go to heaven or not? As Michael Eaton, who grew up in the Westminster Chapel, has observed:

> I found myself reading about the death-bed experiences of 17th century Puritans. I was shattered to discover that their assurance of salvation at such a time was not what I would have expected. Then I came across the remark of Asahel Nettleton ... which expressed the very essence of everything I felt was wrong with the approach to grace that I had grown up with: "The most that I have ventured to say respecting myself is, that I think it possible I may get to heaven." Surely, I thought to myself, there is more joy and assurance in the New Testament than that! Yet I knew only too well that such introspection and doubt was widespread in the Reformed circles I knew.[5]

Respectfully, I wish to say that the failure in regard to 1 John 2:3-4 has been to see the verse in its context. All we have to do is see the three repetitions of "he who says ..." in verses 4, 6, and 9 to know that John is repeating the pattern he established in chapter one with a topic sentence and three responses to it. That would tell us that 2:5 is directly connected to 2:3-4. And though 2:3-4 do not mention "love" directly, 2:5 does. That's the connection—not between keeping His commandments and entrance into life but keeping His commandments and enjoyment of life (it's fellowship, not relationship). And the "know" of 2:4 is again in the perfect tense, which we have explained at length means to know Him intimately, intensely. This too has been overlooked by those who hold the "tests of life" view.

Using these verses as a source of assurance can be dangerous. I once had a discussion with a seminary colleague in which I asked him if he were sure he would go to heaven when he died. He assured me he would.

"How do you know?" I asked.

"Because I can look into my life and see evidence of the Holy Spirit at work: my love for God's Word, my love for people, my hatred of sin, and so on," he replied.

"But couldn't you take a serious fall at some point in the future and lose your love for God's Word, His people, and begin to love sin?"

"Of course," he replied, "let him who thinks he stands take heed lest he falls."

"But if you had such a fall, what would that prove."

"Well," he said, "if I continued in sin, it would prove I never was a genuine believer to begin with."

"Then what could we say of your present assurance based on your love for God, His people, and your hatred for sin?" I asked.

The conversation stopped. The answer is obvious. My colleague's present assurance would be false assurance because his subsequent fall and continuance in sin, according to his understanding, would prove he never was a believer. When would such a person know that he is going to heaven or not? Not until he dies is the only consistent answer.

THE CORRECTION

> But whoever keeps His word, truly the love of God is perfected in him. By this we know that we are in Him (2:5).

It is so very important to keep this verse connected with the previous. In 2:3 we get the main message of 2:3-11. There are three responses, the first of which is in 2:4. The response is an error, of which 2:5 is the correction. The "but" tells us what follows will be contrasted to what preceded. The point is that the promise here is not that if someone keeps His word he will gain entrance to heaven or that he is proving that he has already been given his ticket to heaven. Keeping God's Word in 2:5 is not a sign of regeneration; it is a sign that someone loves God. It is straight out of the Upper Room Discourse, where a bunch of believers are huddled up listening to their Coach tell them that He's about to be transferred to another city. They are going to have to make a go of it on their own. What is their response? Same as any group when the coach or pastor leaves to go to another city: "But don't you care about us? Don't you love us?" They aren't sitting around wondering what will happen to them when they die. They are having heart problems. So, Jesus speaks to their need: "Let not your hearts be troubled ..."

Perhaps we can assign some spiritual meaning to this secular song:

> There is Someone standing behind you;
> Turn around, look at Me.
> There is Someone to love and guide you;
> Turn around, look and see.
> There is Someone who'll love you forever;
> Turn around, take My hand.
> There is Someone who really loves you;
> Turn around, look at Me.

If you don't sense the love of God in your life, perhaps it's because you are not keeping His commandments. You are going down the wrong path in life. But He's right behind you, and He really loves you. And He says, "Turn around. Look at me." He's really there.

The word "keeps" (*tereō*) means a lot more than "has." When we look again at John 14:21 we see that *keeping* His commandments is more than *having* His commandments. "He who *has* my commandments and *keeps* them ...." Loving God is much more than just having His commandments. It's keeping them. This word *tereō* also means more than to just obey. The basic meaning contains the concept of "watching over, guarding, protecting," as a shepherd watches over his sheep, or to protect and guard as a banker his treasure, or a fiancé his bride-to-be.

One of our church members saw a good illustration of this recently. In a trip to visit her parents in Quincy, Illinois, she was looking out the front window and saw a baby bird which had fallen to the ground. The mother bird was coming down to feed it. She would feed the birds still in the nest high above the ground, but then she would swoop down to feed the baby bird on the ground. This went on day after day. Finally, Carol observed that the mother bird was building a protective tent over her baby bird so people passing by wouldn't notice it. Her ritual was to feed the little birds above and then fly to the ground and stay a few feet from the "tent" to watch for predators she might have to ward off should they get near her hidden, baby bird. She was protecting, she was guarding, and she was keeping her little one safe.

That's what "keeps" means here. It's more than just to have a Bible or several of them in your house. It's to treasure God's Word, to guard it, to protect it. It's to realize that many people in this world don't have this book, have never had a chance to listen to its promises or read it for themselves. Outside of our personal relationship with Jesus, His Word may be the most precious thing we have from Him. The person who "keeps" His Word is the one who has His Word, guards His Word, and cherishes His Word. In this person the love of God is perfected.

In the person who so keeps God's Word the love of God is *perfected*. This word (*teteleiōtai*) is another verb in the perfect tense in 1 John. Thus it could be translated "is perfected," "has been perfected," or "is made complete." It's love in its fullness, its completeness. And John says what is in a state of completeness here is the "love of God." This could mean our love for God or God's love for us. We would suppose it means our love for God since this is God's primary love language, that is, the main way He says we can show that we love Him. But we can't rule out His love for us here, since He promises in John 14:21 to love us back if we demonstrate our love for Him by keeping His commandments. Reciprocal love—our love for Him and His love for us. Love is most complete when it is reciprocated. If it is all one-sided, it is still imperfect and incomplete.

CONCLUSION

In 1 John 2:3 we have the beginning of a new principle for fellowship. We saw right living (dealing with our sins) in 1:5–2:2. In 1 John 2:3-11 John looks at right loving (dealing with our brother). Here we learn that God's primary love language is to keep His commandments (2:3). If someone says he is close to God but does not keep His commandments, that person is simply lying (2:4). But when a person chooses to keep God's commandments (Word), the love of God is made complete in that person.

Boris Kornfeld was a Jewish doctor living in Russia.[6] He grew up with Stalin as his god. He was not a practicing or religious Jew. He did not believe in Yahweh of the OT. He believed in Lenin and Stalin and socialism. But one fourth of the people in the USSR were informants for the KGB. It was a terrorist state. Someone turned Boris in. For what, he did not know.

The KGB whisked him off to one of their prison camps. He was dumbfounded. He had not been unloyal to the state. Lenin and Stalin had been his gods. But there he was, a prisoner of the state. And as he sat in his prison camp and saw the senseless death and destruction, he threw off the shackles of socialism. He deposed the god he was worshipping. He said to himself, "This philosophy of life cannot be true."

Kornfeld listened to other prisoners who had put their hope in Jesus. For a Jew to give up socialism or communism was one thing, but for a Jew to embrace Jesus was another. But as he kept hearing about the peace and hope Jesus could bring, Boris decided to try Jesus as his Messiah. Not long after trusting Christ he was in a Bible study and listened to this passage, which gives God's love language: "If you love me, keep my commandments." Boris Kornfeld knew he wasn't keeping God's commandments. On a regular basis he, as a doctor, would sign slips of paper saying a prisoner was fit to go back to work in the mines when he knew this particular prisoner was not fit at all. This is how the prison system thinned their ranks. They just sent an unhealthy person into hard labor. They rarely came out of the mines alive.

Boris had signed hundreds of these slips, these death warrants. He thought, "I'm not going to sign any more slips." He knew he was somewhat protected because they needed doctors, but he really did not know what would happen to him.

Soon after this decision he saw an orderly stealing bread. He could overlook it, but decided the right thing to do would be to report it. The orderly was put into the stockade for three days, but when released Boris knew the orderly would be out to get even.

He began sleeping in the hospital to avoid being caught in the darkness by this vengeful orderly. But he also sensed a new freedom he had not experienced before. He thought, "Being willing to die for Christ, being willing to be punished for Christ—all of a sudden I had a freedom and a peace I had never known in my life. I sensed God was with me and I sensed that He loved me in a special way, and all of a sudden I had to tell someone. I had never told anyone what had happened to me."

A young man came in who had cancer in his intestines. Boris operated on him, and as the young man was coming out of the anesthesia, Boris said to himself, "I've got to tell this fellow." So as the young man was coming out of anesthesia and still in a stupor, Boris began to tell his story of peace and of love and of forgiveness of sins through Jesus Christ. The young man missed most of the beginning of Boris's story because of the drugs lingering in his system, but then he began to understand, and Boris just couldn't stop talking. He went on talking for an entire day.

That night the orderly found Boris and hit him on the head six times with a plasterer's mallet, killing him. But the message Boris shared never left the heart of the young man who heard it, the only man who ever heard Boris's message. This message of good news, peace, and forgiveness burned in his soul until he too trusted in Jesus Christ as his Savior. Ultimately, this young man, cured of physical cancer and the cancer of sin, was released from that prison. He went out and told the world the story of the *Gulag Archipelago*. His name? Nobel Prize winner Alexander Solzhenitsyn.

"If you love me, keep my commandments."

---

[1] Gary Chapman, *The Five Love Languages* (Chicago: Northfield Publishing, 1992).

[2] Chuck W. Colson, *Loving God* (New York: Harper Collins Publishers, 1983).

[3] William Perkins, *The Works of that Famous and Worthy Minister of Christ in the University of Cambridge, Mr. William Perkins*, 3 vols. (Cambridge: n. p., 1608-09), 1:115.

[4] John Owen, *The Works of John Owen*, 16 vols., vol. 3: *A Discourse concerning the Holy Spirit* (1677; reprint, Edinburgh: Banner of Truth Trust, 1965), 45-47, 226-28.

[5] Michael Eaton, *No Condemnation* (Downers Grove, IL: InterVarsity Press, 1995), 9.

[6] Colson, 19-25.

LESSON 6 "GOD'S LOVE LANGUAGE" I JOHN 2:3-5

1. What do you think your "love language" is? Are you able to identify the "love language" of ones you love?

2. Why do you think it is important to consider God's love language? What does Colson identify as God's love language? How does this relate to John 14:15?

3. What commandment(s) may John have in mind in 2:3?

4. On pages 80 and 81, Dave presents an extensive grammar lesson. As you review his points, what do you conclude?

5. How does the Lord respond to us when we "keep His commandments"? Is this response uniform or individual? Explain.

6. Summarize Dave's position on "fruit inspection."

7. What is your understanding of 2:5, "God's love is truly made complete in Him or perfected in Him"?

8. As you conclude this lesson with the story of Alexander Solzhenitsyn, share your thoughts about how you will "keep His commandments."

– 7 –

THE BIGGEST BARRIER

1 John 2:6-11

I suppose the most depressing aspect of September 11 for me was to realize that in a world where we can send men to the moon, there is so much ignorance and hatred within the human race that grown, educated men could fly to their own deaths and take thousands with them and think themselves heroes in the process. It doesn't seem we have come so far since WWII.

And this kind of hatred is not isolated to Muslim terrorists. When I was in Bulgaria, if I spoke English and they found out I was from America, they would ask me to leave their shop. If I spoke German, it was OK to buy because they could not tell I was from America (in Germany they would know from my accent). They were furious at NATO and the Americans for interfering with the religious war which had been going on for centuries in their neighboring Slavic countries. When I went to Kenya, I was told that the same kind of tribal hatred which spawned tribalcide in Rwanda could break out in the more civilized country of Kenya. We find it in Ireland with the religious wars, in India with its caste system, and in Korea with their hatred of the Japanese.

This kind of hatred in our modern world seems out of sync with our advances in technology and supersonic travel. And it is depressing. But, in a sense, those of us who spend a great deal of our time in the church can understand it. After all, it is the world. How can we expect any better of the world? And we can even be a little bit smug, thinking that the church has been sanitized of hatred. And to some degree that is true. We don't read in the newspapers of an attack from First Baptist Houston on First Methodist. The Presbyterians are not sending anthrax letters in the mail to the Episcopalians. It's true—there is no open warfare between churches.

But if I read 1 John correctly, hatred hides behind the pew of every church just waiting for a chance to infect Christians with a disease so debilitating I am going to suggest it is our biggest barrier we face when it comes to getting close to God. What's that barrier? It is one brother hating another or one sister hating another. Of course, since hatred is a sin, it is a specific example of the various sins we might encounter in 1:6–2:2. Any known sin is a barrier to fellowship with God. But my experience as a pastor has shown that this sin of hating one's Christian brother may be the hardest barrier of all for believers to overcome.

Unfortunately, this sin is one of the easiest to rationalize. After all, they hurt us unjustly. There is no defense for what they did. The father abused his daughter—no defense. The former husband deserted his wife—no defense. The Christian partner cheated his brother out of the company—no defense. While I was in Germany, I ran across an old acquaintance who went to Germany as a missionary, spent his life building a successful ministry, only to have the board of that ministry run him off in his old age. Now he remains in Germany, dying of cancer, full of bitterness. Is that the way we want to go out? Carrying the torch of bitterness and hatred toward some Christian who has unjustly hurt us somewhere in the past? Oh, do so if you must, but don't do so and tell us how close you are to God. This passage in 1 John 2 forbids it. Let's take a look at this, perhaps the biggest of our barriers when it comes to getting close to God, and see if there is some way to bust the barrier.

THE LIGHT OF LOVE

> He who says he abides in Him ought himself also to walk just as He walked. Brethren, I write no new commandment to you, but an old commandment which you have had from the beginning. The old commandment is the word which you heard from the beginning. Again, a new commandment I write to you, which thing is true in Him and in you, because the darkness is passing away, and the true light is already shining (2:6-8).

We need to say a word about John's use of the word "abide." To "abide in Him" is a claim to fellowship. It is another of his terms he exports from the Upper Room Discourse. In John 15, for example Jesus says, "As the Father loved Me, I also have loved you; *abide* in My love. If you keep My commandments, you will *abide* in My love, just as I have kept My Father's commandments and *abide* in His love. These things I have spoken to you, that My joy may remain in you, and *that* your joy may be full" (John 15:9-11). Notice the close connection with abiding, love, and full joy. Does this remind you of the stated purpose of this letter: full joy (1:4)? First John is the flower that grows out of the soil of John 13–16.

Even the old/new commandment comes out of John 13–16. We just referenced John 15:9-11. But look at what immediately follows: "This is My commandment, that you love one another as I have loved you. Greater love has no one than this, than to lay down one's life for his friends. You are My friends if you do whatever I command you" (John 15:12-14). The subject matter of 1 John 2:6-8 follows John 15:9-14 with exact correspondence. This is no coincidence. The reason is that the subject matter is the same: intimate fellowship (love and friendship).

Jesus' first reference to the commandment previously given is in John 13:34, the commandment to love each other as He loved us. This commandment is old in that they have heard it from the beginning (meaning the beginning of Christianity). But the commandment to love one another is also new, not in the sense of time, but in the sense of its freshness. The world does not know this love. It is not a sign of relationship, but fellowship, because by this all men will know we are His disciples (fully devoted followers of Jesus).

This present world is viewed by John as darkness. Jesus is the light and has brought light to every man (John 1:4-9). Part of His light is His incredible love, a love the world does not understand, a love which offers forgiveness instead of vengeance. God gave us these words in a Middle Eastern world which only understood an eye for an eye and a tooth for a tooth. They had been taught to love their neighbors but hate their enemies. The concept of turning the other cheek and loving their enemies was completely foreign to them.

The modern problem between the Jews and the Arabs in Israel did not begin with the Jews taking the lands from the Arabs in 1948. At first the Jews tried to purchase land. Sir Moses Montefiore bought land in 1855 for Jewish settlers at Safed, just north of the Sea of Galilee. Then in 1884 Sir Rothschild bought more land for the S. Russian Jews near Ekron. The Jews were trying to escape false accusations brought against them in Russia, Romania, and Bulgaria that they were using the blood of Christian children in their Passover bread. But before 1900 ever rolled around, there were attacks against the Jews by the Arabs in settlements around Jaffa and Tiberias.

Larry Collins' book *O, Jerusalem*, tells how the hatred between these groups escalated until wholesale slaughters of Jewish and Arab villages took place, with raping and castrating on both sides in order to increase the humiliation of the victims. The conflict which continues today knows nothing of the love of Christ. It is a land controlled by Satan and his minions of darkness. Their only hope is the love of Christ.

Yes, Dion Warwick was right when she sang, "What the world needs now is love, sweet love." But she was wrong when she sang, "It's the only thing there is just too little of." The Imperials hit the mark when they sang, "There's a shortage on coal and a shortage on wheat, there's a shortage on corn and a shortage on meat; there's just one thing there is no shortage of—there's no shortage on God's mercy; there's no shortage on God's love."

When we love each other as God loves us, we become lighthouses of His love in this dark world. His light, which will shine around the world when He returns, can shine even now in this dark world. But why is it we so seldom see this kind of love? The biggest barriers of bitterness seem to be within families.

A son had done everything he could do to disgrace his parents. Not only had he deeply insulted them and disgraced their names in the community, when he set out on his own, things did not get better. He wound up spending much of his life in prison. He never did learn to read, so he never got nor expected a letter from home during those years. He didn't even know if his parents were still alive when he was released. But he didn't have anywhere else to go, so he bought a train ticket and headed east from California back to the valley in Oklahoma where he used to live. The train tracks went right by the old family farm, so he'd had another prisoner compose a letter to his parents before he went back home. It gave the instructions to tie a white ribbon around the old oak tree near the tracks if they wanted him to stop by; otherwise, he would just stay on the train and keep on going.

As they got near his old homestead the ex-con couldn't bear to look out the window. Just the thought of seeing a bare tree was more than he could stand. So he asked the passenger next to him to let him know if he saw a white ribbon tied to the great big oak tree near the tracks. When they got near the right place along the route, the ex-con looked away. He waited ... and his fellow passenger grabbed his right leg. "Look," he said excitedly. "Look ... the whole tree is covered with white ribbons." His parents let the light of Christ's love shine through them, a love that is able to overcome former hurts and injustices. The cross of Jesus was a tree covered with white ribbons, flags of forgiveness for all of my sins and yours. The ex-con came home. Their forgiving, Christ-like love transformed his life.

When we love each other in this way, we enter into a deeper fellowship, a closer intimacy with Christ than we knew before. In 1 John 1:5–2:11 we see two levels of fellowship: 1) Fellowship from confession in 1:5–2:2; and 2) Fellowship from loving in 2:3-11. The latter leads us to a deeper fellowship because in this the love of God (God for us and us for God) is perfected (2:5).

But in contrast to the light of love (2:6-8) is the darkness of hate (2:9-11).

THE DARKNESS OF HATE

> He who says he is in the light, and hates his brother, is in darkness until now. He who loves his brother abides in the light, and there is no cause for stumbling in him. But he who hates his brother is in darkness and walks in darkness, and does not know where he is going, because the darkness has blinded his eyes (2:9-11).

The opposite of love is hate. The opposite of light is darkness. Just as loving each other opens the floodgates of fellowship, so hating one another closes them. Thus, the biggest barrier to deep fellowship with God is to hate one's brother. Verses nine and eleven tell us four things about one who hates his brother:

1. He is in darkness;
2. He walks in darkness;
3. He can't figure out God's will (he doesn't know where he is going);
4. He is spiritually blind (the darkness has blinded his eyes).

Obviously, this is not a believer who is close to God. Those who think the book is about the "tests of life" would say this person is not even a believer. After all, he is in darkness. But remember, words like "abide" and "walk" are not terms for relationship, but for fellowship. Yet even if one says that is begging the question, how can an unregenerate man hate his Christian brother? He doesn't have a Christian brother if he's not a brother. It takes a brother to hate a brother.

But what is this hatred? What does it look like? It has different looks:

1. Cold Indifference—this is what we do to people who hurt us. We give them the cold shoulder. We have no intention of giving them the time of day until they come to us and seek an apology for what they have done to hurt us. I met an elder in a church where I was a Spiritual Life speaker who was grieving over broken fellowship with his son and daughter-in-law, who lived a couple of states away. The

parents had not talked to the children or even been able to visit for Christmas. They weren't allowed to see their grandchildren, and they were hurting big time.

"What happened?" I asked.

This elder explained that they had been visiting these relatives in their home, had gone to Wal-Mart to buy something, and he had bought a small gift for his wife. His daughter-in-law chided him for always buying gifts for his wife as though he could buy her love. The elder said he was so taken aback he didn't know how to respond, so he just smiled and said nothing. Well, it turns out that was it.

"What was what?" I asked.

His daughter-in-law thought he had smirked at her when she confronted him with his materialism, so she was not going to speak to him or allow them in their home or to talk to their grandkids until this elder had apologized to her. Cold indifference. That's her revenge.

2. Vengeance—oh, we have lots of ways to do this, don't we? Often this manifests itself in Christians as passive-aggressive behavior. She hurt me, so I won't take out the trash, help with the dishes, or give her any verbal or physical affection.

3. Unforgiving Spirit—how easily this barb gets under our skin. Have you been hurt? Has someone in your past rejected you in such a way that you still hurt when you think about it? Do you become critical of people in your past the minute their names are mentioned? Have you worked hard all your life not to become like your parents? Are there people in your past upon whom you would enjoy taking revenge? Have you made a pastime out of scheming about how you could get back at them or embarrass them publicly? If you can say yes to any of these questions, then you wrestle with an unforgiving spirit.[1]

4. Bitterness (Heb 12:15)—usually beneath an unforgiving spirit is a root of bitterness which Hebrews warns can defile many of those around us and keep us from enjoying the forgiving grace of God. Robert Lewis, in his series called *Quest for Authentic Manhood*, challenges every man to look for what he calls the Father Wound and the Mother Wound. According to him an early wound in our lives often explains much of the dysfunction in our adult lives when it comes to personal relationships.[2]

5. Hatred has any number of different looks. These are just a few. John makes this much clear. A believer cannot know God's will for his life

while he walks in hatred. He is blind to God's path for his life. He must be, for God's path leads him to the brother/sister he hates. Forgiveness leads him back to the light. Indirectly, that's what verse ten is telling us. Two things from this verse are true of the believer who loves his brother: 1) He abides in the light; and 2) There is no cause of stumbling (skandalon = barrier or road block) *in him*.

In other words, hatred of our brother is a big barrier, a stumbling block to intimate fellowship with God. And this barrier is *in us*. We must get rid of it before we can be close to Him and discern His direction and will for our lives.

Here are some steps to remove this ugly stumbling block from within us:

1. Write down the ways the other person has hurt you.
2. Write down a few of the main ways you have hurt Christ.
3. Thank Christ for His forgiveness.
4. Ask Christ to give you a spirit of forgiveness.
5. If possible, sit down with the one who hurt you, explain what you have been holding inside, and tell them you would like to forgive them.
6. If you cannot sit down with them, forgive them as Christ has forgiven you (Eph 4:32). "In Him" is the key. God forgave you *in Him*. You can forgive *your brother* because of your common *position in Him*.

   A brother who is quite a contrast to me in many ways looked up at me (we are even much different physically) and said, "You know, Dave, we're gonna have to live with each other ... FOREVER!" laughing as he said it. Of course, that is true. He was making a subtle appeal based on our eternal position in Him.
7. Don't confuse forgiving with trusting. You can forgive in a moment based on your common position in Christ, but trust must be rebuilt over time. This distinction has tripped up many people. A Christian wife is commanded to forgive her wayward husband (or vice-versa), but she is never commanded to trust him. He needs to earn her trust.[3]

CONCLUSION

Charles Stanley talks about some family problems that developed after he had been in ministry for some time in his book *The Gift of Forgiveness*. Some distance had developed between him and his children. He said he needed to do all he could to rebuild some of these broken bridges. He sat down with his two children, a son and a daughter. His son Andy was twenty-five at the time, already in full-time ministry.

Stanley said, "Kids, I want us to be as close as possible in the latter years of my life. So I want you to tell me if there is something I have done to you in your youth to damage our relationship you haven't already told me about." He says when you ask such a question of your children, you better be seated and ready for their answer. His son Andy opened up and said,

"Dad, there is one thing I can't get out of my mind, and it has affected our relationship."

"What's that, son."

"Do you remember when I was a young teenager and I fell in love with the piano, but I couldn't read music, so I just played chords? I was trying to get better and better, so I just pounded out chords all day long. Remember that?"

"Well, ya, I remember that," replied Stanley.

"Do you remember a day when you walked by while I was pounding out these chords over and over, you started up stairs, stopped, and yelled out, 'Andy, can't you play anything else.' Do you remember that, Dad?"

"Well, no, son, I can't say that I do."

"Well, can you remember that you have never heard me play since?" asked Andy. "I resolved in my heart that I would never, ever play my music in front of you again, and I'm twenty-five years old now and an accomplished musician, and you've never heard me."

Charles Stanley said he humbled himself and said, "Son, I am so sorry for that off-hand comment that has caused you so much pain and damaged our relationship all through these years. Will you please forgive me?"

Of course, his son did forgive him, and now they work together, collaborating on many of his books.[4]

Toward the end of her life in WWI, a Belgian nurse named Edith Cavell became famous for helping the Allied soldiers escape the German army. She was finally caught and executed. Her last words before they killed her were these: "I realize that patriotism is not enough. I must have no hatred or bitterness toward anyone." True, unless you don't want to be close to God.

---

[1] A few of these questions were taken from Charles Stanley, *The Gift of Forgiveness* (Nashville: Thomas Nelson Publishers, 1987), 26.

[2] Robert M. Lewis, *The Quest for Authentic Manhood* (Little Rock, AK: Fellowship Bible Church, n.d.), 10-11.

[3] Charles Stanley, *The Gift of Forgiveness: Put the Past Behind You and Give...* (Nashville: Thomas Nelson Publishers, 1987), 169-170.

[4] Stanley, 22.

LESSON 7 "The Biggest Barrier" I John 2:6-11

1. What is your first thought or reaction to Dave's assertion that the "biggest barrier" to our getting close to God is "one brother hating another or one sister hating another" (p. 91)?

2. How do you see this most? In local congregations? In the larger "Church" with many denominations? Among different religious sects or religions?

3. Why is this "sin" so easy to rationalize?

4. Compare John 15:9-11 with I John 2:6-14. What is Dave's point about the meaning of "abide"?

5. What are the metaphors for the "world" and "love"? Can these metaphors coexist?

6. Dave identifies two levels of fellowship. What characterizes each level?

7. List the ways that "hating one's brother" may look. Dave has identified four. Can you add others to the list?

    1.

    2.

    3.

    4.

    5.

    6.

    7.

8. Are some of these ways more problematic for you than the others?

9. Have you ever tried any of the steps on page 97? What might keep you from trying one of the steps?

10. Reflect on Dave's comment, "Don't confuse forgiving with trusting."

11. Summarize Dave's conclusion to this lesson.

WEAPONS OF OUR WARFARE

1 JOHN 2:12-14

Afghanistan is a long way from the Alamo, and our Special Ops troops are a long way from Davy Crockett. While Davy might have fought with a single shot musket and a Bowie knife, our modern warriors are something to behold. Our Special Ops use the M4 carbine as their basic rifle. It is a shortened version of the standard U.S. M16 with a detachable 40mm grenade launcher mounted beneath the barrel. The weapon can also mount a night-vision sight, and some troops carry night-vision goggles with them. A soldier on sniper duty might lug a heavy Barrett .50 caliber rifle that can hit targets a mile away with a bullet stout enough to pierce armor. Some soldiers also carry the M3 Carl Gustav reusable launcher, a bazooka that fires antipersonnel and antitank rockets.

But the weapons of a believer don't change. The battle may take on different looks, but the enemy is the same, and our weapons of warfare are the same.

First John is primarily a book about our fellowship, not our relationship; our condition, not our position. But it would be a mistake for us to think there is no connection between our position and our condition. In Paul's letters he is careful to give us truth about our position (Eph 1–3, for example) before he confronts our condition (Eph 4–6, for example). He knows that the key to improving our condition is a proper understanding and belief in our position.

John is preparing his people for war. In the Christian life we face three primary enemies: the world, our sin and the devil. John dealt with our sin in the first part of this letter. But we are at a transition point. He is about to lead us against our other two opponents, the world and the devil. We will confront the world in 2:15-17 and the devil in 2:18-25. But to get us ready for the battle, John goes back to remind us of some truth about our position. In doing so, he reminds us of three weapons we will need to be victorious warriors in 2:12-14.

OUR FIRST WEAPON: FORGIVENESS OF SINS

> I write to you, little children, because your sins are forgiven you
> for His name's sake (2:12).

We might wonder about the word order in addressing the 1) little children, 2) fathers, and 3) young men. We would expect it to be: little children ⇒ young men ⇒ fathers, if we were trying to emphasize a progression in growth. But the words are switched up in order to look back at ground already covered and look forward to the battle ahead:

> **Little Children**—Forgiveness; ground covered in 1:5–2:2.
> **Fathers**—Intimacy (deep knowledge of God); ground covered in 2:3-11.
> **Young Men**—Victory over the Evil One; ground covered in 2:15-28.

John addresses the believers as a whole here to tell them that their sins have been forgiven for His name's sake. Two features of this promise tell us that John is turning his spotlight on their position in Christ. One is the perfect tense of *forgiven* (*apheōntai*). Here we see completed action in the past with results that continue right up until the present. If we want to put the emphasis on the present results of this completed action from the past, the present tense translation of the NKJV ("are forgiven") captures that emphasis. On the other hand, it could be John is emphasizing the completed action in the past, in which case a good translation would be "have been forgiven." This may be the better way to look at it. They are about to go into battle. Nothing is more important for the Christian warrior than to be assured of his secure standing before his Maker. Positional truth does just that. They *have been* forgiven—completely! This would be a very strange claim for John to make for readers who need to use this book for "tests of life" or relationship. That (their position/relationship), says John, is secure.

A second feature of this promise also points back to their established position or relationship with Christ. The forgiveness mentioned here is linked with the *name* of Christ. This looks back to the time when these believers first put their faith in Christ. As 1 John 5:13 points out, those who have believed in the *name of the Son of God* are those who possess eternal life.

What we are looking at in 1 John is forgiveness on two levels. One is the forgiveness we receive because of our position in Christ (Eph 1:7 and Col 2:13), which John mentions here; the other is the forgiveness we receive in our condition when we confess our sins (mentioned in 1 John 1:6–2:2). It is essential to see that *the latter is based on the former*.

Let me give you an illustration. When my oldest daughter started to drive, she took Driver's Ed. She was a good student and did well, but on the day she got her license, she was quite nervous. That night she wanted to go to Young Life, and she borrowed our brand new family car to do so. I was out that evening myself, so when I got home I happened to notice that the left side of the car was smashed in and the left rear view mirror was missing. I walked into the house and didn't say a thing. Because I have an eternal relationship with my daughter, she has advanced forgiveness for anything she might do to injure herself, me, or our family. We had insurance on the car, so it was no big deal, but I knew she was going to be feeling very badly.

I just sat downstairs and turned on the TV, waiting for her to come to me. Well, an hour went by. She didn't come. She knew I was home because she could hear the TV. But it wasn't until her older brother called out, "Christie, Dad's home. Don't you have something to tell him?" that she came down the stairs. It was hard for her to get up the courage to tell me. But she finally did so, and started crying.

I said, "Christie, don't worry. You are not hurt, you didn't hurt anyone, and the car can be fixed. But even if we didn't have insurance on the car and you were hurt, I would forgive you. You're my daughter. My love for you will last forever. Come here."

She came over and I gave her a big hug. Then I said, "Hey, why don't we go out and practice some more." So with me at her side, we went out driving.

Christie was still somewhat shaken by her first mistake, so she made a second. She drove at thirty miles per hour right through a four-way stop. A policeman saw and stopped us. As he walked up to the car, he had his head cocked with a curious expression on his face. He said, "You just didn't see it, did you, honey?"

You see, most stop signs are run out of defiance (in which case the car is often accelerating) or with a "roll stop." But Christie just cruised right through at the accepted speed limit for the area. From this the policeman deduced that she had not seen the stop sign at all. He was merciful and only gave her a warning. Now her second mistake wasn't as bad as the first, and she learned even another lesson. Slowly she developed her confidence as a driver and hasn't had any more wrecks (to my knowledge) since then. She is now thirty-one years old.

But in order for Christie to relax and become a better driver, she had to know that she was forgiven for her mistake. And not only the first big mistake, but she had to know that I wasn't going to revoke my forgiveness for the first mistake when she made the second mistake. Because of our father/daughter relationship, because of her position in our family as my daughter, she already has advanced forgiveness for any mistake she may make in life. That's what we call positional forgiveness, forgiveness because of our relationship. But in order to feel close to me, she needs forgiveness not only in her position, but also in her condition. That's why she needed to tell me what she had done, and that's why I reassured her of my love and forgiveness and gave her a big hug. It is very important to see that *our fellowship is based on our relationship.*

My daughter and I have an eternal relationship. As such, she has advanced forgiveness for anything she might do to hurt me. This is relationship forgiveness. But when she does something wrong, she needs to come to me and confess that wrong in order to be reassured of my love and forgiveness. This is fellowship forgiveness. The latter is based on the former. *Any child needs the assurance of relationship forgiveness over and over!* In the passage before us, John is reassuring his little children of God's forgiveness because of their eternal relationship with Him. A knowledge and assurance of this forgiveness is absolutely essential for them to feel confident as they go into battle against the world and the devil. A good soldier cannot operate at his best with the fear that a mistake or two will take him off the front lines.

The problem with positional forgiveness is that so many people have trouble believing and accepting it. Charles Stanley illustrates this with a story from his seminary days:

> One of my most memorable seminary professors had a practical way of illustrating the concept of grace for his students. At the end of his evangelism course he would hand out the exam with the caution to read it all the way through before beginning to answer it. This caution was written on the exam as well.
>
> As we read through the exam, it became unquestionably clear to each of us that we had not studied nearly enough. The further we read, the worse it became. About halfway through, audible groans could be heard throughout the lecturehall. By the time we were turning to the last page, we were all ready to turn the exam in blank. It was impossible to pass.
>
> On the last page, however, there was a note that read, "You have a choice. You can either complete the exam as given or sign

your name at the bottom and in so doing receive an A for this assignment."

Wow! We sat there stunned. "Was he serious? Just sign it and get an A?" Slowly, the point dawned on us, and one by one we turned in our tests and silently filed out of the room. It took the rest of the afternoon for me to get over it. I had the urge to go back and check with him one more time to make sure he was serious.

When I talked with him about it afterward, he shared some of the reactions he had received through the years as he had given the same exam. There were always students who did not follow instructions and began to take the exam without reading it all the way through. Some of them would sweat it out for the entire two hours of class time before reaching the last page. Their ignorance caused them unnecessary anxiety.

Then there were the ones who would read the first two pages, become angry, turn in their paper blank, and storm out of the room. They never realized what was available. As a result, they lost out totally.

One fellow, however, topped them all. He read the entire test, including the note at the end, but he decided to take the exam anyway. He did not want any gifts; he wanted to earn his grade. And he did. He made a C+, which was amazing considering the difficulty of the test. But he could have easily had an A.

This story vividly illustrates many people's reaction to God's solution to sin. Many are like the first group. They spend their lives trying to earn what they discover years later was freely offered to them the whole time. They spend years sweating it out, always wondering if God is listening to their pleas for forgiveness, always wondering if they have finally pushed Him too far. They hope God has forgiven them; they suppose He has. They do all they know to do to get forgiven. But insofar as God is concerned, they do not want to be presumptuous. So they live their lives with doubts.

Many people respond like the second group. They look at God's standard—moral and ethical perfection—and throw their hands up in surrender. *Why even try?* they tell themselves. *I could never live up to all that stuff.* They live the way they please, not expecting anything from God when they die. Often they decide there is no God. Their acknowledged inability to live up to His standard drives them to this conclusion. Instead of living under constant pressure and guilt, they choose to completely abandon the standard. What a shock it will be for them when they stand before God and understand for the first time what was available had they only asked!

Then there is the guy who took the test anyway. I meet people like him all the time who are unwilling to simply receive God's gift of forgiveness. Striking out to do it on their own, they strive to earn enough points with God to give them the right to look to their own goodness as a means of pardon and forgiveness. They constantly work at "evening the score" with God through their good works. "Sure, I have my faults," they say. "But God does not expect anyone to be perfect."

When it comes to forgiveness, there is no room for boasting in one's own ability. As we will see, forgiveness is not a team effort. It is not a matter of God's doing His part and us doing ours. Unlike my professor's test, in God's economy anything less than 100 percent is failing.[1]

When you go into battle, our enemy, the devil, will try to get you to wallow in the past. He will try to get you to focus on your past sins, your failures. This will weaken you when it comes to facing the world with its many temptations. So John reminds his readers that they have been completely forgiven. They stand before God in their position in Christ absolutely purified and secure. Their relationship is eternal. But that is only the first weapon John hands his soldiers. There are two more.

THE SECOND WEAPON: INTIMACY

I write to you, fathers, because you have known Him *who is* from the beginning. I write to you, young men, because you have overcome the wicked one. I write to you, little children, because you have known the Father (2:13).

In addressing the fathers, John uses a word and a tense which we have seen before. He says the fathers have come to know Him, *egnōkate.* We said back in 2:3-4 that the perfect tense in reference to a stative verb like "to know" indicated a deep, intimate knowledge. And now, as he prepares his warriors for battle with this world, he tells them that their close, personal relationship with Christ is one of their strongest weapons. The same claim of intimacy (known = *egnōkate* = perfect tense) is made for the little children.

Marriage counselors differ on many things in their approaches to healing marriages, but one thing they agree upon universally: a marriage is most vulnerable to attack from the outside when the couple stops spending meaningful time with each other. In fact, in his often referenced work *His Needs, Her Needs*, Willard Harley, Jr., gives some fascinating numbers. He claims to have counseled with 10,000 couples by the time of the writing of his famous book. In questioning these couples he asked each how many hours they averaged in meaningful time with each other alone during the year before they married. These couples averaged fifteen hours per week.[2] Then he asked these same couples with marriage troubles how many hours per week they were spending together completely alone. Usually the answer was less than two. Then he asked these same couples if they would have married each other if they had known ahead of time that they would be only spending a couple hours or less of meaningful time together each week. Of course, the answer was no. So in trying to heal these relationships, one thing they work on the hardest is to work back toward those fifteen hours a week.

Do you think it is any different with the Lord? In Revelation 2 the same author who wrote 1 John talks about church members who used to be in love with Jesus, but they had lost their initial love, the love they had for Him in the early days of their Christian lives. Oh, they had their theological "t's" crossed and their "i's" dotted, but their devotional fires were burning very low. His counsel? Do the first works. Go back and do the things you were doing when you were madly in love with Jesus. You know what? I bet that means spending time alone with Him. You can do all kinds of church work, just like a mother and father can do all kinds of things for the family with the kids, but if you don't spend meaningful time alone together, you will lose the intensity of your love relationship.

It took two and a half years after becoming a believer for me to "get serious" about serving Christ. And the moment I joined His army to go into daily battle for Him and His kingdom, I discovered what seemed like a new enemy and a new need. Satan did not like my entering God's army. He intensified his attacks. Thus I found the need for more spiritual food and preparation for each day's battle. My most important time each day became my early devotional time with Him. Without it, failure knocked on my door before ten in the morning.

One of my favorite paintings of Jesus is called "The Good Shepherd." It pictures Christ as a shepherd out in a pastoral setting, surrounded by sheep. But what interests me most about this painting is not the Shepherd as much as the sheep. The Shepherd is holding one little lamb in His arms; a couple more are nudging up against His robe. Others are lying in a cluster not far away. Further back in the scene we see some sheep grazing. But it's the sheep far from the Shepherd that concerns me. Some are looking this way and others that way. They are not at all close to the Shepherd. These are the sheep which are in danger of the wolf and the lion. These are the sheep which could fall off a cliff and break their bones. If you were doing a self-portrait to touch up this painting, where would you place yourself in the picture?

THE THIRD WEAPON: HIS WORD ABIDING

> I have written to you, fathers, because you have known Him *who is* from the beginning. I have written to you, young men, because you are strong, and the word of God abides in you, and you have overcome the wicked one (2:14).

John piqued our interest in the *young men* in 2:13 when he claimed they had overcome the wicked one. The word for *overcome* is another one of these verbs in the perfect tense (*nenikēkate*), which speaks of a complete victory somewhere in the past. This would be another strange claim to make for people whose salvation John questions. It's another word of encouragement based on their position in Christ. In 1 John 5:4 he will remind them that it was their initial faith which gave them victory over the world. When they put their faith in Him, the victory was complete and the results are still there: these people have a secure standing before God in heaven. He encourages them to move out into battle against this world in their condition based on their complete victory in their position.

But now John moves into the present tense and encourages these young men by saying they *are strong*. They are ready for battle. But woe to them if they forget what makes them strong. It is the Word of God abiding in them. Once again John is drawing from the Upper Room Discourse. In John 15:7 he speaks of us abiding in God's Word and God's Word abiding in us. He speaks of this kind of person as being more than a casual believer in Him, but rather a disciple (8:31 and 15:8). When we abide in His Word, we bear fruit and prove that we are His disciples, His fully devoted followers.

Paul describes the disciple with God's Word *abiding* in him in Col 3:16-17 this way: "the Word of Christ is dwelling in him *richly*." Note the parallels between this and Eph 5:18-21:

Colossians 3:16 17	Ephesians 5:18-21
"The Word Dwelling Richly"	"Believer Spiritually Filled"
Teaching ... in psalms/hymns/songs	Speaking ... in psalms/hymns/songs
Singing with grace ... to the Lord	Singing and making melody ...
Giving thanks ...	Giving thanks ...
	Submitting one to another ...

Although Eph 5:18-21 may describe community worship, the parallels between the two passages tell us that Paul must see a connection between being filled with God's Word and being spiritually filled or filled with God's Spirit.[3] In the very next chapter of Ephesians it is the Word of God that is emphasized in the armor of God. The vast majority of the Greek manuscripts of the NT begin Eph 6:16 with the words *epi pasin*, which mean "on top of all." This gives us an important clue to the imagery in Paul's mind when he writes this challenging section on spiritual warfare.

Paul imagines a cohort of Roman soldiers sitting around in their tents waiting for action. Suddenly, the bugle calls them to arms. They are not dressed for battle. Perhaps they have been lying around playing board games. So they don their *inner* armor first: their girdle (leather belt) to hold hand weapons, their breastplate, and their shoes. Then comes the *outer* armor ("on top of all" these other pieces of armor): the shield, the helmet, and the sword.

Now it is interesting that this list of armor contains only one offensive weapon. Everything else is defensive (excepting the shoes, which are neutral). The sword is the only weapon that can be used for offense. And the most common shield during the time of Paul was not small and circular, but large and rectangular. If you saw a Roman soldier coming at you, about all you would see would be this shield, some feet, and the top of a helmet. So, how is the enemy to overcome this soldier? Answer: he must knock the sword out of the soldier's hand.

The sword for the Christian is identified as the Word of God. This is the weapon that can be used for defense and offense. It's the soldier's most important weapon—his first line of defense and his only weapon of offense. When our enemy the devil can take the Word of God out of the hand of a believer, he is well on his way to victory. Conversely, when God's young men and women wield God's Word, there is good reason to expect victory over the enemy.

Here in 1 John 2:14 John tells us what makes the young men strong. It is the Word of God abiding in them. And when we actually go into battle against the world in 2:15-17, we will see the same temptations the devil put in front of Jesus, and we will be reminded that it was through God's Word abiding in Jesus that He found victory against the temptations of this world.

CONCLUSION

While going to seminary, I was privileged to play on a commercial league basketball team with Doug McIntosh, who had two NCAA national championship rings from his college days at UCLA under John Wooden. In the middle of seminary Doug was called upon to join our Olympic team where he won a gold medal. I asked Doug a lot of questions about John Wooden, the man who may be the greatest coach who ever lived according to his record of national championships.

Doug said when the UCLA Bruins went into a game, they just knew they would win. Wooden had their confidence level so high, defeat just didn't enter their minds as an option. Doug attributed this confidence to three things. First of all, they were convinced they had the best coach. He never got rattled. He had covered every detail in his research on the other team. He knew every option for pressure situations at the end of a game. Secondly, Wooden had his team practice their shooting when they were tired. Most teams had their shoot-around at the beginning of practice. Doug said Wooden had them run full-court drills for the first forty-five minutes of practice. Then he let them practice shooting with tired legs. This way they were confident that their shooting would improve during the last ten minutes of the game, just as the shooting of most teams was getting worse because of being tired. And thirdly, because they worked on the fundamentals right up to the championship game so they wouldn't choke under pressure. Even on game day of the national championship, Wooden had them going over the fundamentals of passing, pivoting, and shooting free throws. His theory was that under pressure, your mind won't work quite as well. So, he wanted his team so grounded in the fundamentals of the game that everything came by instinct when the score got tight or they were behind at the end of a game.

In a way, John is doing the same thing with his readers in 1 John 2:12-14. They are about to face the world. The championship of the world is on the line. So he goes back to the fundamentals—positional truth and God's Word. His team needs to be grounded in these fundamentals so they won't have to think about them under pressure. As someone has said, "Victorious warriors win the battle and then go out to war, while defeated warriors go out to war and then seek to win the battle."

---

[1] Charles Stanley, *The Gift of Forgiveness: Put the Past Behind You and Give...* (Nashville: Thomas Nelson Publishers, 1987), 43-45.

[2] W. F. Harley, Jr., *His Needs Her Needs* (Grand Rapids: Fleming H. Revell, 2001), 66.

[3] Lack of the word "holy" is very unusual if the reference is to the Holy Spirit. This construction (*en pneumati* = *en* + dative case) is often translated as an adverb, *spiritually* filled.

LESSON 8 "Weapons of Our Warfare"

1. Review the book of Ephesians. Explain the "truth about our position" (Chapters 1-3) and "confronts our condition" (Chapters 4-6) quotes on page 101.

2. What are the Christians' three primary enemies?

3. What meaning do you attach to the three groups John addresses (page 102)?

   Little Children -

   Fathers -

   Young Men -

4. Why does John list the three groups in this order rather than in chronological order?

5. What do you understand about Dave's statement of "forgiveness on two levels" (page 102)?

6. What most impresses you about the Charles Stanley account (pages 104–106)?

7. What would you identify as the prime factor in "intimacy"? How does this relate to our relationship with the Lord?

8. Where would you put yourself in the Good Shepherd picture? Where would your focus be?

9. Read Col.3:16-17 and Eph.5:18-21. How do these scriptures relate to the believer's third weapon and how do they support John's connecting the believer's strength with the "word of God"?

10. Do you see any parallels to Jesus' interaction with the devil in Matthew 4:1-11?

11. Dave concludes this chapter by reminding us of the two fundamentals that enable us to be victorious in our "warfare." What are they?

9

THE PERMANENT AND THE PASSING

1 JOHN 2:15-17

Years ago I was riding up a chair lift in Beaver Creek, Colorado with a young man who had made it big with Compaq, retiring when he was thirty-nine.

I asked him if he had diversified his stock since retiring. He said, "No. You always have the problem of what to reinvest your money in. Compaq has always been good to me."

The next day we were riding up the lift again and he said, "I should have diversified yesterday. The stock fell about six points."

Turns out our initial conversation was the high point for Compaq. A year later the stock was around fifty percent off (around twenty-five).

"Have you diversified yet?"

"No," he said. "Compaq doesn't have any debt. It will be back."

Another year later and Compaq was at ten.

"Should have diversified," he said.

Of course, he was not the Lone Ranger. During the melt-down of the high-tech stocks billions of dollars were lost. Then the 9/11 tragedy didn't help much. If you were living in Houston, where I live, you saw Compaq, Enron, and Continental slide down that slippery slope toward non-prof-itability. The fortunes of many people went with them.

Where can you find a safe, secure investment? If you think it's difficult in the financial markets, what about your life? Where can you invest your life into something that is safe and secure, something that's permanent instead of passing? We can look out at this world and see the things that are passing away. People pass away. You live a century or less and then you're gone. It's governments, social causes, and nations which seem to endure. But as Haddon Robinson says, "That kind of thinking is all mixed up. We easi-ly fall into the trap of thinking that human beings are part of the passing. They live for less than a century and then they are gone. What is lasting, we suppose, are the causes for which they give their lives—civilizations, cultures, nations, governments. They were here when we arrived; they will go on when we die. They count greatly. But from God's point of view that kind of thinking is all mixed up. It's men, not causes, who will exist some place forever."[1]

Or, to put it in the words of C. S. Lewis, in *The Weight of Glory*: "There are no ordinary people. You've never talked to a mere mortal. It is immortals whom we joke with, work with, marry, snub, exploit—immortal horrors or everlasting splendors." So it's people, not cultures, who last forever. Just that simple observation should tell me if I want to invest my life into something permanent and not passing, somehow I need to connect my life to God, who is eternal, or people, who last forever. And I believe that is exactly what 1 John 2:15-17 is trying to tell us.

Oh, yes, this is a book about fellowship, not relationship. It's a book about finding intimacy with our Maker, our God. We have seen that there are three primary barriers to this intimacy we so desire: 1) personal sin; 2) hating a brother; and 3) enemies in the world. We have looked at John's introduction to the first two barriers. Our outline (see pages 21-22) shows us we are now in his introduction to the third barrier, our enemies in the world.

It has been said that Christians face three enemies: sin, the world, and the Devil. By sin we mean that internal principle of sin which John dealt with in 1 John 1:5–2:2. Our other two big enemies are not internal; they are external—the world and the devil. John addresses both enemies in this third wave on dealing with barriers to fellowship with God (2:12-28). After preparing his soldiers by going over the fundamentals of their position in Christ in 2:12-14, John wants to deal with the world (2:15-17) and the devil (2:18-28). In this lesson we look at our enemy, the world. John gives us three principles to help us overcome the world after our initial faith in Christ (5:4): 1) a principle of love (v. 15); 2) a principle of lust (v. 16); and 3) a principle of life (v. 17). Let's look at the first principle.

A PRINCIPLE OF LOVE

> Do not love the world or the things in the world. If anyone loves
> the world, the love of the Father is not in him (2:15).

The first principle we must learn in order for us to avoid sinking our lives into something which is passing instead of permanent is to know a basic principle of love. What is that principle? *We cannot love God and the world at the same time*—the love of one displaces the love of the other in our hearts. Love is capable of only one primary focus.

Jesus put it this way: "No servant can serve two masters; for either he will hate the one and love the other, or else he will be loyal to the one and despise the other" (Luke 16:13). And James said, "Whoever, therefore, wants to be a friend of the world makes himself an enemy of God" (Jas 4:4).

Frankly, I don't know of another culture in this world where there is a greater temptation to love God and love the world at the same time other than ours. Oh, of course, most of our nation probably could care less about loving God, but for the Christians in our nation there is more of an opportunity and a temptation to try to love God and the world at the same time. But God hasn't changed, His Word hasn't changed, and herein He gives us a timeless principle of love—we can't love God and the world at the same time.

James tells his readers that friendship with the world is enmity with God (Jas 4:4-5). He calls Christians who want to love the world and God at the same time spiritual adulterers and adulteresses. It makes the Holy Spirit jealous. Suppose, for example, a husband comes home one night and tells his wife that he has a sweetheart on the side. How would she respond? Not well, we can be sure of that.

But perhaps he explains, "Oh, honey, it's not so bad. I'm going to split time between both of you fifty-fifty."

How is his wife going to feel about that? But suppose he says, "Well, I'll tell you what, I'll go the extra mile for you. I'll just give her one day a week, and you get the other six."

She's gonna say, "Get out of town, Charlie Brown. I'm not gonna share you with anybody."

Does God have feelings less intense than our wives or husbands? But many Christians don't even split time with God and the world. They pay their respects to God on one day of the week (and only part of that day), while they devote the other six days of the week to the world. Now is it possible to live such a life and still go to heaven? Of course, it is. We can do nothing to deserve our eternal life. Worshipping God seven days a week could not open the gates of heaven for us. But living six days of the week for the world and one day of the week for God will not endear us to His heart; in other words, we will not be very close to Him. He won't feel loved by us; therefore, why should He manifest His love for us? That's what this letter is all about—getting close to God. It won't happen if we try to love God and the world at the same time.

Having established a principle of love, John now goes on a principle of lust.

A Principle of Lust

> For all that *is* in the world—the lust of the flesh, the lust of the eyes, and the pride of life—is not of the Father but is of the world (2:16).

If loving the world is a temptation that can destroy a believer's intimacy with God, then we better know the make-up of the world. That's what John gives us in verse sixteen. The first two areas where the world operates are in the lust of the flesh and the lust of the eyes. This word for *lust* (*epithumia*) is almost always an evil desire in the NT, something which is deceitful (Eph 4:22), defiling (2 Pet 2:10), and controlling (1 Pet 1:14). We never read of these lusts in heaven. In heaven there will be no lust because there will be no sinful nature within us.

These lusts are deceitful to the believer himself. They can trick him into thinking what is wrong is right. "How can it be wrong if it feels so right?" is a siren song from this world system. Or lust can turn something good into something bad. It is good to give money to the Lord's work. But a person can get so consumed with earning money that it becomes a god, when all the while their own lusts have tricked them into thinking how great it will be to have all this money to give to God's kingdom. Here are some good test questions for that lust. When the bottom line is drawn, are you laying up more treasure in heaven than on earth? Does your will leave more to your children than to charities?

I had a businessman in my church who came to me after closing a business deal and said he felt guilty because he was making so much money. How should he deal with this? I told him I had a friend who was a seminary graduate who had also made about fifty million dollars in the last ten years. I suggested we have lunch with him to find out how he deals with it. We did just that.

My wealthy friend said he had a small trust fund for his two daughters. He said the worst thing he could think of was to leave a bunch of money to his daughters. He had seen other girls who had inherited wealth and the problems it brought in terms of their suitors. He didn't want to wish that on his kids. Instead, he and his wife had willed their fortune to Christian charities. That, he said, is how he kept his heart pure.

Well, these lusts can not only deceive us, they can also control us, consume us. I ran into the power of lust last summer when I was on vacation in the middle of Washington State. I stayed for a few days with some friends who had retired from government work to host a bed and breakfast near Wenache. Their place was popular since it enjoyed sunshine most of the summer. When Seattle is still under clouds, people flee to the east just for a peak at the sun.

I have a number of weaknesses when it comes to food: milk chocolate covered caramels, Blue Bell Homemade Vanilla Ice Cream, and … cashews. This couple had set out some mixed nuts for their guests. Over the years I have become adroit at sifting the cashews out of a bowl of mixed nuts. Embarrassingly, I lifted every cashew from this small bowl of nuts. As this dear Christian couple was going to bed, the hostess assured me I could partake of anything they had in their refrigerator or kitchen in general. I told them I thought I would stay up a bit longer to do some reading. My plan was to find the store of mixed nuts and replace the missing cashews in the small bowl before my hostess could notice they were missing.

So about 11 p.m. I slipped down the stairs from the loft where I was reading and began hunting for the nuts. I looked through every cupboard. No nuts. I said to myself, "Nuts!" No, just kidding, but I did keep searching. Frantic from embarrassment I was finally relieved to find the source of nuts in their pantry—a huge container of nuts, enough to supply at least twenty small bowls. As I began to look for suitable cashews to resupply the small bowl I had depleted, I thought, "Well, with such a large supply, what's a few more?"

An hour later I had eaten every cashew in the big container. That takes work. You have to turn the container upside down, shake, sift, surf, all kinds of things to get those cashews. But now the once nearly full container looked odd. It was about a fifth gone, but no cashews whatsoever. I thought, "This looks odd. I better eat the almonds." Well, you can imagine the rest. After three hours I had eaten the entire container of nuts. I turned the container around to see how many calories I had consumed. According to the calories per serving and the number of servings in the container, I had just eaten around 6,800 calories.

Oh, my gosh. Now what? Here I have come into someone's home as a guest, been offered carte blanche in their kitchen, and I have abused the privilege. If I was embarrassed before when I had polished off the cashews in a small bowl, how do you think I felt now? I wanted to find a small hole to crawl into. Well, it was Saturday night, or Sunday morning by this time. I decided I would just pray about it in church that morning and figure out a plan.

I did that very thing. I decided when they went to Sunday night church; I would beg off to do some more reading. After all, I am a preacher, and I am on vacation. I don't have to be in church every time the doors open, do I? Then I would drive to the store, find where they bought the container of nuts, replace the empty container, and they would never know the difference.

So off to the store I went when my host couple went to Sunday night church. But alas, I could not find the kind of container they bought with a gallon of nuts. What to do? I know, I thought, I'll just buy several other small cans of nuts and pour them into the old, empty container. So this I did. But after I had filled the old container and looked at the cashews on top, I thought, "These cashews don't look as big as the others. I better eat the ones off the top so they won't notice." As I began to repeat the process from the night before, I realized there is a serious lust problem here. I felt incredible shame and guilt. There was only one thing to do.

When the couple came home from church, I confessed the whole sordid mess.

She consoled me and said, "Well, Dave, I said you could have anything in our kitchen. You didn't need to replace those nuts."

"Oh, yes I did," I replied. "Otherwise, I couldn't look you in the eye."

And that's the way it is with lust, and sometimes our lusts are quite as harmless as cashews. The power of this world and the devil lies in darkness. While I was sneaking around in the dark gobbling up all the nuts in the house, lust and the devil were reigning over me. I had to come to the light to break that power, just as we saw in 1 John 1:5–2:2.

The Scriptures teach that the Christian has three primary enemies who often operate as a team. Like a fisherman, the devil dangles this world with its lusts in front of us. Our sin(ful) nature goes for the bait. Once we are hooked on this world, the devil draws us into his net. Genesis 3 gives us an example where the devil worked together with this world to defeat Eve, while Matthew 4 gives us an example where the devil dangled the world in front of Christ but lost. What was one of the differences between the devil's victory and his defeat? Let's see.

In Genesis 3 we have a two round boxing match between Eve and two tag-team boxers: the devil and his partner the world. Now, as a side note, it seems to me that Adam has gotten a bad rap lately. I have read a number of authors who tell us in no uncertain terms that Adam stood right beside Eve while the serpent was talking to her and did nothing to defend his wife. Now, I don't wish to minimize Adam's part in our fall. Romans 5 gives him the full responsibility for what happened since (1 Timothy 2) he was not deceived when he sinned and Eve was. But to think he just sat there while Eve had this running conversation with the tempter is not warranted from the text. I realize that Gen 3:6 says Adam was with his wife when she ate and fed him the apple. But it does not say he was with her in Gen 3:1-5.

The first round of the two round match is in Gen 3:1-5. I see this as the devil's work (speaking through the serpent). After he weakens Eve's resolve to obey God in these verses, he leaves the ring and tags his partner, the world, to come in and finish the job. So the serpent weakens Eve with three blows in round one; the world finishes her off with three more in round two (3:6). Notice that each blow from the serpent is some sort of attack on the Word of God. First of all, the serpent *doubts God's Word*: "Has God indeed said, 'You shall not eat of every tree of the garden'?" Then he *denies God's Word*: "You will not surely die." Finally, he *distorts God's Word*: "For God knows that in the day you eat of it your eyes will be opened, and you will be like God, knowing good and evil."

After these three blows, to the midsection, the nose, and the chin, Eve is too weak to resist the world. Do you see all three components of the world system mentioned in 1 John 2:16 here in Gen 3:6—the lust of the flesh ("she saw that the fruit was good for food"), the lust of the eyes ("that it was pleasant to the eyes"), and the pride of life ("and a tree desirable to make one wise")? Adam and Eve did not have a sin(ful) nature as they were originally created. There was no evil within them. That came with their fall. But they did have two enemies: the devil and the world. Both of them worked in tandem to knock Eve out.

So even today the devil's primary attack is against God's Word. The rise of Rationalism erodes the confidence of Christians in the infallibility of God's Word. As their confidence diminished, so did the strength of Christianity in the western world. Even today the strength of the Christian Church is not in Europe and the Western Hemisphere. It's in Africa, Indonesia, and China where attacks against the Word of God by skeptics have not weakened the Church. Remember from Ephesians 6 that our enemy's first tactic in order to defeat the Christian soldier is to knock the sword of the Spirit (God's Word) out of his hand. The young men of 2:14 were strong because the Word of God was abiding in them.

The Word of God was abiding in Jesus when he was tempted by the devil (Matt 4:1-11). When the devil appeared before Christ, he was again twisting and distorting God's Word in his attempt to disarm Jesus. He dangled the world system in front of Christ: 1) Lust of the flesh—Jesus was hungry after forty days of fasting when the devil asked Him to turn the stones into bread; 2) Lust of the eyes—the devil showed Jesus this present world where Satan reigns if Jesus would worship him; and 3) Pride of life—the devil tempted Jesus to prove how important He was to God's kingdom program by throwing Himself off the temple just to watch the angels come to rescue Him. But in each case Jesus overcame the temptation of the devil and this world by His own resolve to be faithful and by a proper use of God's Word: "It is written ... It is written ... It is written." The principle of overcoming lust is transparent: *The war against the lusts of this world is won by God's Word!*

Dr. Lewis Aberson, the Chief Pathologist in Akron, Ohio, has written an article in which he says there is more child abuse in America due to starvation than to battering. Can you believe that? After an autopsy of a six month old baby who died, Aberson and Samuel Gerber (the coroner) said these words: "While battered babies are seemingly a more common occurrence, this is not so. It is only that battered babies are more easily detected. Infant starvation is rarely seen while in progress. Acts of omission, whereby the child is deprived of adequate nutrition, are equally or more dangerous to the child's welfare and equally culpable under the law."

Can you believe that in this country parents would starve their own children to death? Heinous and shocking as this crime may be, are we as shocked by the fact that spiritual malnutrition of children is far more rampant than physical malnutrition? There are churches all across our nation where the people in the pew rarely if ever even hear God's Word, let alone feed upon it. I grew up in a church like that. Never heard anything from God's Word except a two minute reading now and then, and that was always from the Sermon on the Mount. No wonder I got sucked into the world system while still quite young. *The war against the lusts of this world is won by God's Word!*

Three principles we need to understand in order to have victory over the world: 1) A principle of love—we can't love the world and God at the same time; 2) A principle of lust—the war against the lusts of this world is won by God's Word; and 3) A principle of life.

A Principle of Life

> And the world is passing away, and the lust of it; but he who does
> the will of God abides forever (2:17).

If our life is tied to the things of this world (lust of the flesh, lust of the eye, and the pride of life), then our life will simply slip away without any lasting significance. But he who does the will of God abides forever. Isn't that good news? He doesn't say you have to be a preacher or a missionary for your life to have a lasting significance. The qualification for a life that lasts is to do *the will of God*. You can do the will of God every day. Every day can count for eternity. Every day can be significant in His eyes—whether you are a child, an older person, a man, or a woman. Wow! What an equal opportunity system.

But what is God's will? That's not tough. It's keeping His commandments. When I keep His commandments, I prove that I love Him. The love of God is perfected in me (2:5). No, it's not tough to figure out that God's will is to keep His commandments, but keeping them is another matter, especially when things are not going so well. That's why Jas 1:12 promises the crown of life (in this life, not the next) to those who endure in the Christian life in the midst of a trial, for this is how they prove that they love Him. And Rom 8:28, a verse of great comfort, doesn't say that all things work together for good to all Christians, but rather for those who love God. When the Lord is the love of our life, we can interpret the crushing blows from this world in light of eternity, thus giving us a perspective that can help us endure these trials. What are some practical examples of doing the "will of God"? Here are just a few:

1. Finding a life partner without premarital, physical involvement (1 Thess 4:3-6).
2. Staying in a difficult marriage when your emotions are screaming at you to run away.
3. Not being dishonest and unethical in your business even though it would mean a lot more money in your pocket.
4. Not taking that promotion which would double your salary but would also cut your family time in half.
5. Not cheating on the test even though it would help you get a better grade.
6. Not lying to your parents about the parties you're going to and your experimenting with drinking and marijuana.

7. Honoring your mother and father even though their ideas seem so old fashioned and out to lunch.

8. Giving the gift of love to a child who seems impossibly difficult.

So what is the principle of life John shares in 2:17? It's an old adage, but it is captured by the thrust of this verse:

Only one life, 'twill soon be past;
Only what's done for Christ will last.

CONCLUSION

In our war with the world John has given us three principles to help give us the victory. The principle of love says we cannot love God and the world simultaneously. The principle of lust tells us that the war against the lusts of this world will be won by God's Word. And the principle of life is to orient our time on earth around things that will last forever, such as doing God's will. If we are doing His will, we are keeping His commandments; if we are keeping His commandments, the love of God is perfected in us.

Perhaps the most lasting thing we can ever do is to pass the love of Christ along to others. This love can take many forms. It may be to share the good news with a neighbor. It could be adopting an orphaned child. Or it could be what Chad did in third grade.

Chad was new to the neighborhood. He was shy and didn't make friends as quickly as some others. The winter season was coming on, and Chad still didn't have many new friends. Each day after school Chad's mother would listen for the school bus, and then walk to the window to watch for Chad. Most of the children would get out first, laughing and cutting up, arm in arm. Then Chad would come, usually a few steps behind the others—always alone. Thanksgiving and Christmas came and went, but Chad was still pretty much alone.

Then one day in the New Year Chad looked at his mom and said, "Mom, I've got a great idea. Valentine's Day is just a month away. We have about thirty kids in my class. I would like to make a valentine for each one of them. I want each of them to know how much I love them."

Chad's mother thought to herself, "Oh, Chad, I wish you wouldn't do that. It could be a very sad day for you."

But she couldn't discourage that kind of enthusiasm, so she helped Chad buy all the necessary paste and paper and other cut-outs to make some valentines—thirty, one for each member of his class and his teacher.

Well, Valentine's Day came, and Chad bounced up from the table at breakfast, put on his coat and gloves, grabbed his lunch box and his paper sack with all the valentines. He popped out the front door with a skip in his step to meet the bus.

His mother scratched the frost from the front window and watched. "Boy, this is going to be a tough day. I better make some cookies and have some milk ready for Chad when he gets home."

That afternoon she heard the school bus turning around the corner right on time, so she went back to the front window to watch as the kids got off the bus. There they came, laughing and cutting up, valentines under their arms—they had really done well. And here comes Chad, a few steps behind, as usual, not a single valentine in his hand or under his arm. He was walking a little faster than normal, and his mother thought, "Oh, he's going to cry." She opened the door for him and said, "Chad, mommy made some cookies and milk for you. They are sitting on the kitchen table."

But Chad just marched right by that table toward his room, saying as he went, "Not one, mom ... Not a single one ... We didn't miss a single one. Everyone in the room knows how much I love them."

> You see,
> It's not a song until it's sung;
> It's not a bell until it's rung;
> And it's not love until it's given away.

Love is like the magic penny. The more you try to give it away, the more it comes back with extra to spare. Love is the most lasting thing we can do because God says, "Now abide these three: faith, hope, and love; but the greatest of these is love." Don't trade what's permanent for that which is passing.

---

[1] Haddon Robinson, "The Permanent and the Passing," *Sermon on 1 Corinthians 13* (Dallas: Believer's Chapel, 1981).

LESSON 9 "The Permanent and the Passing" I John 2:15-17

1. Did you have any reaction to Dave's discussion of what lasts on page 113 and particularly with his conclusion on page 114, "It's men, not causes, who will exist some place forever"?

2. What parallels might you draw or what differences do you see between financial investments and "forever" investments?

3. Dave presents three principles to help us overcome the world. How can these principles be implemented in our culture? What interferes?

    A Principle of Love 2:15. (Read Luke 16:13 and James 4:4)

    A Principle of Lust 2:16. (Genesis 3:1-5) Define lust.

    In Genesis the serpent used three steps in tempting Eve (page 119).

    1.

    2.

    3.

4. Can you find these same temptations in verse 16? How were they also present in Jesus' temptation in Matt.4:1-11?

5. What are some of current examples to support Dave's contention that "the devil's attack is against God's Word"? (See John 1:1.)

6. A Principle of Life 2:17. What is the qualification for a life that lasts? What is God's will?

7. Pages 121 and 122 list some practical examples of doing "the will of God." What other examples would you add to the list?

8. When you review your life this week (month, year), how do you seem to be doing with respect to "only what's done for Christ will last."

9. How can we be more like Chad? (See the Conclusion.)

– 10 –

GIVE ME THAT OLD TIME RELIGION

1 JOHN 2:18-27

Wwhat American can ever forget the ghoulish grin of Osama bin Laden as he celebrated on tape the destruction of the WTC, sprinkling his glee with the praising of Allah? It all made me sick to my stomach. Then my mind drifted back to the taped interview of a Pakistani youth who was about to cross into Afghanistan to fight for the Taliban. He said it was really the Jews who had orchestrated the implosion of the Twin Towers in order to turn world opinion against the Muslim people and Osama. Given his background and the brainwashing he has received, I could understand his statements.

But then I thought of a former NBA star named Chris Jackson. He had broken the single game scoring record of Pistol Pete Maravich at LSU and went on to lead the Denver Nuggets for several years. Then he converted to Islam, changed his name, and refused to stand during our national anthem. He walked over and sat on the bench in protest. After several trades he is out of the NBA. He has built his own mosque in Louisiana where he leads prayer to Allah five times a day. In an interview he claimed there is no evidence that Osama is responsible for the New York tragedy. He said, "As a matter of fact, there were thirteen Jews found standing on top of a building filming the event, and I think the Jews are responsible." The interviewer looked at Chris Jackson and said, "You know, you're crazy." And this American citizen said, "Well, that's what they said of our great prophet Mohammed, and I am glad to identify with him."

As I watched that documentary, I asked myself, "How does something like this happen right here in our country?" Then I remembered 1 John 2:18-28, part of the third barrier to our becoming close to God. We have already looked at two of the three barriers John wants us to see. The first barrier was our own sin (1:5–2:2). The second barrier was hatred toward our brother (2:3-11). We might say that both of these barriers exist inside the Church. But in 1 John 2:12-28 John moves outside the Church. We face enemies outside the Church who can keep us from getting close to God. Two enemies: the world and the devil. After preparing us for battle (2:12-14), John shows us how to have victory over the world, our first enemy, in

2:15-17. Now he's ready for us to face our second enemy, the devil. And make no mistake about it. When you see thousands of innocent lives being destroyed in the name of God, the devil is at work. Where you see lies and delusion, drugs and pornography, murder and suicide—need we say it?—the devil is at work.

But the devil's primary work, as we have seen, is to attack God's Word. False teaching is the devil's tool to lead people into spiritual destruction. That's why in introducing us to the principles of fellowship in 1 John 1:5–2:28 John spends more time on the third wave than the previous two: right living—dealing with our sins (1:5–2:2); right loving—dealing with our brothers (2:3-11); and right learning—dealing with our enemies (2:12-28). Even in dealing with our enemies, John uses three verses (2:15-17) to deal with the world, but ten verses (2:18-27) to deal with the devil and his false teaching.

As a pastor it amazes me, though it shouldn't, when I find out why people go to this church or that one. It's usually because of the music or the youth program or their family tradition or their friends. Rarely does it have anything to do with the teaching. Most folks don't know what their church teaches—"It's Christian, ain't it?" In fact, a survey used to promote church growth discovered the number one reason people choose a church is for ease of access; second is the nursery; third, the facilities; fourth, the preacher. Way on down the list was the tenth most important reason people pick a church: its teaching.

Now, there are a lot of really good churches with good, solid teaching. If someone leaves my church to attend one of these good churches, I wish them well and hope they continue to grow in grace and the knowledge of our Lord Jesus Christ. But when someone leaves to go to a church where I know the preacher does not believe the Bible is the infallible, inerrant Word of God, I want to yell and scream. One family made such a switch recently because they liked the beautiful music and the choir in the more liberal church. I wanted to ask them, "Have you ever thought of sitting down with the pastor of that church and asking him what he thinks of the Book of Daniel or Jonah or Genesis 1–11?" just to name a few important items. But I don't. I've learned after pastoring off and on for over thirty years that for most people "right learning" is pretty far down the line in their list of spiritual priorities. So I remain silent, and smile on the outside, while I hurt for them on the inside, as John did for his little children, for he knew that the antichrists walk among us.

THE AGE OF THE ANTICHRIST

> Little children, it is the last hour; and as you have heard that the Antichrist is coming, even now many antichrists have come, by which we know that it is the last hour. They went out from us, but they were not of us; for if they had been of us, they would have continued with us; but *they went out* that they might be made manifest, that none of them were of us (2:18-19).

The earliest movie I can remember about it was *Rosemary's Baby*, a sickening Hollywood production about *the Antichrist*. The *Late Great Planet Earth* by Hal Lindsey was selling millions of copies, and people everywhere were speculating that if this really is the end times, then the Antichrist must already be alive somewhere on Planet Earth.

It seems in almost every age believers in the prophecies of the Bible have speculated on who the Antichrist might be. In WWII it would be hard to deny that Hitler met many of the criteria with his attempt to wipe out the Jewish race.

But if we can believe John, his was an age when the Antichrist might well have stepped onto the stage of history. Usually the NT writers will speak of the "latter days" as the end times when the Book of Revelation with its mysterious prophecies would be fulfilled. John gets even more specific, doesn't he? He calls it *the last hour*. Or does he? Just what could be the meaning of the "last hour"?

Well, I don't think we need to make it any more complicated than the usual explanation for the "latter days." If we believe that Jesus Christ could have returned to the earth at any moment after His pouring out of the Holy Spirit, then we must also believe that we have been living in the last hour or the latter days ever since the Day of Pentecost. And we must again mention that the Bible is not a science book. It is not claiming to be a science book. But those of us with a scientific bent are also quick to point out that we do not believe that the Bible conflicts with any of the discoveries of modern science.

Take the "last hour," for example. Does this mean that the Bible has errors in it because the Apostles thought Jesus would return in their lifetime, but they were obviously wrong? Hasn't the "last hour" come and gone? As Zane Hodges points out in his commentary on 1 John,[1] the Bible predicted that scoffers would come in the last days who would deride believers for their doctrine that Christ could come at any moment (2 Pet 3:3-4). "Where is the promise of His coming? For since the fathers fell asleep, all things continue as they were from the beginning of creation." Peter explains that God does not view time as we do. He has a different perspective, or as Hugh Ross would say, a different dimension.[2]

Part of Einstein's theory of general relativity gives time a beginning and makes it relative. In our universe we speak of the dimensions of length, width, height, and time. Time is an effect which had a prior cause. Time exists in a universe of cause and effect. As Ross explains it:

> By definition, time is that dimension in which cause-and-effect phenomena take place. No time, no cause and effect. If time's beginning is concurrent with the beginning of the universe, as the space-time theorem says, then the cause of the universe must be some entity operating in a time dimension completely independent of and preexistent to the time dimension of the cosmos ... It tells us that the Creator is transcendent, operating beyond the dimensional limits of the universe.[3]

According to Ross, our universe operates in half a dimension when it comes to time. That is, time for us has a beginning, but it only moves forward along a single line. It is not reversable. But because God has no beginning, He can go forwards and backwards along the one dimensional timeline with equal ease. And since He is present everywhere at the same time and non-divisible, He views our half-dimensional, linear time from a much different perspective than ours. In fact, if God made time two-dimensional, then time would not be limited to a single line in the first place. It might look something like this.

God is not limited to the half-dimensional time of our universe, which has a beginning and only moves forward (B). Because He created (caused) time, He existed before time and is transcendent with respect to time. And because He has no beginning, He is not limited to the irreversible time of our universe. For Him time could just as well have been two-dimensional, which would allow for

God and Time

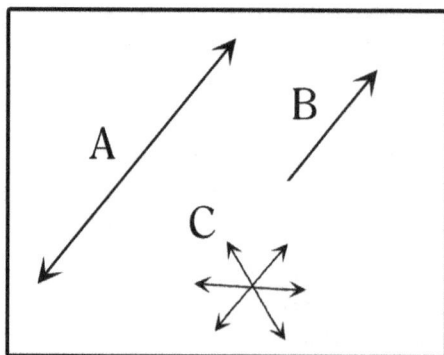

Diagram 4

an infinite number of directions for time and the possibility of existing before and after any single event in time (C). Of course, God can also exist on a time line parallel to the timeline of our universe and never the twain shall meet, unless, of course, He chooses to intervene into human history, or our universe before humans existed (Genesis 1). You might say our God is omni-temporal. All this to say that our God is not limited to our linear concept of "last hour." As Peter said, for God "one day is as a thousand years, and a thousand years as one day" (2 Pet 3:8).

As Hodges points out, in his gospel John uses the word "hour" literally as part of a day (John 1:39; 4:6; 11:9) and also of a time period of undetermined length that has special qualities (John 2:4; 4:21, 23; 5:25, 28; 16:25).[4] The second use makes the most sense here in 1 John. *The last hour* is a time period in the history of mankind where Satan and his forces are finally overthrown. Satan's primary human representative is the Antichrist. Though this period of time lasts over two thousand years of our linear time, to God, this may be just a blip on the screen of eternity.

Of course, John tells us there will be many antichrists before the ultimate Antichrist comes on the scene. He warns of these. The "us" is probably a reference to the apostolic church in Jerusalem. If the meaning of "us" were the Christian church at large, and specifically John's readers, there would be little need for the warning. The false teachers would have left the community of believers and would exist outside the church like the other false religions of the day. But these false teachers did leave the Jerusalem church and went about into the churches of present day Turkey (which were addressed by John in Revelation 2–3). Most of these false teachers were Judaizers (Jews who wanted the Christians to observe the Torah) who went out from the Jerusalem church because they were probably not believers at all.[5] Paul spoke of such "false brothers" who crept into the Jerusalem assembly in order to rob the new church of its freedom in Christ (Gal 2:3-4). Now John says they have spread out, and the believers to whom he writes must watch out. Well, what are they to look for? What is the sign of an antichrist?

THE APOSTASY OF THE ANTICHRIST

But you have an anointing from the Holy One, and you know all things. I have not written to you because you do not know the truth, but because you know it, and that no lie is of the truth. Who is a liar but he who denies that Jesus is the Christ? He is antichrist who denies the Father and the Son. Whoever denies the

Son does not have the Father either; he who acknowledges the Son has the Father also (2:20-23).

With this kind of warning we are wondering what to look for and how we will be able to recognize the sign of an antichrist when it comes. Well, John does tell us how we will be able to recognize this sign. He says, "You have received *an anointing* from the Holy One, and you know all things." Well, what does this mean? Certainly humans are not omniscient. This, however, reminds us of two similar statements Christ made in the Upper Room (John 14:26 and 16:13) where we were promised by Him that the Holy Spirit would *teach us all things* and *guide us into all truth.*

Two items of interest. The word for *anointing* is used only here in the NT. It speaks of a special enablement which comes from the Holy Spirit to discern spiritual truth from error. The word for *knowledge* here is different from the one we saw earlier in 2:3-4 and 2:12-14. It is the second use of *oida* (the first was in 2:11), a word that John now uses fourteen more times in the rest of the letter. It does not refer to experiential knowledge as does *ginōskō*. In the NT it almost always refers to "direct insight" into spiritual or divine truth, although this truth may not yet have been experienced. This truth is the result of the teaching and convicting ministry of the Holy Spirit.

This anointing is used for the "coating of a wall," like plaster. Its use seems to be that of a protective covering, such as in Psalm 23. At the same time, its religious use was to set someone apart for the sacred task to which one was called, such as a priest (Exodus 29–30). It had a figurative use as a symbol of endowment of the Holy Spirit for the duties of the office to which one was consecrated. So both the king (1 Samuel 10, 16; Isaiah 61) and the priest were anointed. It is interesting that only Christ is anointed before Pentecost in the Gospels, and, of course, He was a King-Priest. Only believers are anointed in 2 Cor 1:21 and 1 John 2. Putting it all together, the *anointing* was a protective setting apart by the power of the Holy Spirit for the high calling of serving God. In 1 John 2 it may well refer to the elders, who had this anointing to help protect the flock from false doctrine.

After explaining to his readers how they will be able to spot the sign of an antichrist, he now tells them what to look for: any denial that Jesus is the Messiah. In case this is not clear, he goes on to say the antichrist is the one who denies the Father and the Son. To make things even more serious, if one denies the Son, he also denies the Father. OK, let's bring this into the real world where we live today. Let's apply this lie detector test on Islam. What does Islam say about Jesus Christ? Is He the Son of God or not?

WHO IS JESUS CHRIST?

ISLAM	CHRISTIANITY
Not the Son of God; just a man	The Son of God; equal to the Father
Did not exist in any form before earth	Has existed from eternity past
Did not die on the cross	Died in our place on the cross
Did not rise from the grave	Rose from the grave

So there it is, the lie detector test given by John the Apostle. I was recently sent some mail by someone who listened to my message following 9/11 but who does not attend our church. He was embarrassed and infuriated that there are ministers of Christ who would infer or state straight out that Islam is a fraud and Allah is not God, that is, the same God we worship. He thinks we are all worshipping the same God, but we have different approaches. He thinks we need to respect the Muslim approach as an alternative approach to God. As I read his two letters, I was personally convinced this man knows the Lord. After his first letter, I responded and asked him to check out this passage we are in now and come to his own conclusion. He replied with more ammo, but never addressed this passage. Now I will ask you to do the same thing. If you were twelve years old, what does this passage say about any religious system that denies that Jesus Christ is the Son of God? Two things: 1) It is a lie; 2) It is from the Antichrist. That's another way of saying it is from the devil. But let's go on in the passage.

OUR ARMOR AGAINST ANTICHRIST

Therefore let that abide in you which you heard from the beginning. If what you heard from the beginning abides in you, you also will abide in the Son and in the Father. And this is the promise that He has promised us—eternal life. These things I have written to you concerning those who *try to* deceive you. But the anointing which you have received from Him abides in you, and you do not need that anyone teach you; but as the same anointing teaches you concerning all things, and is true, and is not a lie, and just as it has taught you, you will abide in Him (2:24-27).

Standing on the Faithful Promises

Let's get a grip on the real problem in these verses. Again, it is fellowship, because false doctrine can lead a Christian away from fellowship. That's why John tells them to abide in what they heard from the beginning, that is, the beginning of their Christian lives. It was truth that gave them new life. And only truth will allow them to enjoy their new life.

So in 2:24b John sets up a conditional statement: *if.* And this "if" in the original text meant they might do what he is asking of them, and they might not. He tells them to abide in that which they heard from the beginning. They might, and they might not (I wonder what this says about apostasy). If they do, then they will *abide* (John's key word for fellowship) in the Father and in the Son. Now let's remember the goal of this epistle stated in 1 John 1:3-4. It's that John's readers might have fellowship with the Father and with His Son Jesus Christ. These people came into the Christian life by believing that Jesus Christ was the Son of God who came to save them from their sins. Now, to enjoy their new life in Christ, they must abide in that very doctrine.

Then John reminds his readers of the basic promise which brought them into the Christian family: eternal life. That is God's promise which they received from the beginning. It always amazes me, for more reasons than I can count, why people want to make fruit inspectors of us in order to give us assurance of our salvation, especially in 1 John, when all John himself does is to take the people back to the promises of God. He as much as says right here that when you drift from the promises, you will lose your assurance, simply because you will stop abiding in what you heard from the beginning. You will begin to look at your experience, and that will cause either doubt or false assurance, since you may fall sometime in the future. Then the basis of your assurance has been destroyed.

The gospel promises do not change. Jesus is the Messiah. He is the Son of God. He came from the Father. "For God so loved the world that He gave His only begotten Son." The Antichrist and his representatives deny the deity of Christ. They also deny that salvation is a free gift. Islam teaches the scale-in-the-sky approach to Paradise. For the average Muslim, if he does more good than bad, he gets into Paradise. For the exceptional Muslim, if he dies in battle against the infidels, he gets an automatic pass. But Paul says even if an angel from heaven should preach a gospel other than the one he preached; let him be cursed until Jesus comes (Gal 1:8). That's strong language.

One of the letters I received reacting to my Sept 16 message denouncing Islam and its fundamentalist practitioners said I was preaching Christian hate, not love.

"We need tolerance and love," this letter advised.

Wait a minute. I believe we should love all unbelievers. But I also believe in loving God's children. And I love my physical children. If I say to them, "Stay away from drug dealers," does that mean I hate drug dealers? No. It means I love my children. Drug dealers can destroy their lives. And peddlers of false doctrine can destroy Christian lives.

There is a big difference between intolerance for false teaching and the destruction of people. During the days of the Reformation, all the parties in western Christianity were guilty of the destruction of people for false teaching. The Pope, Martin Luther, Melancthon, and Calvin—all of them sanctioned torture and killing of false teachers. The Anabaptists were killed by other Protestants because they did not believe in infant baptism. Zwingli was viewed by Luther as a heathen because he believed the elements in the Lord's Supper were symbolic. Thousands and thousands were burned at the stake or beheaded. Though Luther and Calvin believed Christ fulfilled the Law and the New Covenant superseded the Old Covenant, they retreated to Old Covenant laws to rid themselves of anyone who did not believe as they did.

There is no justification in the NT for this kind of treatment of people of other faiths. We are told to shun a heretic or a divisive person (the word used is *hairetikos*) after two warnings *in the Church* (Tit 3:10-11). False teachers were put out of the Church and accursed (Gal 1:8). But the NT never condoned killing people for different beliefs or even to be avoided *outside the Church*. False teaching *in the Church* is never to be tolerated. But we are to love the people *outside the Church* who teach and believe differently from orthodox Christianity. Paul says:

> But avoid foolish and ignorant disputes, knowing that they generate strife. And a servant of the Lord must not quarrel but be gentle to all, able to teach, patient, in humility correcting those who are in opposition, if God perhaps will grant them repentance, so that they may know the truth, and *that* they may come to their senses *and escape* the snare of the devil, having been taken captive by him to *do* his will (2 Tim 2:23-26).

It is not clear if this passage deals with those who are in opposition to correct teaching inside the church or outside the church, but it is very clear that the Pastoral Epistles (1 and 2 Timothy and Titus), which have more to say about sound doctrine than any other portion of the NT, do not condone the murder and destruction of those who do not hold to right teaching.

God's promises don't change. That's why the promises of God are the foundation for our assurance of salvation. People who want to teach that 1 John is a book of tests to determine whether you are a Christian or not have gone completely against what John himself uses as his source of assurance: the promises of God.

Standing against the False Prophets

Not only do God's promises not change; God Himself does not change. There are references in this passage to right learning from the Father, the Son, and the Holy Spirit. The attributes of God do not change. That's how we know that Allah is not the same God we worship. His attributes are not the same as the Father, the Son, and the Holy Spirit. How, for example, do we prove that the Father, the Son, and the Holy Spirit are equal and the same? We go to Their essence, Their make-up. That's the same way we show that men and women are equal before God. They have the same essence. Their functions may be different, but not their essence.

My wife thinks I may be losing some of my essence. As I get older, I am doing so many of what I call "firsts." This past week I was getting out of the car very slowly. Since I broke my hip, I have to get out more slowly. As I did so, I was careful to make sure that I had my keys with me, since one of my wife's favorite tricks is to lock her keys in her car. I wouldn't want to be guilty of that kind of fool dodgery. No, not me. So I felt in my pockets, but no keys. I looked back in the ignition, but no keys. Then I saw them in my left hand. Relief. OK, I got the keys. So I closed the car door, walked into the church, and proceeded down the hall to my office. When I reached my office, the door was locked. So I punched the automatic car door opener on my key ring. Nothing happened. My office door was still locked. So I punched the automatic opener again. The door was still locked. *Duuhhh.* When I realized what I was doing, I opened the door with my office key, went straight to the couch and laughed for several minutes. Yes, as time goes on, I may be losing part of my essence. But not God. He never changes (Heb 1:12; Jas 1:17). So, look at this chart on some of the attributes of Allah compared to the Father, the Son, and the Holy Spirit:

ATTRIBUTES OF GOD

FATHER	SON	HOLY SPIRIT	ALLAH
Omniscient (Matt 11:21)	Omniscient (John 1:28)	Omniscient (1 Cor 2:10-11)	NOT
Omnipresent (Ps 139:7 12)	Omnipresent (Matt 18:30)	Omnipresent (Ps 139:7)	NOT
Omnipotent (Rev 19:6)	Omnipotent (Matt 28:18)	Omnipotent (Gen 1:2)	NOT
Holy (1 Pet 1:15 17)	Holy (2 Cor 5:21)	Holy (Lk 11:13)	NOT
Truthful (Rom 3:4)	Truthful (John 14:6)	Truthful (1 John 5:6)	NOT

Essentially, there is little in the Koran devoted to the essence of Allah. This is because Muslims believe Allah is unknowable. He is so "out there" (transcendent) that he is incapable of a personal relationship with anyone. Consequently, little is revealed of his make-up, his essence. Recognizing this weakness, modern Muslim scholars have described him with many of the attributes of the God of the Bible, but none of this comes from the Koran. His essence is only known by his actions, and the Koran clearly teaches Allah is the author of evil and lies. As such, his essence lacks holiness and truthfulness. There are some passages in the Koran from which we might deduce the omni-attributes, but not with the clarity of the Bible when speaking of God.

CONCLUSION

According to John, right learning is very important. False teaching about the Father and the Son is one of the great enemies of Christian fellowship we face in this world. Fortunately, the Holy Spirit has given us an anointing to help protect us from these antichrists. This anointing is certainly given to the church leaders, if not all believers, to enable them to recognize the sign of an antichrist. That sign is a denial of the equality of the Father and His Son Jesus Christ and the messianic mission of the Son.

Well, this is the Christmas message, isn't it? The Father and the Son. "For God so loved the world that He gave His only begotten Son ..." But it's easy to get confused, isn't it? A little boy and girl were singing "Silent

Night," their favorite Christmas hymn, in church just before Christmas. This little boy couldn't remember one of the lines, so he sang, "Sleep in heavenly *beans*." His older sister quickly corrected him and said, "No, it's sleep in heavenly *peas*, not beans." Well, it's one thing to confuse the peas and the beans; it's quite another to deny the Father and the Son.

John Donne wrote:

> Twas much,
> that man was
> made like God before,
> But that God should
> be like man
> much more.
> This is the great news of Christmas: The Father sent His Son;
> That God became man;
> That the Word became flesh;
> That Light entered darkness;
> And the Rich One became poor,
> That the poor might become rich.

There's nothing new in this message. It's old time religion, but it's also good news religion. Give me that old time religion, yes, give me that old time religion. Give me that old time religion; it's good enough for me.

Ruth McBride Jordan graduated from Temple University at age seventy-six. She had raised twelve children in Harlem during the sixties. All twelve graduated from college and some went on to post-graduate degrees. Ruth was a Jewish Caucasian married to an Afro-American, a Baptist pastor who died shortly after the last of his children was born.

According to one of her children (James Jordan, who tells her story in *The Color of Water*), "Ma was utterly confused about all but one thing: Jesus … Jesus gave mommy hope. Jesus was mommy's salvation. Jesus pressed her forward. Each and every Sunday, no matter how tired, depressed, or broke, she got up early, dressed her best, and headed for church."

"Why do you cry so much in church?" James asked his mother one day. "Because God makes me happy … I'm crying 'cause I'm happy." Ruth McBride Jordan had that old time religion. It was good enough for Paul and Silas, and it was good enough for her.

[1] Zane C. Hodges, *The Epistles of John: Walking in the Light of God's Love* (Irving, TX: Grace Evangelical Society, 1999), 106-107.

[2] Hugh Ross, *The Creator and the Cosmos* (Colorado Springs: NavPress, 1993), 76.

[3] Ibid.

[4] Hodges, 107.

[5] The Judaizers fell into two categories: 1) Those who believed converts to Christianity must keep the Law of Moses to be justified, and 2) Those who believed converts to Christianity must keep the Law of Moses to be sanctified. Although those in the first category most probably were unbelievers (since their gospel was clearly wrong), those in the second category may well have been believers who were confused on the means of progressive sanctification. Legalism is a huge problem for believers, and we have no reason to think born again Christian teachers are immune to its attraction.

LESSON 10 "Give Me That Old Time Religion" I John 2:18-27

1. This lesson deals with the third barrier to our becoming close to God. What were the first two barriers?

    1.

    2.

2. What would you say is the third barrier? How is it different from the other two barriers?

3. Dave summarizes the three barriers as three "rights." List the three and the focus for each.

    Right _____ dealing with _____

    Right _____ dealing with _____

    Right _____ dealing with _____

4. Dave cites research that indicates "teaching" is not a high priority for people when they choose a church. What were your priorities in choosing your church?

5. Explain the concept that God is "omni-temporal" (page 129)?

6. How does the discussion of time relate to John's use of the term "last hour"?

7. In what sense does the scripture address both antichrists and Antichrist?

8. What seems to be a common theme of the antichrists (false teachers)? Identify some of the false teachings or false religions that flourish in our world?

9. In verse 20, John references an "anointing." What do you understand about the meaning of the word in this context?

10. What is the source of the believer's "assurance of salvation"? Why is it so important to understand this?

– 11 –

SPIRITUAL MONOVISION

1 John 2:28–3:3

When I was forty-eight years old, I needed to buy new contacts, but my prescription had expired, so I went to see an optician. After an eye exam he looked at me seriously and said, "You need bifocals."

I was incredulous. "This can't be," I assured him. "I see just fine. All I want to do is to renew my prescription."

He explained to me very patiently that from birth on we, meaning everyone, loses one third of a diopter every four years, so that by the time we are forty, we have lost one half of our power to focus. He said I can still see OK, but that my eye muscles are working overtime to focus.

The doctor convinced me. But I still enjoyed playing sports and didn't see how I could do that with bifocals. Then he introduced me to "monovision." With monovision one eye is fitted for reading, while the other eye is fitted for distance. The dominant eye is fitted for distance, and the brain adjusts over a period of about three weeks to switch back and forth between the eyes as the need may be. Well, it worked, and I have been using monovision ever since.

In the spiritual life we also need monovision. I'm not sure we can successfully navigate the treacherous waters of this life without keeping one eye on this world and another eye on the world to come, simultaneously. The two of them together will help us deal with the trials of this life. Our divine optician wants to help us with monovision. We may be tempted to argue with Him. We may want to tell Him we see just fine. We don't need this dual vision thing. His answer will be, "Trust me. You are straining without it. You will wear out your spiritual eye muscles until the events of this world become blurry and you can't see up from down. Let me give you spiritual monovision."

We will get a lens for distance vision (2:28), a lens for seeing up-close (3:3), and in-between a description of what it's like to have perfect vision (2:29–3:2).

ANTICIPATION OF HIS COMING— A LENS TO SEE FAR OFF

> And now, little children, abide in Him, that when He appears, we
> may have confidence and not be ashamed before Him at His
> coming (2:28).

Some have suggested that 2:28 is a theme verse for the entire letter.[1] What are some of the reasons they might think this? The first is the word *menō*. As we have suggested already, this word is a word about fellowship, not relationship. Just to reinforce our understanding here, let's look at John's use of the word in John 15:5-11. The word is used seven times in these verses and always connected to fruit-bearing, love, and answered prayer. Can you see that a word tied to fruit and love is a statement about condition, not position—fellowship not relationship? It is so important, once again, to see the context of the Upper Room Discourse. We are in the Holy Place. This is truth for believers, not unbelievers. And it's truth for believers whose hearts have been cleansed. Just as the hearts of the disciples were cleansed symbolically by Jesus as He washed their feet before He got into the deep truth of fruit-bearing in John 15, so in 1 John cleansing of the heart is the first thing John discusses (1 John 1:5–2:2) before he goes on to "abiding" truth.

But now we come to the phenomenal statement that those who abide in Him will have confidence when He appears and not be ashamed. To understand this we need to plug fellowship into the picture. The one who abides in Him, that is, the one who seeks to walk in the light, to have fellowship with Him—this is the one who will have confidence when He appears. To understand this further, we need to see the separation of the two great judgment seats, one for believers and the other for unbelievers.

Other passages (2 Cor 5:10 and Rom 14:11-12) make it clear that the Judgment Seat of Christ is designed to judge the works of believers for the purpose of rewards. It is not a judgment seat about destiny. This is why the Millennium is so important. It keeps the judgment seats separate. Otherwise, they are collapsed and there is only one Great White Throne (Rev 20:11-15) judgment seat to determine destiny and reward. All those whose names are not written in the Book of Life are thrown into the Lake of Fire. But these people are also judged according to the works of each one, the works that are recorded, not in the Book of Life, but in "the books."

The two judgment seats mentioned in Scripture, the Judgment Seat of Christ and the Great White Throne have one thing in common. At each judgment seat a person is judged according to his works, not according to his faith. For the dispensationalist who believes that the Millennium (thousand-year reign of Christ on earth from Jerusalem) separates these two judgment seats, there is no problem. Because the born again people have believed, they show up at the Judgment Seat of Christ. Their eternal destiny is already secure. They appear before Christ to be judged for the works since they became believers to see how much of their life will glorify God forever and ever (rewards).

For the dispensationalist only unbelievers show up at the Great White Throne. They show up there because they did not believe in order to have the sin barrier between them and God removed. Their eternal destiny is set before they appear at the Great White Throne. Because they did not believe their name is not in the Book of Life. Their destiny? The Lake of Fire. Why then the Great White Throne judgment? There the unbelievers are judged for their works to determine their rewards (in a negative sense).

But for the person who does not believe in a literal thousand-year reign of Christ on earth from Jerusalem (an amillennialist), the spiritual waters get muddy very quickly when the two judgment seats are collapsed. It is inescapable that the basis for judgment at each of these seats is the works of the person being judged. No wonder the people in the pews of churches that do not believe in the Millennium are confused on the relationship between faith and works. Both are thrown together at these judgment seats, although it must be admitted that neither faith nor lack thereof is mentioned at either judgment seat. It is my belief that this confusion in "future things" begun by Augustine has also caused confusion in the requirements to go to heaven.[2]

The dispensationalist (one who believes Jesus will really come back to set up an earthly kingdom which will last one thousand years) understands that his relationship with the Lord is settled and secure. But the life of the believer (works) will be judged to see how much of it will glorify God. The believer who has sought to walk with Him has nothing to worry about when He comes, that is, he will "not be ashamed before Him at His coming."

This brings a whole new light to the thinking of most believers about the Judgment Seat of Christ. There is the concept of *shame*. Yes, there will be shame at this time for His children who have lived their lives for the flesh and in the flesh. Does this threaten their eternal destiny? No. No more than you may be more proud of some of your children than others. Maybe one of your children has taken the gifts he has been given, worked hard to develop them, and is doing something productive with his/her life. You are proud of that child, and rightly so. Perhaps another child even more gifted has buried his gifts in the sand, has not worked hard to develop his God-given abilities, and is not doing anything productive with his life. Of that child you may be ashamed. Is he still your child? Yes, but you probably would not wish to reward him for his slothful life.

Of course, the shame in 1 John 2:28 is in reference to the believer, not God. I do not see the shame lasting beyond the Judgment Seat of Christ. But because we will have no sin(ful) nature when we see Him, we will also not be hardened to sin and not be rationalizing it. For those who have not been abiding in Him, the remorse, sorrow, regret, confession and repentance that should have been on earth will come at the Judgment Seat. At that time some will wish God would give us a mulligan (a do-over, if you are a golfer), but it will not be so. Confess now. Abide now. Or as James put it, "Draw near to God, and He will draw near to you. Cleanse *your* hands, *you* sinners; and purify *your* hearts, *you* double-minded. Lament and mourn and weep! Let your laughter be turned to mourning and *your* joy to gloom. Humble yourselves in the sight of the Lord, and He will lift you up" (Jas 4:8-10).

But let's not be so negative. The hope of 1 John is positive. John is writing that we might have fellowship, abide in Him, and have confidence before Him when He appears. He anticipates the day when we will have perfect vision.

GLORIFICATION AT HIS COMING—PERFECT VISION

> If you know that He is righteous, you know that everyone who practices righteousness is born of Him. Behold what manner of love the Father has bestowed on us, that we should be called children of God! Therefore the world does not know us, because it did not know Him. Beloved, now we are children of God; and it has not yet been revealed what we shall be, but we know that when He is revealed, we shall be like Him, for we shall see Him as He is (2:29–3:2).

A glance at our outline tells us that John has completed the first section of the body of his letter. He has introduced the three principles of fellowship: right living, right loving, and right learning. First John 2:28 serves as a swing verse to take us from the first section of the body to the second: Principles of Fellowship Developed. Here John takes the same three principles to which we were introduced in the first section of the body and goes further (see pages 78-79).

If 2:28 is a thematic verse, then 2:29 begins a new section which runs all the way through 3:10b. It's about right living—dealing with our sins. It tells us how children of God can manifest who they really are as "born-again" people. Of course, the answer is—only one way. That's by being righteous. Now this righteousness is not humanistic do-gooding. It's to keep His commandments, and we have already seen that His commandments involve loving other believers. We saw that in 2:3-11. But we will see it again in 3:23-24a: "And this is His commandment: that we should believe on the name of His Son Jesus Christ and love one another, as He gave us commandment. Now he who keeps His commandments abides in Him, and He in him." Again, it's not about relationship. If it were, then the only way to get to heaven would be by keeping His commandments. It's about fellowship.

The *righteousness* of 2:29 is to believe in Jesus and love one another. By this definition of righteousness, *only a Christian can do it.* So, this verse tells us that God is righteous, and anyone doing the kind of righteousness we have talked about here is "a chip off the old block." As Zane Hodges puts it, "… John is clearly concerned with the deduction which we can make if we know that God is righteous. If *that* is known, it follows that one who to any extent reproduces His righteous nature is actually *manifesting* that nature and can rightly be *perceived* as born of Him."[3]

This is a theme that will carry John for the next ten verses. But as he is building up to how God's children can make visible the fact that they are born again, He talks about what a privilege it is just to be called a child of God. The thought of *new birth* (and this is the first reference to the new birth in 1 John) in 2:29 brings an exclamation of wonder from John. The Greek word translated "what manner of" (*potapēn*) sometimes carries a sense of intensification, like "how great," "how wonderful," and the standard Greek dictionary suggests for this place the words "how glorious." And the word translated *behold* is a plural (*idete*) as opposed to the standard *idou*. This is an actual call to really take a look at how glorious this love is.

John is slowly getting around to the new nature we have in Christ. He is saying that God's nature is righteous. So we can be born of God and share in His nature. We can be righteous. It stupefies John that God would love us enough to let us share in His nature. This is the same nature that came into Mary in the form of Jesus and was born on Christmas. Part of this same divine nature was passed along to us at new birth. It has changed our entire character and make-up. Now we are truly the children of God. That's who we really are.

The world doesn't know (*ginōskō*) this because it has not experienced God. Until someone has experienced the new birth, it's even hard to explain what it is like to have this new nature within. But in verse two John goes on to explain that one day this new nature is the only nature that we will manifest. Why? Because someday our evil nature, our sin(ful) nature passed down to us congenitally, will be taken away. That will be when He appears. At that time we shall be completely like Him, for we shall see Him as He is. This is the final stage of sanctification of the believer (perfective sanctification), or glorification. This is when all the effects of the fall are reversed for us. We have glorified bodies which don't wear out ... but best of all, no more sin(ful) nature to contend with. We shall be like Him.

I believe this is what the "wretched man" of Rom 7:24 longed for. It's as though his new nature and his true identity in Christ have been obscured by a body that wears out and an evil nature which from time to time raises its ugly head to lash out like a king cobra to paralyze our Christian lives. He longs to be rid of that thing. He cries out for deliverance.

> When all my labors and trial are o'er,
> And I am safe on that beautiful shore,
> Just to be near the dear Lord I adore,
> Will through the ages be glory for me.
> Oh that will be glory for me, glory for me, glory for me;
> When by His grace, I shall look on His face,
> That will be glory, be glory for me.

PURIFICATION FOR HIS COMING—A LENS TO SEE UP CLOSE

And everyone who has this hope in Him purifies himself, just as He is pure (3:3).

Even now, beholding the glory of the Lord has a transforming effect upon us (2 Cor 3:18). We don't have to wait until He comes to be transformed. As we anticipate His future coming and manifestation, we have *a purifying hope*. We want to be like Him now. All believers will be like Him when He appears. So we don't want to be ashamed at that time because we have been unlike Him now.

That John speaks of this hope as a purifying hope is one of the reasons we believe the rapture will occur before the Tribulation begins. If the rapture takes place after the Tribulation, as many teach, I could wait until the middle of the Tribulation to start cleaning up my act. I could just wait around until the Man of Sin reveals himself, and then I could start getting serious about my Christian life. After all, I could count the days until His appearing. It will be 1260 days from the revelation of the Antichrist.

No, we believe the NT teaches Christ can come for His bride at any moment. We don't know when that will be. It's as though you were a personal friend of President Bush and he said he planned to drop in to see you on one of his trips to his ranch here in Texas. You ask, "Do you know when that will be?" "Why?" he asks. "Well, I want to make sure the house is clean when you come." "Oh," he says, "well, I want to surprise you. Just keep it clean." That's what he is saying here.

The Bible teaches four kinds of sanctification (Prospective—Jer 1:5; Positional—1 Cor 1:2; Progressive—Heb 10:14; and Perfective—1 Thess 5:23). For the past few months I have been getting headaches on Mondays. They last all day. Not good. So I thought it might have something to do with preaching three sermons on Sunday morning, since starting another service seems to coincide with these headaches. So I thought perhaps a bigger breakfast on Sunday morning would do it.

I have a regular ritual on Sunday mornings, and part of that ritual is to drive by Burger King for breakfast. So I got my usual healthy Burger King breakfast, but then I thought I might need something else. So I drove over to the Texaco station near Burger King. I went in and looked over the candy section and selected a Twix Bar. I pulled it off the shelf from the other Twix Bars and took it up to the cash register to buy it. But I noticed I had left my money in the car. So I told the lady at the cash register to hold that Twix Bar for me, and I would be right back. That's what we call *prospective sanctification*. That Twix Bar was *set aside for my use* from all the other Twix Bars in the store. But I still hadn't paid for it.

After getting my money from the car, I went to the lady at the cash register, paid for the Twix Bar I had previously selected, and put it in my shirt pocket. When I went out of the store, the Twix Bar went with me. When I got into the car, so did the Twix Bar. I drove to the church, and the Twix Bar went right along with me. That's what we call *positional sanctification*. In my pocket the Twix Bar was taken out of its former position in the store. It no longer belonged to the store. It belonged to me. I paid for it. It went where I went.

But, then, I unwrapped the Twix Bar and began to eat. Slowly, but surely, the Twix Bar disappeared into my mouth and stomach. I was using it as I had intended to use it from the moment I bought it. I purchased it in a moment, but it took a little while to eat. This is what we call *progressive sanctification*. Unlike positional sanctification, progressive sanctification is a process that requires time.

Finally, the entire Twix Bar was in my mouth, in my stomach, and digested into my blood stream. It had been completely transformed. You might even say it did not have its old nature. And this is what we call *perfective sanctification*. In 1 John 2:29–3:3 we have referred to two of these four types of sanctification. Can you identify which two?

CONCLUSION

Recently I needed to go in to see my optician to renew my prescription again so I could order some more contacts. I see fine with my current contacts, so I didn't want to go through the eye exam. And two years ago when I renewed the prescription, we bypassed the eye exam, so I thought I could do it this time as well. I told the girls at the front desk, "Let me just see Dr. Russell first, and if he thinks I need an eye exam, we'll do it."

Well, Dr. Russell said, "Oh, ya. We need the exam. It's been five years. You could have glaucoma. Not safe to skip it this time. Besides, your eyes may have changed."

Well, I was sure it was a waste of time. But, the doctor was right once again. I don't have glaucoma, but I did need my prescription tweaked a bit. He gave me some new contacts with the new prescription to try, and it was amazing. I saw much better with the new ones. No telling what I have been missing during the past year or so.

Perhaps you have been a believer for quite awhile. Maybe even a prophecy buff. You can decipher the difference between pre-trib, pre-mill dispensationalism and post-trib pre-mill covenant theology. But constantly staring at this world can get you to change your focus. We don't have much choice but to look at this world. But we will lose our Christian balance if we don't put one eye on the world to come. Spiritual monovision is what we need. But even if we have it, let's not forget a regular eye exam to see if we are keeping both worlds in proper focus. And let's all look forward to the day when we don't need this monovision thing anymore. That's the day we will be like Him, for we will see Him as He is and have perfect vision.

I stand amazed in the presence
Of Jesus the Nazarene,
And wonder how He could love me,
A sinner, condemned, unclean.
How marvelous! How wonderful!
And my song shall ever be:
How marvelous! How wonderful
Is my Savior's love for me!
When with the ransomed in glory
His face I at last shall see,
'Twill be my joy through the ages
To sing of His love for me.
How marvelous! How wonderful!
And my song shall ever be:
How marvelous! How wonderful
Is my Savior's love for me!

---

[1] Zane C. Hodges, *The Epistles of John: Walking in the Light of God's Love* (Irving, TX: Grace Evangelical Society, 1999), 124-25.

[2] David R. Anderson, "The Soteriological Impact of Augustine's Change from Premillennialism to Amillennialsim," *Journal of the Grace Evangelical Society* 15 (Spring 2002): 25-36.

[3] Hodges, 127.

LESSON 11 "Spiritual Monovision" I John 2:28-3:3

1. Explain the metaphor "Spiritual Monovision." Name the two lenses that accomplish this for the believer.

2. Read John 15:5-11. What is the common theme in that scripture and I John 2:28?

3. When will a believer have "confidence and not be ashamed"?

4. Who will appear before the "Judgment Seat of Christ"? Who will appear before the "Great White Throne" judgment? What is common in the two judgments?

5. What is the meaning of "everyone who practices righteousness"? (See verse 29.)

6. Share your thoughts about "Behold what manner of love the Father has bestowed on us, that we should be called children of God!" What did John think?

7. John says that when Jesus appears we "shall be like Him." In what ways will we be like Him?

8. How would you explain the four kinds of sanctification described on page 145?

   Prospective (Jer. 1:5) -

   Positional (I Cor.1:2) -

   Progressive (Heb.10:14) -

   Perfective (I Thess.5:23) -

9. Which two of these types of sanctification are referred to in verses 2:29-3:3?

10. How can we maintain our Christian balance?

– 12 –

THE CANCER OF SIN

1 John 3:4-6

After getting back from my ski accident in Colorado and the subsequent operation on my broken hip, I was weaker than I expected. I lost thirteen pounds in the hospital in just four days. My Denver surgeon told me to get with an internist as soon as possible after arrival in Houston so he could regulate my coumadin and an orthopedic specialist within a week so he could monitor success or failure of my operation. Well, I got back on a Wednesday, so I got a Friday morning appointment with an internist who is a member of my church.

Now, what he didn't know was how weak I was and how much effort I had to exert just to get showered and dressed in the morning. It left me sweating. So I was still sweating after I got to his office as his first patient. When he walked in, he took one look at me and said, "Whoa! You look awful."

He felt my arm and face. "You're all clammy," he exclaimed. "I think you might have a blood clot. We're putting you back in the hospital right now." So, that's what we did. Fortunately, tests revealed I did not have a blood clot, but I was getting the distinct impression that blood clots after hip surgery are a major concern.

When I got back to the internist's office that afternoon, he asked, "How much coumadin are you taking?"

"Well, 2.5 mg/day for two days in a row; then I take a one day break before two more days of 2.5 mg/day," I replied.

"Well, that's not much coumadin. We usually start people on 10 mg/day and work it down to 5. Let's double your dose, but come in Monday so we can look at your blood."

Of course, I complied.

Now, you know when you are taking a serious drug when they give you a twenty-five page booklet about the drug to read before you start taking it. I had glanced at the booklet back in the hospital in Denver and learned enough to know that coumadin was a blood-thinner to keep me from getting clots after the operation. I recognized it from newspaper articles about

Hakeem Olajuwon when he was having trouble with blood clots in his legs. I knew I had to follow the doctor's instructions carefully, so I took 2.5 mg in the morning and 2.5 at night. The weekend passed without my early demise, so I went in Monday for a blood test. This time I was ready for my doctor. Hearing him coming down the hall, I crossed my eyes, stuck my tongue out the side of my mouth, and began a twitching motion.

He took one look, laughed, and said, "Now that's the Dave I know and love. Everything looks OK from your blood test Friday, but I am curious why you broke a hip at this early age. You need a bone density test."

"OK," I replied obediently.

The next morning, Tuesday, I got a call from his nurse around 7:30 a.m. "Have you taken your coumadin yet today?"

"No."

"Well, don't take it. Your blood is too thin."

"OK."

Well, the next day was Wednesday, and I had an appointment with the orthopedic guy. As he is looking at my x-rays from before and after the surgery, he looks at my chart, and asks, "What are you doing taking this cummadin?"

"Well," I said, "the surgeon in Denver said to take it for a month and my internist here in Houston said a month to six weeks."

"No more coumadin," he said with a scowl on his face. "This is not a benign drug."

"But what if I get a blood clot?" I asked.

"We give this to people in the hospital when they are immobile. But now that you are moving around, you don't have any more chance of a blood clot than I do."

The next night, Thursday, I was at a picture party from a trip I had led to Israel, sitting next to another doctor in our church who had been on the trip. I shared with him my coumadin story. He nodded silently, and then said, "Well, now you're in it."

"In what?" I asked.

"We doctors don't really know what we are doing with coumadin. I have seen two patients die from taking coumadin. They die of internal bleeding."

As you can imagine, hearing so many opinions from so many different doctors about a drug I had been taking to avoid blood clots was somewhat discomforting. Nevertheless, one thing was for sure. They all agreed that the risk of blood clots after hip surgery was greater than the risk of well-monitored use of coumadin for a brief period of time to keep the clots from forming. A blood clot can end your life prematurely. One small coagulated blob of blood can clog up the arteries to your heart and cause you to die.

And one small sin in your life, that you know about, can rob you of your spiritual vitality, your spiritual life. I didn't say it would rob you of heaven, but it can rob you of the full, abundant life Jesus wants you to have on earth. And that's what John is trying to prevent at this point in his letter. We said this is a letter about fellowship, not relationship. It's not a book about the way; it's a book about the walk. It's not about how to get to heaven; it's about how to have a little bit of heaven on earth. We are in John's second section on right living—dealing with our sins. He introduced this principle of fellowship in 1 John 1:5–2:2. But now he develops this principle. He takes our understanding of sin in our lives, even though we have already been justified (declared righteous in God's court room in heaven), to a new level.

It is this section in 1 John, more than any other, which keeps expository preachers from trying to present this little book to their congregations. This section about sin in our lives is hard to reconcile with his first section on sin in 1 John 1. Here, I am going to present an understanding which makes the most sense to me, but my intent is not to be dogmatic. Before we go through the text verse by verse, let's see if we can spot the main issue in the text.

In verse six John says, "Whoever abides in Him does not sin. Whoever sins has neither seen Him nor known Him." As the Dixie Chicks would say, "There's your trouble."

Many well-known preachers say this verse means if a person who claims to be a Christian "sins," he simply professes Christ but doesn't possess Christ. That statement has a nice ring to it, but it should be a problem for anyone who has read 1 John from the beginning.

Back in 1 John 1:8 we were warned that the Christian who claims he has no sin in his life is self-deceived. Of course, those who say the person in 3:6 is not a Christian also say the person in 1:8 is not a born-again believer. But we pointed out that the subject of 1:8 is "we," a "we" which includes the apostles (when "we" is traced from 1:1 through to 1:8). To say the "we" in 1:8 does not refer to believers does all sorts of violence to the text. You might as well say the apostles were not born-again believers. But if these are believers in 1:8, then it appears we have a contradiction between 1:8 and 3:6.

"There's your trouble." We have to explain this apparent contradiction somehow.

OK, we are going to get a little bit academic. Bear with me. We haven't done this since 2:3-5. Those who say 3:6 is not referring to born-again believers have to do something with the fact that all humans still fall short of the absolute holiness of God. In other words, they are still sinful. This includes Christians and non-Christians, possessors and professors, the elect and the non-elect. Therefore, 3:6 could not mean absolute sinlessness. So when we can't explain the text from the apparent meaning in the English translation, we like to retreat to Greek grammar. No problem. Sometimes that is very helpful (such as in 2:3-5). But we need to be sure our Greek grammar is correct.

Those who want to get the born-again person out of 3:6 tell us that the present tense of *hamartanō*, the Greek verb used in the original text, is in the present tense. So far, so good. But this is where some get off track. They want to tell us that the basic meaning of the present tense in the Greek language is *continuous* action. In other words, a true believer does not *continue* to sin. Anyone who claims to be a Christian but *continues* to sin has neither seen nor known Him, that is, he's simply not a genuine believer.

You can see this interpretation without going to a commentary by just looking at the NIV. The NIV translates 3:6 as such: "No one who lives in him keeps on sinning. No one who continues to sin has either seen him or known him." Here they not only change the word "abides" to "lives" (these are two different words in the Greek language), but they reveal their interpretation of the present tense as *continuous* action when they translate the verb *hamartanei* as "keeps on sinning." They translate it this way in the first half of 3:6 and in the second half (the same root verb) as "continues to sin."

Unfortunately, there is nothing inherent in the Greek present tense that tells us this is *continuous* action. For example, Jesus refers to His single act of coming to the earth at His incarnation in the present tense in John 6:33 when He says, "For the bread of God is He who comes down from heaven and gives life to the world." Is there anyone who would like to tell us that the present tense here means *continuous* action, that is, that Jesus is continually coming down from heaven? I don't think so. The present tense *can* mean continuous action, but that is only one of its ten different uses, and it's a fairly rare usage. There need to be other indicators in the context of the verb before we conclude that the meaning is *continuous* action.

So, I hope you see the problem. What is our suggested solution? We will present that shortly, but let's back up. Let's go back to 3:4 and set the stage for the rest of these verses in this section. John discusses the character of sin (3:4), the cancellation of sin (3:5), and the contradiction of sin (3:6). Let's go verse by verse.

THE CHARACTER OF SIN

> Whoever commits sin also commits lawlessness, and sin is lawlessness (3:4).

Many think that John was facing a group of opponents who were the beginners of a heresy called Gnosticism, though it was another hundred years in the history of Christianity before this heresy was completely developed. One of their teachings was that light and darkness, sin and righteousness were all part of the divine experience, that is, sin was not a problem.

John says that whoever commits sin also commits lawlessness, which may be too limiting as a translation of *anomia*. This Greek word is used to translate twenty-four *different* Hebrew words in the Septuagint (the Greek translation of the Hebrew OT). Most frequently it is used to translate the Hebrew word *'awon,* which means "wickedness" or "iniquity." The Confraternity Version (imprim. 1961) probably gives the best translation: "Everyone who commits sin, commits *iniquity* also; and sin is *iniquity.*"[1]

John is trying to open their eyes to the wickedness of sin, all sin. Obviously, anyone who condones or excuses sin in his/her life is not purifying himself as 3:3 urges. Now John is going back to verses 1:5–2:2 to pick up the problem of sin once again. Here he expands on what he introduced there and takes his discussion on our battle against sin to another level. Here, for example, he is getting into a discussion of the very nature of sin itself: wickedness.

Because sin seems inevitable for the human being, we like to white-wash it, make light of it, excuse it. "Well, nobody's perfect, you know." John wants us to know that any sin is just plain wicked.

> Man calls it an *accident*; God calls it an *abomination.*
> Man calls it a *blunder*; God calls it *blindness.*
> Man calls it a *defect*; God calls it a *disease.*
> Man calls it a *chance*; God calls it a *choice.*
> Man calls it an *error*; God calls it *enmity.*
> Man calls it a *fascination*; God calls it a *fatality.*

> Man calls it *infirmity*; God calls it *iniquity*.
> Man calls it *luxury*; God calls it *leprosy*.
> Man calls it *liberty*; God calls it *lawlessness*.
> Man calls it a *trifle*; God calls it a *tragedy*.
> Man calls it a *mistake*; God calls it *madness*.
> Man calls it a *weakness*; God calls it *wickedness*.

There is a small tree which grows in SE Asia known as the Judas Tree. Long before its leaves appear, gorgeous blossoms grow on its branches. Looking like scarlet sunbeams caught among the boughs, the brilliant beauty of the crimson flowers attracts thousands of tiny insects. The wild bees also seek to draw honey from the exquisitely shaped cups.

But every insect—bee or butterfly—that comes to rest upon the edge of its blossom is overcome by a fatal, curious sort of opiate, or drug, which the flower-juice contains, and drops dead upon the ground below! So, when walking around Judas Trees, a person sees the soft grass covered with dead and dying, bright-winged insects.

The Judas Tree reminds us of sin. Sin may look bright, pleasant and attractive to our eyes; it may appear harmless to indulge in it. But lurking behind the "pleasure of sin" is a fatal poison. And sin is a poison, a wickedness that acts as a drug to take away all our motivation for the Christian life, or worse. Wickedness: that's the character of sin. But what about its cancellation?

THE CANCELLATION OF SIN

> And you know that He was manifested to take away our sins, and
> in Him there is no sin (3:5).

Christ's Purpose

Christ came to take away (to cancel out) the sins of the world (compare 2:2). For us to continue in our sins after being justified is completely inconsistent with His purpose in coming. To place us into His army in order to defeat the kingdom of darkness, when we ourselves are walking in darkness, is a contradiction in terms, or at least purposes. It would be like Billy Graham going into business with Larry Flint, or George Bush asking Osama bin Laden to be his running-mate. It doesn't compute.

This isn't to deny the reality of sin in our lives. This verse is not a statement of reality or unreality; it is a statement of purpose. Christ's purpose in coming to earth was to take away sin. Now that our sins have been washed away by His blood in our position, we should also desire to see them wiped away in our condition. Known sin in the condition of a believer is incongruous with Christ's purpose and Christ's purity, which is the emphasis of 3:5b.

Christ's Purity

The purpose of Christ's coming was to take away our sins. But now He lives within us. He is absolutely pure, absolutely clean. During my stay in Germany I was impressed with the desire of the people to keep their country clean. I used the home of a missionary who was back in the States on furlough. He was not charging me rent, but did ask me to keep his yard mowed. When I first got here, the grass had not been mowed for at least three weeks. It was an eye sore to the neighborhood. So I got out the lawn mower, was thankful it was light because my broken hip had not healed well, and mowed the yard. There was no grass-catcher attached to the mower, so grass just went everywhere. When I finished, I was about to go in the house, knowing I'd pleased my fastidiously clean German neighbors, when I saw an old lady across the street with her broom. She was sweeping away the grass I had blown onto her side of the street. She wasn't sweeping my side of the street; just hers. Of course, since I had made the mess, I took the hint, found a broom, and swept the grass off the street. My, these people are concerned about cleanliness.

Are we that concerned about cleanliness? Oh, I'm not talking about external cleanliness. You know what I mean. The absolutely pure Savior lives within us. Do we want to throw beer bottles, dog manure, and pornography all over His yard? Do we care more about the cleanliness of our material homes than we do our spiritual hearts?

The character of sin is wickedness; cancellation of sin is harmony with the purpose and purity of Christ; and known sin in the life of a believer who is close to Him is a contradiction.

The Contradiction of Sin

> Whoever abides in Him does not sin. Whoever sins has neither
> seen Him nor known Him (3:6).

One of the main reasons many expositors assume the *continuous* nuance of the present tense in verse six is the obvious incongruity between ongoing sin in the life of a professing Christian and the very purpose for which Christ came, that is, to take away sin. Here are just a few examples of what mystifies pastors, in general, no matter what their theological stripe:

1. How a man can come to church, claim to be a Christian, and go out and cheat like crazy in his business.
2. How kids from Christian homes, who claim to know Christ, can come to church and go to youth groups while they act the same as their non-Christian friends with their drinking, drug experimentation, and pre-marital involvement.
3. How couples, who are successful in business and come to church, can claim to be Christians, use the church facilities, let their children be nurtured by the church staff, but give less money to their church than their non-Christian friends give to their secular charities.
4. How women who claim to be Christians can spend more time reading romance novels than quiet time in the Scriptures.
5. How people can claim to be Christians yet show no desire and spend no time in community with other believers in church, Sunday school, or Small Groups.

These selected examples mystify pastors because each example speaks of an activity or lack thereof which is so very far from the heart of God. The difference in perspective, however, is that some of these pastors would say the people in the above examples simply are not genuine Christians, while others would say they might not be genuine Christians, or they might be genuine Christians who are not very close to God (they are living for this world).

Why might an informed interpreter think the issue in this verse is fellowship instead of relationship? The first clue is the word *abides*. We have seen over and over that this word should be a clue that John's subject is fellowship instead of relationship. We saw how he used the word in John 15:5–11. So, when we see it in 1 John, we should begin with the working assumption that he is giving us some more truth about fellowship unless there is strong evidence to the contrary.

Our second clue is John's choice of the *perfect* tense for the verbs *seen* and *known*. Just as in 2:3-5, especially for verbs describing a state of being (*to know*) as opposed to verbs of action (to hit), the perfect tense expresses an intensified state. In other words, "to know" in the perfect tense becomes "to know intensively" or intimately. "To see" in the perfect tense becomes "to see very closely." These are verbs of *close fellowship* with the Savior.

A Christian in close fellowship with Jesus wants sin out of his life. The Christian who can dismiss the sin in his life as no big deal has never caught a close vision of the Savior and does not know Him very intimately. It is *a contradiction* to claim close fellowship with the Savior and to sin without remorse, confession, or repentance.

But how can we reconcile this claim in 1 John 3:6 that Christians in fellowship (abiding) do not sin when 1 John 1:8 says they do? Well, as we have already discussed, one approach is to say that the present tense of the verb "to sin" means "to continually sin." However, as mentioned, that meaning is not inherent in the present tense. To mean continual action, the text will employ other words along with the present tense to make that meaning obvious, such as: 1) *diapantos*—"continually" (Luke 24:53; Heb 9:6; 13:15); or 2) *eis to diēnekes*—"continually" (Heb 7:3; 10:1).

J. P. Louw ["Verbal Aspect in the First Letter of John," *Neotestamentica* 9 (1975): 99-101] demonstrates convincingly that the present tense in 1 John has no such meaning. It is, in fact, "a zero tense of factual actuality." We will look at this again when we get to 3:9, which would be a direct contradiction to 1:8, if the *continual* meaning of the present tense is imported into both verses. Thus the NIV demonstrates questionable scholarship on this point when it imports the "continual" translation here. That is an interpretative choice made by the translators, but the choice comes from a theological point of view they have imported into the text, not from a careful study of Greek grammar.

And who of you really wants to take the verbs in verse six as continual action? Have any of you wrestled with an on-going problem with a particular sin? Better asked, who of you has not? The only people who can raise their hands are the hypocrites or self-deceived, which is precisely the errors of the Christians in 1:6 (hypocrites) and 1:8 (self-deception). Going down that road can lead into deep darkness.

While sitting in Germany writing these words, it occurred to me that I had never read *Mein Kamf*, Adolf Hitler's totalitarian manifesto. It amazed me as I read his autobiographical account that he had no antipathy for Jews growing up. He only knew one or two and thought it unfair when they were denigrated by others simply for their religion. After all, the Jews he knew were Germans. But after his parents died, he was forced to move to Vienna in order to eke out a living. Even though Vienna was 10% Jewish (200,000 out of two million), he hardly noticed them. It wasn't until he was exposed to the Christian Socialist Party and their propaganda that he began to look upon the Jews with jaundiced eyes.

Now, if you didn't already know it, let's remind ourselves that Hitler was no atheist. He considered himself a God-fearing Christian. And it was through other Christians that he learned to hate the Jews and hold them responsible for promoting Democratic Socialism or Marxism (Karl Marx was a Jew). Finally, Hitler saw the Jews as non-Germans, a blight on society and the cause of all the anti-nationalistic sentiment in the former German Reich. Who could deliver his beloved nation from this cancer? Voila. Hitler began to see himself as God's messiah, not an antichrist in any sense of the word, but rather a servant of Christ to cleanse Germany and the world of Jewry, the bacteria of the human race. But, here, read his words:

> The Jewish doctrine of Marxism rejects the aristocratic principle of Nature and … the result of an application of such a law could only be chaos, on earth it could only be destruction for the inhabitants of this planet.
>
> If, with the help of his Marxist creed, the Jew is victorious over the other peoples of the world, his crown will be the funeral wreath of humanity and this planet will, as it did thousands of years ago, move through the ether devoid of men.
>
> Eternal Nature inexorably avenges the infringement of her commands.
>
> Hence today I believe that I am acting in accordance with the will of the Almighty Creator: *by defending myself against the Jew, I am fighting for the work of the Lord* [emphasis his].[2]

Please, please do not misunderstand me. I am not suggesting that Adolf Hitler was a born-again Christian. Though I cannot prove it, it would not surprise me to discover in eternity that Satan himself, instead of one of his minions, possessed Adolf Hitler, since Satan's tactic to keep Christ from returning in accordance with His promise from Matt 23:30 has been to wipe out the Jewish race. But this does illustrate how deeply into the darkness of depravity one can wander when he deceives himself into thinking the wholesale slaughter of human beings is the "work of the Lord."

The explanation that 1 John 3:6 teaches a genuine Christian cannot continue in sin throws us right back to the "sea of subjectivity" we ran into back in 2:3-4. We begin to ask all those questions about what commandments, how long is "continuing," and so on. Instead of the Bible teaching absolutes, we become conditioned to think in terms of relative truth. We then begin to deny, excuse, or rename our sins. This is walking in darkness.

A better approach is to stay with what John has already taught. In 1:7 he told us that the believer walking in the light (in fellowship) is constantly being cleansed by the blood of Christ for the purpose of continued fellowship with the Lord. This refers to all those sins we are committing we don't even know about as we walk in the light. His rose-colored (blood of Christ) *Son-glasses* filter out all that sin so that God the Father sees us as completely clean and free from any charge of iniquity. By contrast, the believer who does knowingly and defiantly sin "has neither seen Him nor known Him" intimately.

CONCLUSION

John can never be accused of white-washing sin. Though he recognizes the cleansing blood of Christ as God's provision for our relationship and our fellowship, John never excuses sin nor takes it lightly. Sin is serious stuff. Just one willful, known sin in the life of a believer can act as a blood clot in a vein to rob him of his spiritual life, his vitality, his joy, his fellowship with the Lord. John urges believers to keep the clots out of their system.

The character of sin is wickedness. To knowingly practice sin is diametrically opposed to the purpose and purity of Christ who came into this world for the cancellation of sin. Known sin in the life of a believer in Jesus is a contradiction. He cannot willfully, knowingly sin and be close to Jesus at the same time. Chances are such a child of God has never really seen Jesus up close and personal. He is in desperate need of a close-up of Christ. After getting a close look at Him and His absolute holiness, the Christian's appetite for sin wanes in a hurry.

Many think John 1:29 was in the back of John's mind when he wrote 1 John 3:5. Both verses use the same verb "to take away" (*airō*). In the gospel John the Baptist sees Jesus coming to him and says, "Behold! The Lamb of God who takes away the sin of the world!" We remember in 1 John 2:2 the apostle John tells us that Jesus' work was the propitiation for the sins of the whole world. And in this passage (1 John 3:4-6) John calls us to sobriety with a biopsy of the malignant tumor of sin, but he also reminds us that our Savior came into this world to take sin away.

On the Day of Atonement there were two goats and an urn presented to the high priest. He reached into the urn to draw out one of two lots. One lot said, "For the Lord," while the other said, "For Azazel." It was considered a special blessing if the high priest reached into the urn with his right hand and pulled out the lot which said, "For the Lord." Then he would lay his hand upon the goat which was to take away the sins of the people. Upon the horns of the other goat the high priest would tie half of a crimson sash. The other half of the sash, torn in two for this occasion, was nailed to the temple door.

This second goat is mentioned only four times in Scripture. Its name is Azazel. Twelve different men arranged in relay form, a "goat express," escort Azazel away from the city, proceeding east into the Judean Wilderness, each man walking one mile before the goat is handed off to the next man. When the appointed precipice is reached, the crimson sash is once again torn in two. One half is tied to the edge of the cliff, while the other is retied to the horns of the goat. Then the goat is pushed off the cliff. This is the "Scape Goat" which *takes away* the sins of the people.

According to the Mishnah, the oral tradition of the Jews recorded around A.D. 200, which was combined with the Gemorrah (a commentary on the Mishnah written from A.D. 200 to A.D. 500) to form the Talmud, if the Lord accepted the sacrifice of the Scape Goat (Azazel), then the crimson sash nailed to the door of the Temple would turn white.[3] Also in the Mishnah (Yoma 39) it says that for forty years before the Temple was destroyed the crimson sash did not turn white and for forty years in a row the high priest reached into the urn and pulled out the lot which said, "For Azazel." (That's like flipping a coin and having it come up tails forty times in a row.)

For those of you who have trusted in Christ as your Savior, the sash has turned white. The Father has accepted the sacrifice of His Son. "Though your sins like scarlet, they shall be white as snow; though they be red like crimson, they shall be as wool," for the Lamb of God has taken away the sins of the world.

---

[1] Zane C. Hodges, *The Epistles of John: Walking in the Light of God's Love* (Irving, TX: Grace Evangelical Society, 1999), 132.

[2] Adolf Hitler, *Mein Kampf*, trans. Ralph Manheim (Boston: Houghton Mifflin Company, 1943), 65. (This was the fifteenth printing, Sentry Edition C, a renewed copywrite in 1971.)

[3] Mitch and Zhava Glaser, *The Fall Feasts of Israel* (Chicago: Moody Press, 1987), 107.

LESSON 12 "The Cancer of Sin" I John 3:4-6

1. What lesson can we draw from the discussion about blood thinners and blot clots?

2. On page 151, Dave says of I John, "It's not a book about the way; it's a book about the walk." What is your understanding of that quote?

3. Let's look at verse 6. This verse is interpreted in various ways and even Dave says he is not dogmatic about his view. What do you think John means? What is the position that Dave presents?

4. What do you think is the main point of the discussion of "The Character of Sin" on pages 153-154? Any connection?

5. Dave engages in some lengthy discussion of grammar, translations, and context. To really understand 3:6 one has to do the hard work following his discussion and conclusions. List the key components of his position regarding this verse.

6. Why do you think Dave titled this lesson "The Cancer of Sin"?

7. Having studied Lesson 12, how would you explain verse 6?

– 13 –

ROOTS AND FRUITS

1 JOHN 3:7-10A

First John is book about fellowship, deep intimacy with God, soaring in the heavens. It talks about the barriers to that kind of life, the barriers which keep us chained to the earth, keep us from flying as God has designed us to fly. John wants to remove those barriers. He wants us to live as God has created us to live, to live according to our new birth.

Right now we are in the most difficult section of 1 John for all interpreters. Our outline shows it to be about the "Fruit of Fellowship." As such John introduces three crucial principles of fellowship in the first couple of chapters: right living, right loving, and right learning. Each of these sections deals with a different barrier to close fellowship with God. After an introduction to these three principles, John develops them more deeply. Like surfacing porpoises, he follows these three principles through three successive waves in the waters of 1 John. This is our second look at the porpoise of right living. In our introduction to right living (1:5–2:2) we learned that known sin in the life of a believer is a barrier to a close walk with God, but through genuine confession of that sin, the barrier is removed. In this further development of right living (2:29–3:10a) we learn that when a Christian knowingly sins, he is acting out of character. He is living contrary to God's design for him. He's a golden eagle living like a prairie chicken, chained to the earth.

We said this is a difficult, controversial passage. Why? Because in 3:4-6 it appears to say that a born again Christian does not sin, and in 3:7-10a it appears to say that a born again Christian is not able to sin. This presents two obvious problems, one in the text and one in our experience. The problem is the text comes from the fact that 1:8 seems to contradict 3:6-9. In 1:8 it says Christians are self-deceived if they claim they have no sin in their lives, but in 3:6-9 it appears to say that Christians are not capable of sin. The problem in our experience is simply that all but self-deceived or hypocritical Christians will admit that they have more or less sin in their lives, and if 3:6-9 says a true Christian is not capable of sin, then doubts about the validity of our salvation abound. In verse nine we read, "Whoever has been born of God does not sin, for His seed remains in him; and he cannot sin, because he has been born of God."

Do you have any problem with that verse? You should. If I were to ask for a raise of hands in a typical evangelical church to indicate if a person thinks he is a genuine Christian, certainly the majority of the people would raise their hands. If I followed the first question with a second asking how many people in the audience still wrestle with sin in their lives, the majority would still raise their hands, assuming only a minority of the congregation is made-up of hypocrites (1:6) or self-deluded people (1:8). The honest admission of on-going sin in the life of a genuine believer appears to contradict our present passage in 1 John. Is there a satisfactory explanation? That's what we hope to present. We will look at what the child of God does do in verse seven and what the child of God does not do in verse nine. In between we will look at what the child of Satan does (3:8). We will conclude with how we reveal our roots in the first part of verse ten. In a word, we will study "Roots and Fruits."

THE CHILD OF GOD—WHAT HE DOES

> Little children, let no one deceive you. He who practices righteousness is righteous, just as He is righteous (3:7).

The word *righteousness* throws us back to 2:29, which I suggested is the key to understanding our present passage. Why shouldn't it be? In 2:29 we have the first verse of a new section, John's second section of right living—dealing with our sins. We should expect the initial verse of a new section to have some bearing on the proper interpretation of that section. Perhaps this syllogism will help us understand what John is saying in 2:29:

> **Major Premise:** Divine righteousness comes from God's divine nature.
> **Minor Premise:** Someone produces divine righteousness.
> **Conclusion:** Therefore, someone, who produces divine righteousness, must have God's divine nature (born of God).

John is saying that "God is light and in Him is no darkness at all" (1:5). That's His nature—perfect holiness, perfect righteousness. So if you see someone doing divine righteousness (not human righteousness *á la* Isa 64:6) you can know it is coming from God's divine nature in that person. Somehow God must be living in that person and performing His divine righteousness through His divine nature within that person. In simple terms, the person doing divine righteousness must be born again, that is, he must have God's divine nature. In 3:7 we have the same concept with slightly different words:

> **Major Premise:** Someone producing divine righteousness is righteous.
> **Minor Premise:** God's divine nature is righteous.
> **Conclusion:** Therefore, someone who produces divine righteousness must have God's divine nature (born of God).

So, all this verse is saying is that God's nature will produce God's righteousness; therefore, if someone is producing God's righteousness, he must have God's nature. John goes from the deeds to the character, from the fruit to the root. And this is just another way of saying, "A certain kind of root will produce a certain kind of fruit." *Divine roots produce divine fruits.* Or you can go backwards. If you see divine fruit, then it is produced by a divine root. John goes from the outside to the inside.

John is simply saying that a "born of Him" (2:29) person is a person who has been given part of God's nature. This is expressed more explicitly by Peter. In 2 Pet 1:3-4 we read,

> … as His divine power has given to us all things that *pertain* to life and godliness, through the knowledge of Him who called us by glory and virtue, by which have been given to us exceedingly great and precious promises, that through these you may be partakers of the *divine nature* (emphasis mine) …

Having His divine nature does not mean that we are exactly like God. We are not omnipotent, omniscient, omnipresent, immutable, and so on. But we have some of His nature, a nature given to us when we were born again, born of God. Some of His attributes cannot be passed along to us, as mentioned. But some of them we can share and He can produce through us: love, truth, holiness, and so on. His divine love (*agapē*) is produced by His Spirit (Gal 5:22) in our new, born-again-with, divine nature.

The principle should be clear: *Divine roots produce divine fruits.* This is what should characterize the child of God. He was designed to soar in the sky, to display the glory of God (an open, public display of His character). The child of the devil cannot produce divine fruit. What does he do? The next verse tells us.

THE CHILD OF SATAN—WHAT HE DOES

He who sins is of the devil, for the devil has sinned from the beginning. For this purpose the Son of God was manifested, that He might destroy the works of the devil (3:8).

Another simple syllogism restates the conclusion of this verse:

Major Premise: The devil produces sin.
Minor Premise: Someone is sinning.
Conclusion: Therefore, someone who sins has the nature of the devil.

And this is just another way of saying, "A certain kind of root will produce a certain kind of fruit." *Satanic roots produce satanic fruits.* Or you could go backwards. Where you see Satanic fruits, there will be Satanic roots. If someone is doing the works of the devil, he must have a nature within him like the devil's. We believe this was one of the results of the fall of man. This is the sin(ful) nature inherited from Adam. It was not given to Adam by birth. Neither did Satan receive his fallen nature by birth. Somehow the choice of personal sin by these individuals so twisted their make-up that, in Adam's case, this twisted, perverted nature could be passed down to the human race through his seed (Ps 51:5). However, the likeness of man's fallen nature and the devil's is so similar that Jesus says the father of unbelievers is the devil (John 8:44), and Paul says unbelievers are "sons of disobedience" and "by nature the children of wrath" (Eph 2:2-3). This is why the unbeliever cannot keep from producing the works (fruit) of the devil. It's in his nature, his make-up.

Ocean's Eleven is a remake of an old movie by the same name starring the infamous "Rat Pack" (Frank Sinatra, Dean Martin, Sammy Davis, Jr., Joey Bishop, Peter Lawford, and Angie Dickenson). In the remake George Clooney plays the same part as Frank Sinatra, Danny Ocean, an ex-con, who jumps parole to organize eleven friends to rob the "central bank" of some Las Vegas casinos. At one point in the movie Ocean's former wife, who divorced him when he went to prison, appeals to him to mend his ways and live a straight life. Ocean replies, "This is what I do." End of conversation. He's saying, "I'm a crook. This is my nature. I couldn't mend my ways if I wanted to. And I don't want to."

In essence, this is what John claims for the unbeliever with his Adamic/Satanic nature. He's a "thief and a robber" (John 10:1). This is what he does. He couldn't change his ways if he wanted to. Oh, our Satanic roots are capable of a variety of Satanic fruits. Every sin(ful) nature does not characteristically produce the same sinful fruit. But it's all rotten.

THE CHILD OF GOD—WHAT HE DOES NOT DO

> Whoever has been born of God does not sin, for His seed remains in him; and he cannot sin, because he has been born of God (3:9).

Like verse six, this verse appears to say that a genuine, born again Christian does not sin and cannot sin. But that contradicts 1:8, which says Christians do sin. Suggested solutions:

1. The people in 1:8 are not genuine, born-again Christians. But, then, as we have asked before, who are the "we" of 1:1-7? It includes the apostles. Surely they are genuine, born-again Christians.

2. The present tense of 3:9 means a genuine, born-again Christian does not and is not able to *continually* sin. As in verse six, this is the approach of the NIV: "No one who is born of God will *continue* to sin, because God's seed remains in him; he cannot *go on sinning*, because he has been born of God" (emphasis mine). But, as we saw in 3:6, the present tense in 1 John does not mean continual action. Try sticking the "continuous action" present tense in 1:8—"If we say that we do not continually have sin, we deceive ourselves, and the truth is not in us." If the present tense means continuous action in 3:9, consistency argues for continuous action in 1:8. But that makes 3:9 a direct contradiction to or inconsistent with 1:8. Consistency cannot breed inconsistency. The law of non-contradiction prevails.

3. Perhaps the best answer lies in *His seed*. This is a reference to God's nature. His divine nature is passed down through His divine seed. The new birth places His seed in us. Just as my physical seed cannot produce something outside its genetic code, so God's seed cannot produce something contrary to His nature, that is, sin. God's nature cannot produce sin. God's nature in us (His seed) cannot produce sin.

This passage may be best understood as a parallel to Paul's statements in Rom 7:14-25. The evil which I do is done by me, but not really; it is done by my sin(ful) nature. So, the divine good which I do is not done by me; it is done by my divine nature. Both of these Natures dwell in the child of God simultaneously.¹ However, even though the sin(ful) nature from our "B.C. days" stays with us after we are born again (as does our physical body, our personality, our core intelligence, et cetera), the addition of God's divine nature with the indwelling Holy Spirit changes our identity forever. We are radically, fundamentally different from the Old Man (all we were before we met Christ or were born-again). We now have the mind of Christ (1 Cor 2:16). "For I delight in the law of God according to the inward man" (Rom 7:22). When I obey the lusts of the flesh, my new inner-man (the divine nature) is disgusted and repulsed. I can only cry out with Paul, "Oh, wretched man that I am!" when I choose to follow the lead of my sinful side.

This inner disgust was not present in my Old Man. Conviction from the Holy Spirit, yes; disgust and anguish such as Paul was reeling from in Rom 7:24, no. The new creature in Christ (2 Cor 5:17) knows that when the believer knowingly sins, he is not acting in accordance with this fundamental change which has taken place within him when he was born-again. He longs with the mind of Christ to act in harmony with his new identity. In fact, that is the only way he can manifest or make visible who really is a child of the King. And that's what the first half of verse ten tells us.

CONCLUSION—REVEALING OUR ROOTS

> In this the children of God and the children of the devil are manifest (3:10a).

This verse makes more sense if we understand it as a conclusion to all that has preceded in 1 John 2:29–3:9. This verse looks backwards. We would suggest that the last half of verse ten begins a new section on right loving—dealing with our brothers. The first half of verse ten concludes this developed section on right living—dealing with our sin. John's been trying to motivate us to godliness by pointing out how sin in the life of a believer is incongruous with Christ's purpose in coming and the new nature of the believer. It goes against who he really is at the core of his being.

The *children of God* only demonstrate or make visible (*manifest*) who they really are when they produce divine righteousness. The *children of the devil* only demonstrate or make visible (*manifest*) who they really are when they produce sin. So, remember, the sin(ful) nature we were born with remains with us until death. But when you sin, you are revealing only what you were before you were born-again. It does not mean you are not born-again with a divine nature. But it does mean you are keeping the divine nature hidden. We summarize the truth of this passage with these thoughts:

1. When a Christian sins, he is acting contrary to who he really is and what he really desires. It's against who he is at the core of his being. Though he may still have a sin(ful) nature, he is fundamentally a new creature in Christ whose inner man (his human spirit where God the Father [Eph 4:6], the Son [Col 1:27], and the Holy Spirit [1 Cor 6:19] have come to live) screams outs with the mind of Christ to do God's will.

There's a story of a man with a bizarre problem who went to see a psychiatrist.

"What's the trouble?" asked the psychiatrist.

"Well, doc, I know this sounds crazy, and I guess that's why I'm here, but whenever I go into a grocery store and get near the dog food, I have an overwhelming desire to tear into the Alpo and start eating."

With a quizzical frown the psychiatrist replied, "Well, I must say, I haven't run into this before. How long have you wrestled with this desire?"

"Well, doc, I guess ever since I was a little puppy."

We tend to act in accordance with how we see ourselves. If we don't understand our fundamental make-up as Christians, we may be going after Alpo instead of steaks. We may be scratching around for insects like a prairie chicken instead of soaring in the heights. You may even like the initial taste of chocolate covered ants or even chocolate covered Alpo, but the aftertaste is awful. Sin may taste good initially, but the aftertaste is terrible.

2. When a Christian sins, he is hiding God's glory. God was not created for our glory; we were created for His glory. We are put here to reveal His glory. We can only do that as we allow Him to live through us. We cannot display His glory and His character when we knowingly sin. Verse ten is about revealing who we really are.

Someday I hope to take a romantic trip with my wife up into New England to look at all of the beautiful leaves after they have turned from their summer green to a kaleidoscope of variegated colors. But you know what I've learned? Leaves really don't change color. The color is already there, but in spring and summer cells of chlorophyll cover up the true colors of the leaves. In the fall the chlorophyll cells fall away, and the true colors of the leaves are revealed. There is no changing of the colors; it's an unveiling of the colors.

And so it is in our Christian life. We can allow our true colors to be covered over with the chlorophyll of sin. That hides the glory of God. But progressive sanctification is becoming who you already are. As the work of the Holy Spirit in our lives progressively peels away the chlorophyll of sin, there is an unveiling of Christ in us, the hope of glory. The world sees an open expression of God's divine nature in us. We become a prism for His light to shine through us so the world can see His various colors (His attributes in us).

3. When a Christian sins, it is contrary to Christ. Isn't that what verse eight tells us? "For this purpose the Son of God was manifested, that He might destroy the works of the devil." As we allow Christ in us to be made visible for the world to see, we are helping to destroy the works of the devil. It is contrary to Christ's purpose to do anything else.

A psychiatrist thought he would do an experiment on self-image, so he got ten volunteers, brought them into his office one at a time, and briefed each on his assignment. He explained to them, "I want to see how people will respond to someone with a hideous, ugly deformity." Then the psychiatrist brought in a make-up artist who put an ugly scar on the right cheek of each volunteer. Before sending the volunteer out, they got a chance to look at themselves in a mirror. After the volunteer had gotten a good look, the mirror was taken away and the make-up artist was told to put the final touches of make-up on the scar. But, unknown to the volunteer, the make-up artist was instructed to pull the scar away before sending the volunteer out. The volunteer did not look any different when he left than when he had come in.

Each volunteer was told to sit for twenty minutes in the waiting room with other patients to observe their reactions to the phantom deformity of the volunteer. Then their job was to come back into the psychiatrist's office after observing the reactions and report how people had treated them. Ten different volunteers, with ten different perspectives resulted in reports that were all the same. According to the volunteers who thought they had ugly scars on their cheeks, the other patients in the waiting room were rude to them. People shunned them, and worst of all, if you can believe it, the other patients stared straight at the scars—the scars that weren't actually there.

The point of the experiment was to demonstrate that other people react to us in response to how we see ourselves. When you look inside yourself, what do you see—a big, hideous scar, or the Lion of the Tribe of Judah? When you look into the mirror, do you see a prairie chicken or a golden eagle?

As John Calvin said, "The responsibility of the Christian is to make the invisible world visible."

---

[1] Again, I do not wish to debate whether we have one nature or two natures once we become Christians. Call the "flesh" of Gal 5:21 and "the" sin of Rom 6:12ff whatever you wish. This remains within us after we are born again, and this is the sin factory. It really does not matter to me if we call this "our tendency toward sin," "our proclivity toward sin," "our residual sin pattern," or whatever. I choose to call it our Sin(ful) Nature. Whatever it is, it will not go away until Christ comes.

LESSON 13 "Roots and Fruits" I John 3:7-10a

1. Why is this scripture so controversial and difficult to understand?

2. List the rationale Dave sets forth for understanding 2:29 as a preface to 3:7.

    Major Premise:

    Minor Premise:

    Conclusion:

3. Now list the logic for understanding 3:7.

    Major Premise:

    Minor Premise:

    Conclusion:

4. How does 2 Peter 1:3-4 relate to 3:7?

5. What is your interpretation of 3:8 in light of Psalm 51:5, John 8:44 and Eph.2:2-3?

6. Review the suggested solutions to understanding 3:9. Which of these makes sense to you? Why?

7. How does Paul's statement in Romans 7:14-25 help us understand 3:9?

8. When believers become aware of their "sinful side," how do they react?

9. In 3:10a, John concludes the previous discussion. Dave summarizes this chapter with three statements that begin, "When a Christian sins ___ ." Write the three summary statements:

    When a Christian sins, he is acting _____

    When a Christian sins, he is hiding _____

    When a Christian sins, it is contrary to_____

10. How is sin like chlorophyll?

– 14 –

THE NECTAR OF LIFE

1 JOHN 3:10B-18

We have entered the *second wave* in John's presentation of the principles of fellowship. These were introduced in the first section of the body of this letter, and now he is developing these principles. In each principle he deals with one of the primary barriers preventing us from getting closer to God in our Christian walk or fellowship. Our sin is a major barrier. He has dealt with that twice: 1 John 1:5–2:2 and 1 John 2:28–3:10a. Now he wants to develop the second principle of fellowship, right loving, or how to deal with our Christian brothers. Yes, believe it or not, our Christian brothers can do more to keep us from walking close to God than people in the world. "To dwell above with saints we love, O, that will be glory; but to dwell below with saints we know, well, that's a different story." We saw this in 1 John 2:3-11, but here in 1 John 3:10b-23 John takes this principle, the principle of right loving, to another level.

But not all love is the right kind of love. In 1 John 3:10b-18 John explains just what right loving is all about. He gives us an exhortation to love (10b-11), an explanation of love (12-16), and an expression of love (17-18).

EXHORTATION TO LOVE

> Whoever does not practice righteousness is not of God, nor *is* he who does not love his brother. For this is the message that you heard from the beginning, that we should love one another (3:10b-11) …

There is a big difference between saying "not of God" and "not *born* of God" or "not *a child* of God." John uses "of God" in a way similar to Gamaliel in Acts 5:38-39, where in speaking of Christianity he said the work is either "of men" or it is "of God." If it is "of men," it will come to nothing, but if it is "of God," it cannot be overthrown. He speaks of who is behind the work, men or God. It's like saying the believers are either on God's side or man's.

And so in 1 John 3:10b God is not behind someone who does something unrighteous; nor is He behind the person who does not love his brother. Likewise, the one who does something unrighteous or does not love his brother is not on God's side, that is, he is not doing God's kingdom work, especially if he does not love his brother. (And, by the way, who is the person who does not love his brother? Certainly not a non-Christian. Do we need to be reminded of the obvious? Non-Christians *don't have Christian brothers!* In other words, this is not a test to see if you are a Christian or not.)

Again, the source of the concepts and wording in 1 John is important. It comes from the same author who wrote the Upper Room Discourse. In preparation for that intimate setting and the intimate truth shared, Judas did not belong. He had to be sent out of the room. What Jesus was about to give was not evangelistic truth. He had already done that, and John 1–12 reflects exactly that. Jesus cleared the room of the only unbeliever because what He had to say in His final hours was for those who were His own (John 13:1).

The message which they had heard from the beginning about loving each other came from those early years of their Christian lives when He walked with them, and specifically from the Upper Room. In John 13:34 He gave them the new commandment that they were to love each other as He had loved them. Now look at the connection between this kind of brother to brotherly love, Christ's commandments and joy:

> As the Father loved Me, I also have loved you; abide in My love. If you keep My commandments, you will abide in My love, just as I have kept My Father's commandments and abide in His love. These things I have spoken to you, that My joy may remain in you, and *that* your joy may be full. This is My commandment, that you love one another as I have loved you. Greater love has no one than this, than to lay down one's life for his friends. You are My friends if you do whatever I command you (John 15:9-14).

This is 1 John. It's truth for believers. For people to claim that this book is written to a mixed audience to help separate the sheep from the goats is to say Judas is still in the Upper Room. No. Judas has been sent out. The Upper Room truth and 1 John truth is unadulterated truth for an unadulterated audience of believers.

So, this is John's exhortation that we love one another. Why is this a barrier between us and God? Or why is it so hard to love our brother? Could it be that our brother has more potential to hurt us than the world? Could it be that we expect evil from the world, but not from our Christian brother? It hurts when a Christian brother does us wrong. It hurts deeply. And we go out of our way to avoid pain.

John says God calls us to love. But what does that mean? We need an explanation.

EXPLANATION OF LOVE

… not as Cain who was of the wicked one and murdered his brother. And why did he murder him? Because his works were evil and his brother's righteous (3:12).

Cain and Abel had a genuine relationship of brotherhood. It was physical, all right, but the parallel John is drawing is brotherhood. One brother is having problems with another brother. Cain killed his brother out of envy. Are Christians capable of murder and envy? Of course they are. Otherwise we wouldn't have passages like: 1 Pet 4:15 ("Let none of you suffer as a murderer, a thief, an evil doer …") and Jas 3:14; 4:2 ("You murder and covet and cannot obtain."). These verses are sure a waste of inspired text if they don't refer to Christians.

I have spoken in most of the prisons around the Houston area. I will never forget one inmate south of Houston in the unit called Ramsey 2. It's where they hold David Wayne Henley (the serial killer of teenage boys in Houston) and many other violent offenders. I went with a team to minister several times and got to know a fellow pretty well who had only one eye. I finally got comfortable enough with him to ask him how he lost his eye.

He said, "I was killing the man who raped my wife, and while I was strangling him, he gauged my eye out."

I thought a lot about him as we drove away that night. I could visualize myself doing the same thing if I caught the man who had raped my wife. And I realized, then, that I am capable of murder. So are you, whether you are a Christian or not.

Are you happy for your Christian brother or sister who receives a blessing like a new house, car, a promotion, raise or public recognition? Do you rejoice when your brother makes a coup in business? If you really love someone, you're just happy for them. Any other response is *of the wicked one*. It could be envy, jealousy, judgmentalism or any number of evil attitudes, but this is for sure … it's not love.

> Do not marvel, my brethren, if the world hates you. We know
> that we have passed from death to life, because we love the
> brethren. He who does not love his brother abides in death (3:13-
> 14).

Here is another passage which appears, at first blush, to be a test of whether we are genuine Christians or not. "We *know* that we have passed from death unto life because we love the brethren." So, it would appear that our love for other Christians is an indicator that we are truly God's people. But, what if we have a problem with a Christian or two, or three or four? If we don't love these brethren, does that mean we aren't Christians? Suddenly we are floating around in the limitless universe of subjectivity again.

Well, once again, our help may be in the use of the verb "to know," although this verb is different from those we have seen before (*oida* instead of *ginōskō*). The verb "to know" has numerous OT parallels in which it either speaks of a special intimacy or a deeper kind of understanding. In Gen 4:1 Adam "knew" his wife Eve and she conceived. Obviously, he had more than a casual knowledge of her. "To know" in this case is an example of physical intimacy. Hosea gives us several examples of spiritual intimacy. Gomer has been unfaithful and exemplifies the unfaithfulness of Israel. Both Gomer and Israel are in covenant relationships, one with a prophet and the other with Yahweh, respectively. But after she (Gomer/Israel) has played the harlot, God claims He is going to woo her back and says to her in Hosea 2:19-20,

> "And I will betroth you to Me forever;
> Yes, I will betroth you to Me in righteousness and in justice,
> In lovingkindness and in compassion,
> And I will betroth you to Me in faithfulness.
> Then you will *know* the LORD."

This use of "know" speaks of a deeper experience with the Lord than she had known before, that is, spiritual intimacy.

And Gen 22:12 gives us another example of "to know" as a deeper experience of understanding. God has asked Abraham to offer his son on the altar as a sacrifice. Abraham is obedient. Just before the knife is plunged into Isaac's heart, the Angel of the Lord says, "Do not lay your hand on the lad, or do anything to him; for now I *know* that you fear God, since you have not withheld your son, your only *son,* from Me."

Wait a minute, didn't the Lord know before Abraham went up the mountain what was in Abraham's heart? Sure He did; He was omniscient, all-knowing. But after Abraham raised the knife, God experienced Abraham's faith on a deeper level. There was a deeper kind of understanding.

Obviously, "to know" in the OT had many uses which took the knower beyond a superficial experience. That may well be what's going on with the meaning of *know* in 1 John 3:14. A new believer can have assurance that he will spend eternity with God when he dies based on God's promises (1 John 5:13). But when he has an experience of outrageous, triumphant love (loving someone who has hurt him), he enjoys the fact that he has passed from death unto life in a fuller, deeper way.

We must remember that the emphasis in eternal life is on *quality*, not *quantity*. All people exist forever. It's the *quality* of their existence which differs. And we can experience this improved quality of existence (eternal life) right now (1 John 5:11-12) as we love our Christian brothers and sisters. Our passage from death to life (John 5:24) can be experienced and appreciated right now when we share our Christian love for one another.

But if a believer hates his brother, his experience *on earth* is death. He abides in death. Don't forget the significance once again of "abides." We are talking fellowship here, not relationship; condition, not position. In this case, the believer is out of fellowship and experiences the *living death* of the Christian widow who lives for pleasure (1 Tim 5:6), or the Christian miserably aware of the battle within himself between his sin(ful) nature and his desire to do what is right (Rom 7:24), or the believer whose mind is filled with things of the flesh (Rom 8:6). The believer who walks around with hatred in his heart is miserable and often depressed.

> Whoever hates his brother is a murderer, and you know that no
> murderer has eternal life abiding in him (3:15).

"Murderer"—when we hate another Christian brother, we have the same attitude as Cain, who murdered his brother. Eternal life does not abide on such a person. We are not talking hell here; it's not relationship truth. This person is clearly not enjoying the wonderful, abundant life Christ offers on earth. His quality of life on earth is less than spectacular. Sitting around eaten up by the cancer of hatred for another is a miserable existence. It was Lord Tennyson who said,

> He that shuts Love out, in turn shall be
> Shut out from Love, and on her threshold lie
> Howling in the outer darkness.

Ben Wallace painted this pathetic picture on the canvas of life in his best selling novel, *Ben Hur*. The main character, Juda ben Hur, returns to Israel intent on one thing, revenge. Because of one man, he spent the best years of his youth as a slave in the galley of a ship. He had lost both position and wealth. And because of this one man, his mother and sister were dying as they rotted away in a cave outside Jerusalem as lepers. Ben Hur lived only for the hope of revenge. His enemy? Messala. That name burned its way into the brain of Ben Hur like a branding iron on cattle. So tightly did this passion for vengeance grip Ben Hur that his sweetheart, Esther, looking into his tortured eyes, said, "Juda ben Hur, you have become Messala."

It's the same old story. You become what you think about. If you think of how your enemy hurt you, you become like your enemy. Unfortunately, too many of our "enemies" are Christian brothers and sisters.

> By this we know love, because He laid down His life for us. And
> we also ought to lay down *our* lives for the brethren (3:16).

The opposite of Cain is Christ. Cain took a life; Christ gave His life. Does this not have echoes of John 15:13—"Greater love has no one than this, than to lay down one's life for his friends." Those who have experienced His sacrificial love understand what love is all about. As we live out this kind of sacrificial love, God's abundant life will abide in us—full joy (see 1:4).

Craig Phillips is an heir to the Wrigley fortune, and he talked about how he found joy and peace in Chicago when we was twenty-three years old. He was walking to work where he had a prominent job with a Fortune 500 company. He saw a poor man lying in the gutter, walked past him, and then recalled a faint voice from his youth when he had responded to a call to ministry. He went back to help the poor man. Since that "turn around" in his life, he left the prominent job, has founded two churches, and now in his mid-eighties volunteers at the wayside Cross Mission in Aurora, Illinois. What nectar of life did he find that caused him to leave a life of luxury? He describes his life since the "turn around":

> Since then my life has been a joy because there are so many broken things in life that Jesus can fix. When you let Him do it, you share in that joy. It's greater than any riches you could ever have.

It's greater than any material thing. One word with somebody has the power to pick him up and show him Jesus, and let him know that Jesus loves him. No amount of materialism can ever replace that. That lasts for eternity. That's where your treasure is. That's where your heart will be. And no one can take it from you. You can never lose that.[1]

Well, after his exhortation to love (3:10b-11), I'd say John has given us a pretty good explanation of what kind of love he is talking about (3:12-16). But what we need now is a good example or tangible way to express our love, and he gives us just that.

EXPRESSION OF LOVE

But whoever has this world's goods, and sees his brother in need, and shuts up his heart from him, how does the love of God abide in him? My little children, let us not love in word or in tongue, but in deed and in truth (3:17-18).

Here's a little test. Most of us will never have the opportunity to lay down our physical lives for our brethren. But we have opportunities almost every day to live a life of sacrificial love. Giving of the necessities of life is one expression of sacrificial love. If we hoarded these things, we might prolong our own lives in time of emergency. But our brother's emergency may be now. If we pass up the opportunity before us, the love of God does not *abide* (hint, hint—fellowship, not relationship) in us.

To *say* (word and tongue) we love our brother without meeting his emergency needs is pure hypocrisy. Divine love, sacrificial love, does not operate in such people. But they are the losers, for they miss out (lose) on the quality of life described herein. True, divine, sacrificial love as demonstrated by Christ is "in deed" (action is required) and "in truth" (genuine concern for the other person as opposed to some self-serving motive).

George Santayana said, "Love, whether ... parental or fraternal, is essentially sacrificial, and prompts a man to give his life for his friends." And Elbert Hubbard concluded, "The love we give away is the only love we keep."

CONCLUSION

What oasis in the desert did Craig Phillips find on the streets of Chicago? John has been instructing us in right loving, especially as it deals with our Christian brother. The message he gives over and over in his explanation of true love and his expression thereof is that genuine love is sacrificial.

Two Americans were challenged to go to Russia and spend some of their time in ministry to orphanages. They weren't professionals, and it cost them a pretty penny to leave their jobs and pay their own way. They sacrificed, but as they gave their love, they too found love in return. They came to one orphanage of about a hundred kids where the Christmas story had never been told. So they shared the story of Bethlehem, and the inn, and Mary and the manger, and you know the rest. Then they gave each kid some cut-outs to build their own little manger scene. They used brown flannel to make baby Jesus, some cardboard for the manger, and some yellow scraps of paper for straw.

As these women went around to look at the work of each child, all went well until one of the women got to the table where little Misha sat. He was about six years old, and everything was in perfect order until she looked into the manger. There were two babies in the manger. She thought, "Oh, my gosh. What's happened here?" So she asked the translator to come over so she could find out where Misha had gotten mixed up.

As Misha told the story, everything was accurate. He had all the details in place until he got to the very end, and then he began to ad lib. He said, "And when Maria laid the baby in the manger, she looked at me and asked me if I had a place to stay. I told her, 'I have no mamma and I have no pappa, so I don't have any place to stay.' Then Jesus told me I could stay with Him. Then I told Him I couldn't because I didn't have a gift to give like everyone else did.

"But I wanted to stay with Jesus so much, I thought, what do I have that I could give as a gift? I thought maybe if I keep Him warm, that would be a good gift. So I asked Jesus, 'If I keep you warm, would that be a good gift?' And Jesus said, 'If you keep me warm, that would be the best gift anyone gave me.' So I got into the manger, and Jesus looked at me and told me I could stay with Him in the manger ... always."

As little Misha finished his story his eyes brimmed with tears and they began to splash down his little cheeks. Then he put his hand over his face, his head dropped down to the table, and his shoulders shook as he sobbed and sobbed. The little orphan had found Someone who would never abandon or abuse him, Someone who would always stay with him. The American finished her story by saying, "And I learned it's *not what* you have in your life, *but who* you have in your life, that counts."

What did Mother Theresa find, and Craig Phillips, and this unnamed American? Isn't it that unmeasured giving reaps unlimited living. To give is to live. That's the nectar of life.

---

[1] Joseph M. Stowell, *Loving Christ* (Grand Rapids: Zondervan Publishing House, 2000), 162-63. Stowell shares this story by permission of Craig Phillips.

LESSON 14 "THE NECTAR OF LIFE" I JOHN 3:10B-18

1. What are your thoughts about the following quote? "To dwell above with saints we love, O, that will be glory; but to dwell below with saints we know, well, that's a different story" (page 173).

2. What importance do you attach to John's saying "not of God" in verse 10 rather than "not born of God" or "not a child of God"? How does Acts 5:38-39 help us understand the point that John is making?

3. How do we know that 10b is talking about believers?

4. Before Jesus talked to the disciples about loving each other (John 15:9-14), he sent Judas out of the room. Was that significant? Why?

5. John urges us to not be like Cain, and Dave then explains what it means to "love our brother." How would you summarize the Explanation of Love (pages 175-179)?

6. In the discussion that follows the heading, Expression of Love (page 179), there are several key ideas about love. List the ones that you identify.

    1.

    2.

    3.

7. What did little Misha (page 180) teach you?

8. So, what is the Nectar of Life?

– 15 –

JUST DO IT

1 JOHN 3:19-23

Valentines Day is a great time to practice Christian love, especially if you are married. Husbands are supposed to love their wives as Christ loved the church, which, of course, was sacrificial love, as we saw in 1 John 3:10b-18. So, I thought I would take Betty out to eat. Now I like candlelight and roses, being a hopeless romantic, but Betty is much more practical than I, so, wanting to be sacrificial, I offered to take her to Burger King. Don't laugh. Burger King is one of the few places you can get into on Valentines. I suppose there is a reason for that … but anyway I was looking for sacrificial things to do.

Now, in the course of my studies through the years I have learned to translate a number of different languages, most of them Indo-European and biblical languages. Oddly enough, I have never studied the two languages closest to my home: Spanish … and Female. So, after thirty-five years of marriage I decided it was time to study Female. This would be a good way to show sacrificial love. So I got a Female Dictionary. I'm just starting out, but already I have learned some good stuff. For example:

1. "Fine"—this is the word women use at the end of any argument when they feel they are right but can't stand to hear you argue any longer. It means that you should shut up. (Never use "fine" to describe how she looks. This will cause you to have one of those arguments.)
2. "Five Minutes"—this is half an hour. It is equivalent to the five minutes that your football game is going to last before you take out the trash, so women feel that it's an even trade.
3. "Nothing"—usually the answer given in answer to the question, "What's bothering you, sweetheart?" "Nothing" means something, so you should be on your toes. It usually is used to describe the feeling a woman has of wanting to turn you inside out, upside down, and backwards. "Nothing" usually signifies an argument that will last "Five Minutes" and end with the word "Fine."

4. "Go Ahead" (with raised eyebrows)—this is NOT permission; it's a dare! If you mistake it for permission, the result will be the woman will get upset over "Nothing" and you'll have a "Five Minute" discussion that will end with the word "Fine."

5. "Go Ahead" (normal eyebrows)—this is NOT permission either. It's resignation. It means "I give up" or "do what you want because I don't care." You will get a raised eyebrow "Go Ahead" in just a few minutes, followed by "Nothing," and "Fine" and she will talk to you in about "Five Minutes" when she cools off.

6. "Loud Sigh"—this is not actually a word, but is still often a verbal statement. Very frequently misunderstood by men. A "Loud Sigh" means she thinks you are a complete idiot and wonders why she is wasting her time standing there arguing with you over "Nothing."

7. "Soft Sigh"—again, not a word, but a verbal statement. "Soft Sighs" are one of the few things that some men actually understand. It means she is momentarily content. Your best bet is to not move or breathe in the hope that the moment will last a bit longer.

8. "That's OK"—this is one of the most dangerous statements that a woman can say to a man. "That's OK" means that she wants to think long and hard before deciding what the penalty will be for whatever you have done. "That's OK" is often used with the word "Fine" and in conjunction with a raised eyebrow "Go Ahead." Once she has had time to plan it out, you are in for some mighty big trouble.

9. "Thanks"—the woman is thanking you. Don't faint and don't look for hidden meaning. Just carefully and sincerely say, "You're welcome."

10. "Thanks A Lot"—this is dramatically different from "Thanks." A woman will say "Thanks A Lot" when she is really ticked off at you. It is usually followed by the "Loud Sigh." This signifies that you have hurt her in some callous way. Be careful not to ask what is wrong after the "Loud Sigh," as she will only tell you "Nothing."

Well, I am just beginning to learn Female and wish I had gotten this dictionary earlier in my marriage. Hopefully, Betty will see this as an attempt at sacrificial love. Sacrificial love. Perhaps the bigger problem is not the act as much as the attitude. How do we really know that we have the right motive? After all, some day the thoughts and intents of our hearts will be judged by the Lord. And we are told that we can give our bodies to be burned, but if we have not love, it profits us nothing. Because of the motive problem, doubts often creep in, even in the midst of Christian service. We begin to question our own motives. Why am I doing this? Is it to be seen and admired by other people? Is there some self-serving reason here? And we begin to question the motives of others. These doubts are daggers in the heart of Christian service.

It was Shakespeare who said, "Our doubts are traitors, and make us lose the good we oft might win, by fearing to attempt."[1] One of the greatest problems facing the human being is doubt. It is a measure of our insecurity. Security is surety. If we are secure, we are sure. If we are insecure, we are unsure. And we are all insecure to some degree. One of our greatest insecurities deals with our worthiness to be loved and our capacity to display love.

Inside of us hides something so dark, so depraved that we are scared to death someone will discover who we really are and what we are really like. We fear if they did, no one would like us, and no one would love us, precisely because it is this part of ourselves we detest, we dislike, and we abhor.

John wants to help us with this problem of insecurity and doubt about our self-worth caused by this evil within us. He realizes that we are still impure in our condition, that it is not until Jesus comes back that we will be completely sanctified (purified). Until then we still wrestle with this depraved aspect of our "humanness." He has tried to encourage us by explaining the fundamental change that took place in us when we were born of God and received His incorruptible seed with us. Instead of trying to correct the evil within us, he encourages us to release the Good (Jesus and the Holy Spirit whom we can quench and grieve).

Part of releasing the Good sounds like the Nike commercial: "Just do it." The word "Nike" is the Greek word for "victory." And although it is a secular company trying to sell shoes and other athletic wear, their motto isn't too far from what John is saying in this passage in regard to sacrificial love. "Just do it." That's what he says in 1 John 3:19-23. In the previous verses on sacrificial love (3:10a-18) we were told not to love in word and in tongue, but in deed and in truth. Here John explains what he means by "in truth." In order to get his point across John will explain to us the problem of a corrupt conscience (3:19-20) and the blessing of a clear conscience (3:21-23).

Problem of a Corrupt Conscience

> And by this we know that we are of the truth, and shall assure our hearts before Him. For if our heart condemns us, God is greater than our heart, and knows all things (3:19-20).

Of the truth is a reference back to the word "truth" in v. 18. We are to love in deed and in *truth*. We said that meant to love genuinely, that is, sincerely, with the right motive. It is precisely when we set out to do something to help another that our heart may condemn us and accuse us of false motives, our own unworthiness, or any number of doubts.

Now a legitimate question here would be why I have labeled this section "The Problem of a Corrupt Conscience" when the word "conscience" is not found in these two verses. We see the word "heart" a couple of times, but not "conscience." The answer to this is the use of the word "heart" in the NT. Sometimes the conscience is that part of the human spirit often referred to in Scripture as the heart (see Acts 2:37 and Heb 4:7).

Where did the conscience come from? It became part of the spirit of Adam and Eve when their relationship and fellowship with God was restored after they sinned. The first dispensation or administration in God's dealing with man is often called *Innocence*. But after they sinned, they did have some knowledge of good and evil. God incorporated this knowledge into a new feature of man's spirit to help them distinguish between good and evil. We call this new feature man's conscience and the second dispensation *Conscience*.

But man's conscience is not omniscient (all-knowing). That was part of Satan's lie to Eve, that is, he implied that she would have knowledge of good and evil on the same level as God. Adam and Eve got some knowledge of good and evil, but it was different from God's in at least too ways: 1) Experiential—God knew about sin but had never committed a sin; and 2) Incomplete—Eve now knew experientially the difference between good and evil, but she certainly was not omniscient like God. Even her knowledge of the difference between good and evil in *all things* was incomplete.

Paul points out the problems of a conscience which has incomplete knowledge in 1 Corinthians 8, where he contrasts the weak conscience and the strong conscience based on the amount of knowledge the conscience possesses. The strong conscience in a certain area (meat offered to idols) has God's knowledge about good and evil in that particular area. The weak conscience lacks that knowledge. The person with incomplete knowledge did not know God had declared meat offered to idols clean, that is, all right to eat. Paul urges the brother with that knowledge, the brother with the informed or strong conscience, not to use his freedom to eat meat offered to idols in such a way that his brother with incomplete knowledge, a weak conscience, is unable to progress in his Christian life.

What, you might ask, does all this have to do with 1 John 3:20? Simply this. Not all believers have strong (educated) consciences in the same areas. I might be able to do something with a clear conscience, while my brother might get a boat load of guilt for doing the same thing. Though the gift of conscience is from God, our consciences do not possess complete knowledge of good and evil. Some times we need to appeal to God's greater knowledge.

Here is a suggested translation of verse twenty: "*That* if our heart condemns us, *that* God is greater than our heart and *knows all things.*"[2] The important point here is that God is omniscient (all-knowing), whereas our consciences are not. We can assure or persuade (*peithō*) our heart by realizing that our own consciences do not have a perfect understanding of the thoughts and intents of the heart. God does. At the Judgment Seat of Christ He will sort out the act-intention complex (the deed and the motive behind the deed). Don't let the doubts of your own conscience keep you from acts of sacrificial love.

I can never forget when I was a young pastor starting my first church. We did not have a church building yet, so we rented a little office in a commercial building near the town square. I didn't have a secretary to help, but I did have a nice, reclining easy chair to sit in when my desk chair became uncomfortable. I also liked to sit in this particular chair or kneel before it when I prayed. I especially liked to kneel because kneeling is just uncomfortable enough to remind me that I am supposed to be praying. When I sit, my mind seems to wander more quickly. If I am on my knees and my mind begins to wander, sooner or later the discomfort reminds me that I am on my knees. From there I ask why am I on my knees, and then I remember that I am supposed to be praying. Am I the only one who wrestles with stuff like this?

Oh well, one day I was kneeling in front of this chair praying when I realized I had not locked the door of my office. People were used to dropping by on a pretty regular basis. Someone could walk in and see me praying. I thought, "Oh, I better get up and lock the door so they won't think I'm trying to be showy like the Pharisees." Then I thought, "No, this could be good. They will open the door and say, 'Oh, my, isn't our pastor spiritual?' and spread the word." Then I thought, "You scumbag. How could you have a thought like that? Why don't you just quit praying?" Then I thought, "Uh oh, that thought was from Satan. He won't get me. I'm just going to keep on praying." Then I thought, "But the door is still unlocked. Better lock." And then I thought, "No, this could be good ...." And so on.

Now I realize that most of you don't wrestle with stuff like this, and I don't know if my Sin(ful) Nature is worse than most, but it is pretty sickening. What do you do in those cases? You know what you do? *Just do it.* And that's what I think this passage is saying. You bow before the Lord and say, "Lord, I am going to do this because I think it is sacrificial. I am not aware of any false motives I have. But if they are there, I trust the blood of Christ will cleanse me from these unknown sins. So I am committing myself to you to sort these things out in your own time."

What does this mean in practical terms? Here are some typical situations where we tend to be plagued with doubts:

1. Second guessing yourself after you made a decision with all the info you had at the time. The job, marriage, the investment turned out to be a disaster. Now you are kicking your self to sleep at night. Stop it. Don't do that.

2. You see evidence of some spiritual gifts in your life. You feel the tug of the Holy Spirit to do something of eternal value with your life. But you doubt that you are worthy. You hold back. John would say, "Just do it."

3. You're like the rat in Skinner's experiment. You go to the food at one end of the cage and get burned by an electric shock. So you go to the food at the other end and get burned by another electric shock. Back and forth. You're hungry, so you want to feed, but every time you take a bite, you get burned. Finally, you sit down in the middle of the cage, immobile, afraid to make another choice. Perhaps you have been burned by love or Christian service. You're hungry for love, or you want to serve, but every time you seem to get burned. Now you sit at home and vegetate, afraid of getting burned again. John would say, "Love again." John would say, "Serve again." The only one who wins is Satan, the great accuser of the brethren, the great developer of doubt.

4. You're an approval seeker. You need strokes from people to feel good about yourself. The fact that the Lord sees you and is pleased is not enough. You serve and serve without the appreciation from your superiors or your peers that you deserve. You do love the Lord and want to serve him, but you crave the approval of men. Your mixed motives have you all mixed up. You're tempted to quit. Confess the desire for the approval of men and move forward. Serve Him. Just do it.

5. You love the Body of Christ. You want to serve sacrificially. But the stars in your eyes always turn to sand. Sooner or later you get caught in a church conflict, you get misunderstood, and the very people you have tried to help the most wind up your accusers. You're conflicted. You think your motives are right, but you're not sure. If you really were serving as unto the Lord and not men, then why does it hurt so much when you get dumped on? You're on the side-lines, confused, conflicted.

Joseph Stowell tells a moving story in his book on *Loving Jesus* about one of God's servants in Union Grove, Wisconsin. His name is Bud Wood, and he runs Shepherds Home, one of the finest facilities in America for dealing with mentally challenged children and adults. Wood said one of the greatest problems they had at the home was maintenance. You would think his reference would have been to spilled drinks on the rugs or structural damage to beds, chairs, and tables. But he said, "No, it's the cleaning of the windows. You see, we share Christ with every single child and adult in this facility. We don't know how much they understand. But we know that a high percentage of them profess faith in Jesus Christ. And you can go up and down the halls of this facility any time of day and see all kinds of children and adults with their noses, and fingers, and hands pressed against the windows ... because they are looking for Jesus ... and they are waiting for Him to come ... and to take them home."[3]

When I read that story, I thought, "Man, we who lack the mental impairment of these people are so sophisticated and get so balled up in attitudes and actions and how we will look to others, but these children seem to be able to just see straight through ... just pure faith ... a direct link ... a direct pipe. They are just looking to the author and finisher of their faith." Oh, how I long for that day, the day when I no longer have this sickly, Sin(ful) Nature, when I am pure as He is pure, for I shall see Him as He is. But until that day comes, I am not going to allow my accusing heart to keep me from making a difference, because I know that my God is greater than my heart, and He knows all things.

So, John has told us about the problem of a corrupt conscience. That's the bad news. The good news is that there is a blessing which goes along with a clear conscience.

BLESSING OF A CLEAR CONSCIENCE

> Beloved, if our heart does not condemn us, we have confidence
> toward God. And whatever we ask we receive from Him, because
> we keep His commandments and do those things that are pleas-
> ing in His sight. And this is His commandment: that we should
> believe on the name of His Son Jesus Christ and love one anoth-
> er, as He gave us commandment (3:21-23).

The opposite of doubt is *confidence*, especially before God. James 1 tells us that the one who doubts when he comes to God in prayer: 1) Will not receive what he is asking for; and 2) Is a double-minded man, unstable in all his ways. But the blessing of a clear conscience is confidence before God. There is no need to cower before Him in shame, as did Adam and Eve after they sinned. We can walk with Him in the garden because He is our Lord, but He is also our friend. He is our Father in heaven, but He is our Abba on earth.

The confident Christian can also be assured of a fruitful prayer life. The one with a clear conscience can come boldly before the throne of grace. Why? Because he is keeping God's commandments, and the most important of these commandments is the command to believe on the name of His Son Jesus Christ and to love one another. The focus here is not on the ten com-mandments, though nine of them have been carried over into the New Covenant, the Law of Christ. The focus here is on a commandment only Christians can keep because the command includes believing on the name of Jesus as well as loving Christian brothers. Non-Christians do not believe on the name of Jesus, which is why they are non-Christians, and therefore cannot love their Christian brothers. Remember, non-Christians don't have Christian brothers. They aren't part of the same family.

When we love one another, we are doing the kind of sacrificial acts men-tioned in 1 John 3:16-17. Such a person will undoubtedly be praying unselfishly as well, according to the needs of those he is helping. God delights in answering such prayers. Quite often these prayers are according to His will (1 John 5:14).

In his concluding thought to this section of right loving, John comes back to the commandment Christ gave us to love one another as He loved us in John 13:34. This commandment has been in the back of John's mind throughout the letter. And there is a direct link between our conscience and our ability to love (1 Tim 1:5): Sincere Faith + Good Conscience + Pure

Heart ⇒ Sacrificial Love. When my conscience is clogged with guilt, not only is there a barrier between me and God, but I am also unable to love others as He loved us. My motives are impure. I cannot love in deed and in truth (sincerely).

CONCLUSION

What am I trying to say out of all this? The cure for self-condemnation is self-sacrifice.

If it is a question of morality, when in doubt, cut it out. But if it is a question of sacrificial love, when in doubt, *just do it* and commend yourself to the One who knows your heart better than you do.

The story comes from Denmark in the days after Hitler put forth the decree to round up the Jews from the nations surrounding Germany.[4] Are you aware that far more Jews were killed from nations outside of Germany than in Germany itself? There were less than a million Jews in Germany when the persecutions began, but as we all know, more than six million Jews were destroyed by the Nazi war machine. In Denmark every Jew was commanded to wear a yellow arm band to identify his lineage. Then they were picked up by the Gestapo to be railroaded into the death camps.

This was more than the king of Denmark could bear. Yet he had to read the decree or be killed himself. So Christian X stood up in the palace in Denmark and read the decree from the Nazi government. Then with tears in his eyes he pulled out a yellow arm band, though he had no Jewish blood in his own lineage, and put it on his own arm. Then all the people listening to and watching the king did the same thing. You see, news of the king's plan has spread all around Denmark, so the Gentiles in Denmark decided they too would wear yellow arm bands. So both the Jews and the Gentiles were wearing yellow arm bands, thus confusing the Gestapo and preventing them from singling out the Jews for extermination.

Christian X did this at the risk of his life. But greater love has no one than this, than to lay down one's life for his friends. And you know, all of us came into this life with yellow arm bands, not signifying our Jewishness, but rather our sinfulness. It's in our lineage from Adam. But the great mystery of it all is that the King of Heaven, with love and with tears in His eyes, came down to earth, marched up to Galgotha, and put on a yellow arm band for us. He identified with us and offered to take our yellow arm bands from us, so that whoever would believe in Him could take off his yellow arm band

and nail it to the cross that we might not be marched off to Satan's death camp, but that we could be free and live forever.

---

[1] William Shakespeare, *Measure for Measure*, I, IV, 78.

[2] Zane C. Hodges, *The Epistles of John: Walking in the Light of God's Love* (Irving, TX: Grace Evangelical Society, 1999), 164.

[3] Joseph M. Stowell, *Loving Christ* (Grand Rapids: Zondervan Publishing House, 2000), 203.

[4] Ibid., 204-205.

LESSON 15 "JUST DO IT" I JOHN 3:19-23

1. If you are a man, what "female language" would you add to the list on pages 183 and 184?

    If you are a woman, what "male language" would you put in your "Male Dictionary"?

2. How are sacrificial love and motive related? Explain what it means to "love . . . with actions and in truth" (verse 18).

3. "And we are all insecure to some degree" (page 185). Why do you think Dave made this statement in the context of this lesson?

4. How would you counsel a person who says, "I just need to let my conscience be my guide"?

5. On pages 188-189, you will find five typical situations where one might be plagued with "doubt." Can you identify with any of the five? How might the Nike slogan apply?

6. In what sense is God "greater than our heart (conscience)" (verse 20)?

7. "If our heart does not condemn us, we have confidence toward God" (verse 21). What are some of the benefits of this "confidence"?

8. On page 191, Dave states the cure for self condemnation. What is it?

9. Verse 23 gives us a two-part command. What are the two parts and how can you demonstrate them in your life this week?

FIREFLIES OR ROACHES?

1 JOHN 3:24–4:6

Being from Houston I'll have to admit, I'm not much of a bug lover. I'll never forget my first week in Houston after moving from the hills of Tennessee. It was early September but still hot and muggy. But worse, I was a freshman living on the third floor of a dormitory with no air conditioning. That's right. Rice University was free in those days for everyone who was admitted and the richest private school in the nation (they even owned Yankee Stadium), but they couldn't seem to afford air conditioning for their on campus students (this has changed, but they also started charging tuition). We survived those early weeks (barely) with window fans. But open windows meant, guess what, roaches. I'd never seen a roach fly. The first time one took off it looked light a black Boeing 747. I ducked. Hate those things—ugly, squishy, gratuitous, no redeeming values.

And then there are the mosquitoes banditos. If roaches are 747s, then Houston mosquitoes are dive bombers, Intruders. They descend with an annoying whine and land like a Harrier. But they rarely come at you solo. No, there are squadrons of these blood-sucking monsters. Without protection they will carry you away—take you to their house for dinner.

There are centipedes, fleas, fire ants—I could go on and on. So this summer I am enjoying Germany. What a place to be in the summer. It's 65–75° twenty-four hours a day. The people in the country live in bunched up little villages, so the country-side is either all woods or beautiful fields of barley and wheat. On top of that, they have walking or bike riding trails all through these woods and wheat fields. Gorgeous. Reminds me of Tennessee, only cooler. And guess what? You got it—no bugs. I haven't seen a roach, a mosquito, an ant, a centipede—anything.

I take that back. There is one bug I have seen over here. But, then, even this bug is not ugly. In fact, it may be the only bug I've ever found attractive. Can you call a bug attractive? Well, I think you'll agree with me, this one is. In America we call it a firefly or lightning bug. Same in German—Leuchtkäfer. It stays light until eleven in the evening in Germany, so I enjoy taking a long walk into the woods, come out onto the edge of a giant wheat field, sit on a bench with a good book, and watch. Just before dusk the deer come out—a beautiful reddish colored deer. And then, the fireflies.

I remember as a boy we kids would run around with a glass jar catching the lightning bugs, putting twenty or thirty in a jar with holes for air in the top. It was fun to watch them glow. Or even to let them walk around on your arms or fingers. Harmless little creatures. They mind their own business, don't carry diseases, don't leave fang marks, not stealth vampires, and they don't steal your food. Best of all, as the young Robert Louis Stevenson said, they punch "holes in the darkness."

Now, I ask you, would you rather be a roach or a firefly? Is there really a choice there? Scripturally speaking, I'd say we are born roaches, but born again fireflies. As roaches we can be a menace to society, but as fireflies we have the potential to put holes in the darkness. Jesus said we are the "light of the world." But He also said we can put our light under a bushel basket.

What is it that makes some Christians glow in the dark, while others blend in so that they are indistinguishable from the darkness around them? Is there something that can light up the life of a Christian so that the world can see a difference and be drawn to that light? Is there anything a former roach can do to let his light shine. I'm now a firefly instead of a roach, but my blinker's not turned on. How can I be a firefly for Christ?

John speaks of a sustained joy in 1 John 1:4 which comes from fellowship with the Father and with His Son Jesus Christ. In 1 John 3:24–4:6 we learn about the power source which helps sustain this joy and turns our blinker on.

John has been developing the principles of fellowship he introduced in chapter one. He runs through the same three principles in three successive waves. In 1 John 3:24–4:6 we come to his second treatment of right learning—dealing with our enemies. We are right back with the Antichrist, who was introduced in the last section on right learning (1 John 2:18-27). False teachers and false prophets can be very deceptive. That's how they gain a following. Often times they deceive born again Christians. We need help to overcome them. So John thinks back to the Upper Room promises from Jesus, in particular the promise about a Helper who would guide them into all truth. Of course, as God's revelation to man progressed though the giving of more Scripture, we know this Helper to be the Holy Spirit. Here John talks about living with the Holy Spirit (3:24), looking for the Holy Spirit (4:1-3), and listening to the Holy Spirit (4:4-6). Frankly, I know very few subjects more confusing to believers than the different ministries of the Holy

Spirit, so at the end of our lesson we will try to sort out the baptizing, leading, and filling ministries of the Holy Spirit. But right now let's follow John's introduction to the Holy Spirit.

LIVING WITH THE HOLY SPIRIT

> Now he who keeps His commandments abides in Him, and He in him. And by this we know that He abides in us, by the Spirit whom He has given us 3:24).

With the key word *abides* we return once again to our theme of fellowship, not relationship. The word in noun form means "home, abode." This use of "abiding" began in 2:6 and continues as a picture of fellowship. In 1 John 2:3 knowing Him intimately/intensely is equated with keeping His commandments. In the verse before us abiding in Him is equated with keeping His commandments. That should tell us something. If A = B, and B = C, then A = C. To abide in Him is to know Him intimately. Need we repeat it? Abiding in Him is not a statement about our position, but our condition; not our relationship, but our fellowship. This word is used almost as much in John 14–15 (fourteen times) as all the rest of John, and it is used twenty-four times in 1 John. If we remember that John 14–15 was intimate truth for the ears of believers only (Judas was sent out), just the parallel use of *abide* in 1 John should tell us that the latter is truth for believers as well, that is, truth about their fellowship with God, not their relationship with God. It's about edification, not evangelism.

But this is the first mention of *Spirit* in 1 John. The anointing of 2:20 was probably the Holy Spirit, but John did not use the word *Spirit*. In his Gospel John tells of Jesus' promise to send the Holy Spirit to guide, testify, glorify, convict, and disclose (John 15:26-27; 16:7-15). The thought here is that the Holy Spirit will be a sign to us that we are in fellowship with God. We know that He *abides* in us by the *Spirit* whom He has given us. But how will the Holy Spirit manifest Himself to us so that we know we are listening to the Spirit of Truth and not a spirit of error?

LOOKING FOR THE HOLY SPIRIT

> Beloved, do not believe every spirit, but test the spirits, whether they are of God; because many false prophets have gone out into the world. By this you know the Spirit of God: Every spirit that confesses that Jesus Christ has come in the flesh is of God, and every spirit that does not confess that Jesus Christ has come in the

flesh is not of God. And this is the spirit of the Antichrist, which you have heard was coming, and is now already in the world (4:1-3).

Jesus said the Holy Spirit would be the Spirit of Truth who would testify on behalf of His person and work (John 15:26). This Spirit glorifies Jesus (John 16:13-15). Thus the Holy Spirit confesses that Jesus came in the flesh. It is generally thought that the opponents of John were teaching that the spirit of Christ came upon Jesus the man at his baptism and left at the cross, but never really mixed with human flesh.

Platonic and Neoplatonic philosophy put a great deal of pressure on Christian doctrine from the beginning of Christianity. After all, Plato was the primary philosophical influence in the Mediterranean world and had been for three hundred years before Jesus. He emphasized perfect ideals in a spiritual world, which had corresponding (but imperfect) representations in the material world. Plato's philosophy had a variety of offspring, which elevated the spiritual over the material. Most of them saw the human soul as eternal and good, but it was clothed in a material body which was not good. The goal was to get the spirit or soul of man released from its bondage in his evil body.

Of course this approach to the material and spiritual worlds is not biblical for a fistful of reasons, not the least of which is that God created the material world, including the human body, and declared this material world good, not evil. The view that the body is evil led to all sorts of ascetic (denying the flesh) practices and a prohibition of marriage for clergy that we have with us even today. Augustine, who studied the works of the philosopher who most influenced that era, Plotinus, imported this view of man right into his theology. He led an ascetic seminary in which he viewed any sexual relations between a man and wife to be sinful unless it was for procreation only. I have people in my church who were raised on that philosophy. We are indebted to Augustine for many wonderful emphases he brought into our understanding of Christian theology, but his neoplatonic influence is not one of them.

Plato was still the primary philosophical influence in Christianity during the days of the early reformers. Melanchthon, the friend and teacher of Luther, actually put Plato and Aristotle on an equal level during the first twenty years of the Reformation. Thus we find this huge emphasis in Western Christianity on going to heaven, on doing whatever is necessary to make sure our spirit and soul spend eternity in heaven when we die.

This all began in earnest with Augustine. He is the one who said we spend our entire lives being made righteous (being justified) so we can go to heaven when we die. If we don't attain the acceptable level of righteousness God requires (perfection), then we go to Purgatory to suffer an appropriate length of time before we go to heaven. This entire concept became a huge fund raiser for the church because they could sell indulgences (forgiveness) to people who wanted to buy their poor suffering parents out of Purgatory after their death. It was this very issue which prompted Luther to protest the sale of indulgences in his ninety-five theses.

But the preoccupation with trying to get to heaven did not cease. The English Puritans and their followers who came to establish America spent much of their spiritual efforts in meditation and introspection to determine if they were elect or not, that is, would they go to heaven after they died or not.

Now, I don't wish to alarm you. Obviously, it is very important whether we go to heaven when we die. That's relationship. There is no fellowship without relationship. Christ died to remove the sin in our lives which separated us from God. Unless that separation is removed, there is no relationship or fellowship. BUT, it is interesting to look at the OT to see where we find this emphasis on getting to go to heaven when we die. It's not there, and that is the vast majority of our Bible. The emphasis in the OT is on having a long, prosperous life in the land, meaning Israel.

And what about the NT? Where would you go in Matthew, Mark, and Luke to get me to heaven? It's not the *emphasis* of those three gospels. Oh, I didn't say it's not in there. But just the fact that you have trouble connecting the dots in those three gospels with faith, forgiveness of sins, and eternal life in heaven tells us this is not the *emphasis* of those books. When most people start thinking about how to go to heaven in evangelical circles, their minds wander over to parts of John, a little bit of Romans, a little bit of Ephesians, a little bit of Galatians. But even in these books there are only a few explicit verses about how to be in heaven when we die. And it certainly is not the emphasis of the rest of the NT.

What then is the emphasis of the NT? It's to glorify God through becoming like Christ. That involves discipleship, or teaching people how to be *fully devoted followers* of Jesus Christ. Even the well-known Great Commission of Matt 28:19-20 puts the emphasis on discipleship: "Go, therefore, and make disciples …." It never mentions evangelism, per se.

"What's the point here?" you ask. "Are you going to downplay the most important decision of my life, the decision to trust Jesus Christ as my Savior." Not at all. It is the most important decision or step of faith any of us will ever make. But I am going to call it the "starting blocks." What would you think of a camera man who was doing the TV work for the 400 meter Olympic finals if the gun went off to start the race, and he left the camera on the starting blocks? You would jump up and down in front of your TV about what an idiot he was for not panning his camera on the runners as they go around the track.

Well, Christians and preachers who spend all their time focusing on "getting people to heaven" are like that camera man. They are putting all their attention on the starting blocks and missing out on the race. The biblical emphasis is on the race. Could this be one reason why there are so many complacent Christians who are content to have their ticket to heaven but live like hell? If so, this is the legacy of Plato and his troops. It all developed out of his emphasis on an ideal, perfect spiritual world as opposed to an imperfect, evil material world.

John was facing some variation of this same theme. That's why he made sure we understood that Jesus really could be heard, seen, and touched (1 John 1:1-2). And that is also why he is concerned that people confess or agree (*homologeō*) that Jesus Christ came *in the flesh*. His body was not just an appearance. It was real flesh and blood, and it did not make Him sinful. Such errors about the person and work of Christ do not come from the Holy Spirit, but rather from false prophets and the spirit of Antichrist within them.

Well, it stands to reason if the Holy Spirit is living in us, and we now know what to look for to recognize the voice of the Holy Spirit, how do we recognize someone who is listening to the Holy Spirit?

LISTENING TO THE HOLY SPIRIT

> You are of God, little children, and have overcome them, because He who is in you is greater than he who is in the world. They are of the world. Therefore they speak *as* of the world, and the world hears them. We are of God. He who knows God hears us; he who is not of God does not hear us. By this we know the spirit of truth and the spirit of error (4:4-6).

The contrasts in this passage are many and as strong as black versus white: 1) *You* versus *them* or *they*; *He who is in you* versus *he who is in the world*; *of God* versus *of the world*. And notice the subtle shift from *you* in verse four to *we* in verse six. It's another situation of A(*You*) = B(*of God*) and C(*We*) = B(*of God*); therefore, A(*You*) = C(*We*). Of course, these are not really equations. The *you* refers to the *little children*, and the *we* has to include the apostle who is writing the letter. But at least the *we* must include the little children along with the apostle. The point is that the apostle identifies with his readers. It's not a *we* versus *you* contrast. The *we* and the *you* combine into one group against the *them*. It wouldn't even be necessary to mention these obvious facts if there weren't so many preachers and commentaries of the reformed persuasion out there who will tell us that John is writing to a mixed audience of believers and unbelievers so they can figure out who are the sheep and who are the goats. That kind of introspection was a Puritan preoccupation. John Owen wrote a 650 page book just to help his readers look within to figure out if they were elect or not.[1] The NT teaches preoccupation with Christ, not with yourself. As long as I focus on myself, there will always be doubts. When I focus on Jesus, the doubts disappear.

Those who are not of God will listen to the false prophets who spread false doctrine about the person and work of Jesus. Those who are of God will listen to the voice of the Holy Spirit as He speaks the truth about the person and work of Jesus. Correct doctrine about Christ is one way to distinguish between the Spirit of Truth and the spirit of error. So this is how we can recognize the Holy Spirit within us.

There is so much confusing teaching about the Holy Spirit in evangelical circles today. Many of the charismatic persuasion tell us we must get the baptism of the Holy Ghost (Spirit) at least once if not twice in order to have enough power to live a victorious Christian life. They contrast Peter before and after Pentecost and tell us we are like Peter before Pentecost. That's why we fail so much. But look at Peter after Pentecost. He got the Holy Ghost and never looked back. That's what you need—more power.

Others will tell us the key to a victorious Christian life is the filling of the Holy Spirit. The campus ministry that discipled me, for which I will ever be grateful, also had what we called the "Bird Booklet." It had a picture of dove on the front, which symbolized the Holy Spirit, and gave us five steps on how to be filled with the Holy Spirit. If we were filled, we were told, we would be in fellowship with God and enjoy the fruits of the Holy Spirit, but especially we would have the results of filling, which were speaking to one another in psalms, hymns and spiritual songs, singing and making melody in our hearts to the Lord, giving thanks for all things always to God the Father, and submitting one to another in the fear of God (Eph 5:19-21).

People sometimes call our church to check it out and begin with the question, "Is this a Spirit-filled church?" That's a tricky question to answer because "Spirit-filled" means different things to different people. The believers in Acts 2 were Spirit-filled and spoke in tongues. So to some a Spirit-filled church is a charismatic church where they try to practice all the gifts of the Holy Spirit. To another group Spirit-filled just means you are walking in fellowship with Jesus.

Though this subject deserves a book unto itself, I've put together a little chart comparing the three primary ministries of the Holy Spirit in the life of a believer. This chart has helped many distinguish these ministries more clearly and understand their own pilgrimage with the Holy Spirit in a more biblical light.

MINISTRIES OF THE HOLY SPIRIT

BAPTIZING	LEADING	FILLING
Rom 6, 1 Cor 12	Rom 8, Gal 5	Luke 1, Acts 2
Fact	Faith	Feeling
Indwelling	Enabling	Intoxicating
Permanent	Progressive	Periodic

The Baptizing Ministry of the Holy Spirit

The NT does not reference two different baptisms of the Holy Spirit. A distinction between being baptized by the Holy Spirit into the Body of Christ and baptism with the Holy Ghost for power does not exist. "With" or "by" is the same word in Greek, as is the word for "Spirit" or "Ghost." There is only one baptism and one Spirit (Eph 4:4-5). And that baptism occurs when a person trusts Christ and is baptized into the Body of Christ by the Holy Spirit (1 Cor 12:13). That baptism must be the experience of all Christians (new or old, carnal or spiritual) because the church at Corinth included all varieties of believers, but Paul says they all had the baptism of the Holy Spirit.

Now this baptism took place whether the Christian knew it or not. It was a fact. The Holy Spirit placed that person into Christ and came to dwell in him (1 Cor 6:19). At that point the new believer got all the power he will ever get for a victorious Christian life (2 Pet 1:3). Now Paul prays that his spiritual eyes will be opened so he can see how much power he has been given (Eph 1:18-19). And this indwelling of the Holy Spirit is permanent (Eph 4:30). He cannot be taken from us. This ministry is quite a bit different from the leading ministry of the Holy Spirit, one which we don't hear that much about.

The Leading of the Holy Spirit

Sometimes I ask a class of students to pick out the big "victory" chapters for the Christian life from the NT. They will usually get around to Romans 8 and Galatians 5. Then I ask them if they find the word "filling" in any of these chapters. Of course, it is not there, which leads to another question: If Romans 8 and Galatians 5 are the most important chapters in the NT on the victorious Christian life and the filling of the Holy Spirit is never mentioned in these chapters, then what is the relationship between a Spirit-filled life and the victorious Christian life? Could it be that there is none?

Now before you brand me a heretic, hear me out. The Holy Spirit is certainly referenced in these two chapters. There is no victory in the Christian life without the power of the Holy Spirit. But these chapters do not speak of the filling ministry of the Spirit. They speak of His leading ministry. Is this being picky? Not if every word in our text is inspired by God.

The Christian life is described as a walk, a journey in Romans 8 and Galatians 5. From our perspective, we walk with the Spirit. From His perspective, we are led by the Spirit. If we are led by the Spirit, we will not fulfill the lusts of the flesh (Gal 5:16). In other words, we are victorious Christians. What are the lusts of the flesh? They are the works of the flesh mentioned a few verses later. But, if we walk with the Spirit or are led by Him, we will enjoy the fruit of the Spirit which are also mentioned a few verses after Gal 5:16. This is the victorious Christian life. It is not a permanent occurrence like the baptism of the Spirit. Rather, it is progressive. As we continue growing in our Christian lives, we follow Him (are led by Him) more and more consistently.

Nor is the leading ministry characterized by the word "fact" as is the baptism of the Spirit. It is better characterized by "faith." The Christian life is a life of faith. Jesus was *led* by the Spirit into the wilderness to be tempted by Satan. I'm sure that didn't *feel* good. It took *faith* for Him to go through that experience. But by faith He was victorious. He left us an example of limiting the use of His own power and depending on the power of the

Spirit for His walk and His works (Matthew 12). If the baptism of the Spirit could be described as "indwelling," then the leading ministry of the Spirit can be described as "enabling." He supplies the power for victory.

The Filling Ministry of the Holy Spirit

This is probably the most confusing of the three ministries of the Spirit because people and preachers seem to use "filling" interchangeably with "baptizing" and "leading." The charismatics have a good argument that filling involves speaking in tongues at least once since the people at Pentecost were filled and spoke in tongues. And in Acts 10:43-47 those of the household of Cornelius spoke in tongues as a sign that they had received the Holy Spirit (although it does not use the word "filled" in this case).

Other evangelicals who are not of the charismatic stripe get their understanding of filling from Eph 5:18-21 where the believers are commanded to be filled. Various "formulas" have been suggested as to how this might be accomplished. What is missing in this approach are three observations: 1) The word "holy" is not connected with "spirit" as it is every other time filling and the Spirit are mentioned; 2) The Greek construction "be filled with" is not found in this passage (a construction which requires the verb to be followed by "Holy Spirit" in the genitive case); and 3) The following participles which give us either the results of being filled or the means by which to be filled are addressed to a church worship experience such as you would find in 1 Corinthians 14 (how, for example, can you "submit" to yourself? "Submitting to one another" is the fifth result or means of filling.).

Another relevant observation not directly connected with Ephesians 5 is that in every case where filling of the Holy Spirit is mentioned with the verb *pimplēmi* (Luke 1:15, 41, 67; Acts 2:4, 4:8, 31; 9:17; and 13:9), there is a definite physical manifestation of that filling so that both the one(s) filled and any listeners or observers knew something special was going on. Usually someone was preaching or giving some testimony. But it was not some fact hidden away from the eyes and ears they had to take by faith. In as much as the manifestation of the filling was physical, you might say you could "feel" the filling. It was described in Acts 2 like something intoxicating. It also seems to come and go without any sin either being committed or confessed (Peter, for example, was filled in Acts 2 and again in Acts 4; but we do not have any record of sin on his part between Acts 2 and 4 which would have taken away his filling and required confession to get it back).

"But what about Ephesians 5:18-21?" someone will ask. "Aren't we commanded to be filled with the Spirit?" I've explained part of this. It isn't "with the Spirit," and there is no clear evidence that this is the *Holy* Spirit. This construction is often translated as an adverb; that is, *en pneumati* = spiritually. A suggested translation here, keeping the church worship context in mind, would be: "Allow yourselves to be spiritually filled by means of speaking to one another in psalms, hymns, and spiritual song, singing and ...." We can quench the Holy Spirit in our worship services, or we can allow ourselves to be filled (*plērousthe* as a middle-passive form can speak of allowing something to happen or be done to ourselves). The type of worship described in the following verses may be more conducive to spiritual filling than the more ritualistic approach.

Putting all these observations together, it looks as though the filling ministry of the Holy Spirit was a special, sovereign act on the part of the Holy Spirit to empower the one filled for a unique ministry at the moment. When that ministry was over, the filling left. In some cases we have no record that the filling ever returned (Elizabeth and Zacharias). In others it seemed to return when necessary (Peter and Paul). There did not appear to be any formula they went through to affect the filling. About all we can observe along those lines is that as a general rule the Lord does not fill people He is not leading, and He does not lead people He has not baptized.

Putting this all together, some whom the Holy Spirit baptizes, He also leads; and some whom He is leading He chooses to fill. The baptizing ministry is a fact; the leading is by faith; and the filling can be felt. The baptizing is an indwelling; the leading is enabling; and the filling is intoxicating. The baptism of the Holy Spirit is permanent; the leading of the Holy Spirit is progressive; and the filling of the Holy Spirit is periodic.

CONCLUSION

How does all this help us with 1 John and what we might call the "abiding" ministry of the Holy Spirit? First John 2:6 connects "abiding in Him" with "walking as He walked." Thus "abiding" is related to walking with the Holy Spirit or the leading ministry of the Holy Spirit. When we do this we do not fulfill the lusts of the flesh (Gal 5:16), but rather we enjoy the fruits of the Spirit: love, joy, peace, patience, kindness, goodness, faith, meekness, self-control.

When we are enjoying these fruits, we can know that we are abiding in God and He in us, that is, we are in fellowship with Him. As such, we are like fireflies. His fruit is in us and we are enjoying it. We are minding our own business, not harming anyone, not annoying anyone, not sucking anyone's blood or stealing their food.

And from time to time the Holy Spirit may have a special ministry for us to help someone in darkness. Perhaps they need the gospel; perhaps they need a word of encouragement; perhaps a word of counsel. That's when we light up. We help them find their way in the darkness. This is the filling of the Holy Spirit. The fruit of His leading is mainly internal. We are aware of it even if others are not. But the light of His filling can be seen by all.

While I was in seminary, I also served as a Youth Pastor in Scofield Memorial Church in Dallas. During the summer the church used a camp on the edge of the city called Camp El Har, the "Mountain of God." One summer during a break from activities I overheard a little girl of about six playing with a little pet she called, my "Darling." She was having such fun, I couldn't keep from watching at a distance. Her "Darling" was a huge, black, ugly roach she had in captivity. She had drawn a circle with a two foot diameter, and this was the roach's prison yard where he was free to roam. Once he started to cross the line in order to escape prison, this little girl would block the roach with her hand and say, "Oh, no, my Darling." The frustrated roach would scurry off in another direction, always looking for a way out, but the little girl was enjoying her sovereign role over the roach too much to let it escape.

Finally, the little girl's mother called her for lunch. She said, "OK, just a minute." Well, it was only a moment before her "Darling" attempted a prison break. This time the little girl said, "Oh, no, my Darling" as usual, but with a move as fast as a karate expert she stomped on the roach and said, "You shouldn't have done that," and without another thought marched off to lunch.

Aren't you glad you aren't a roach in God's eyes and when you cross the line, He isn't just waiting there to squash you with His foot? We used to be roaches in God's eyes—scavengers, disease spreaders, worthy of being squashed. But as redeemed roaches, we become fireflies in His eyes. We can punch holes in the darkness. But even the world won't see our light shine if we don't come out at night.

---

[1] John Owen, *The Works of John Owen*, 16 vols., vol. 3: *A Discourse concerning the Holy Spirit* (1677; reprint, Edinburgh: Banner of Truth Trust, 1965), 45-47, 226-28.

LESSON 16 "Fireflies or Roaches" I John 3:24-4:6

1. What were some of your thoughts about the roach/firefly ideas in the introduction to this chapter?

2. Note the three areas John covers in this scripture related to the Holy Spirit.

   a. _____ with the Holy Spirit

   b. _____ for the Holy Spirit

   c. _____ to the Holy Spirit

3. What truth is illustrated by "If A =B, and B =C, then A =C" (page 197)?

4. How would you contrast the ancient philosophies cited in this chapter with John's teaching in the scripture for this lesson?

5. When is a believer "baptized by the Holy Spirit"?

6. Review the chart on page 202. How would you explain the words, "Fact, Faith, Feeling" as they relate to the terms at the top of the respective columns?

7. How is the leading of the Holy Spirit "progressive"?

8. Using the scriptures cited on pages 204 and 205, as well as the discussion of "The Filling Ministry of the Holy Spirit," how would you explain the "Filling Ministry of the Holy Spirit" to a new believer?

9. Should a believer (who has been baptized by the Holy Spirit) be more focused on being led by the Holy Spirit or being filled with the Holy Spirit? Why?

– 17 –

PERFECT LOVE: PART 1

1 JOHN 4:7-12

Can you remember the first time you fell in love? I remember it as though it were yesterday. I saw her on the other side of a crowded room. She turned toward me, and her eyes looked like Bambi's girlfriend. Her hair, the perfect length and color. Her cheeks with dimples and just a pinch of rose. It seemed to be love at first sight. And we were with each other almost every day—from third grade all the way through fifth grade. We did everything together. Walked home from school, rode horses, came over for dinner, introduced her to my parents—I even took her along one of my underground sewer paths.

But then it went away as fast as it came. The first day of school. Sixth grade. Everything seemed OK. We did not have an argument. But she had changed. She had cut her pig tails. I really can't explain my feelings. I just didn't seem to be able to love her anymore without her pig tails. Now we can smile at that kind of puppy love; but it's real to the puppy. And I have seen adult relationships end on a series of things which don't seem a lot more consequential than vanished pig tails.

We would all like to find a perfect love—a love that accepts me as I am, understands me, someone I don't have to perform for, someone who knows the good side and bad side but stays with me. But can you find that kind of love on this earth and in this life? What's in your mind when you think that "Love Is a Many Splendord Thing"? Is it a couple standing arm in arm staring out over the Pacific Ocean from the edge of a cliff?

Maybe you don't see a man and woman at all. Perhaps you visualize an old man and his grandson with their backs to you walking side by side, hand in hand down a dusty road, one holding the fishing poles, the other with the bait and tackle. Or perhaps you imagine a Norman Rockwell scene at Thanksgiving with the immediate family and relatives all gathered round the long dining room table. The turkey is served, the dressing is prepared, and the gravy is hot. Everyone has a smile on his face and a family anecdote in his mouth.

But, then, this is all in our imagination and our Land of Wishes. Though we do get glimpses of that kind of love from time to time, little snap shots of dreams come true, sound bites of perfection, is there any source of love like that which really lasts? John is here to say yes. Such love does exist in the universe. But it is not sourced in humans, or angels, or animals. It comes from God, and He wants to share it with us, so we can share it with others. That's what our passage is about as we enter the third wave of John's presentation of the principles of fellowship.

As you can see from our outline (see pages 78-79), we are suggesting that these three waves get successively bigger as we go along. The principles of fellowship are introduced, developed, and climaxed. Just so, this is the third time John presents the principle of right loving—dealing with our brothers, but this time it is the climax. That is precisely why we would expect him to be teaching us about perfect love in this passage. If you look at verse twelve it says, "No one has seen God at any time. If we love one another, God abides in us, and His love has been *perfected* in us." He mentioned this kind of perfect love in his first section on right loving (1 John 2:3-11), but he did not develop the concept. But that's what this final section on right loving is all about. Look at verse eighteen: "There is no fear in love; but *perfect love* casts out fear ...." So John is coming to his crescendo of love in this passage, but it has been in the back of his mind all along (1 John 2:5). Now he doesn't hold back. Here we get a portrait of perfect love. In the first part (4:7–12) of the portrait John gives us a mandate to love (4:7-8); then comes a manifestation of love (4:9-10); and finally he offers a motivation for love (4:11-12).

MANDATE TO LOVE

> Beloved, let us love one another, for love is of God; and everyone
> who loves is born of God and knows God. He who does not love
> does not know God, for God is love (4:7-8).

In this command for Christians to love one another, a command we have seen referenced numerous times already in this letter (2:7, 10; 3:11, 14, 15, 23), we get a key clue as to the nature of perfect love: *Love is of God*— this means it is sourced in God; it comes from God; it is divine, not of human origin. If I understand this correctly, this kind of love is not something the non-Christian can understand or produce. I'll get even more radical just to see if you're awake. I don't think a Christian can produce this kind of love either. He can understand it, to some degree, but he can't produce it at all. It comes from the Holy Spirit. It is a fruit of the Spirit (Gal 5:22). In fact, after his mention of perfect love in verse twelve, John mentions the Spirit for only the second time in this book in the very next verse. This kind of love comes from His Spirit; it is a spiritual love.

The reference is to a particular kind of love, *agapē* love. Perhaps you have seen a chart like this before:

LOVE

eros	*philē*	*agapē*
Body	Soul	Spirit
Physical	Emotional	Spiritual
Selfish	Half & half	Selfless
Getting	Getting & giving	Giving

The Holy Spirit comes to live inside our human spirit. That's why we speak of an unbeliever as spiritually dead. Death in this sense is separation from God. But when we trust Christ as our Savior, the separation ends because the barrier of our sins is removed. This opens the door for God to live within us. So the Holy Spirit enters and makes His home away from home in our heart. He indwells us.

Unfortunately, the average Christian has let the world paint the picture of perfect love for him. Hugh Hefner and his copycats portray perfect love in terms of eros or erotic love, physical love. It's a valid kind of love and quite good as originally intended by God, but it can easily be perverted. Without its companions of *philē* and *agapē* it is wholly inadequate, shallow, and not satisfying. Fabio and friends peddle their version of love to the better half of our race in terms of *philē*, or love of the soul, especially the emotions. And because of her softer more compassionate side, the world easily defrauds a woman into thinking this kind of love will fulfill all her dreams. But this love operates on a *quid pro quo* MO. If I give a little, you need to give a little. No give; no get. And, as Thornton Wilder said, "There may be two equally good, equally gifted, equally beautiful, but there may never be two that love one another equally well."

I suppose you might say I was love-challenged back in grammar school. After losing the first love of my life when Judy cut her pig tails, I was scanning the prospects for a replacement. We used a messenger system in those days, but to maintain privacy we also communicated through notes. Now I guess the messenger is a computer and they communicate through chat rooms. Well, I spotted a likely candidate, so I sent a note to her through my messenger buddy which said, "Cathy, I'll like you if you like me." Cathy sent a return note which said, "Sorry, Dave, I don't like you." Well, that kind of response elicited a return note to her return note. It said, "Then I don't like you either." I think you get the picture. That's how it goes with human love. It's not wrong; it's just not perfect.

Again, there is nothing wrong with *philē*. We were created in God's image, and God has deep emotional love for us. That's why He can get angry at us and be provoked to jealousy. It's because we can hurt Him by our callous rebellion, which says, "I don't love you." But again, this kind of love by itself can so easily turn into a *cul de sac* of disappointment and pain. It was only designed by God to be part of a three man backfield. *Agapē*, or spiritual love, is the blocking back for the other two. *Agapē* opens the holes for *eros* and *philē* to run through. When they function as a team, they are unbeatable.

And *agapē* love is perfect. Why? It comes from God, and *God is love*. This is the second character statement concerning God we have read in this letter. Earlier John said, "God is light; in Him is no darkness at all" (1 John 1:5). Here it says *God is love*. But it also says *He who does not love does not know God*. So we are right back into our discussion of "tests of life." Does this mean if a person does not love, he is not a Christian. So many commentaries go in that direction, but invariably they are amillennial commentators (do not believe in an actual thousand year reign of Christ on earth after the Tribulation Period). Let's be more careful with the text. Look at the preceding statement in verse seven: *everyone who loves is born of God and knows God*. If a person has *agapē* love, we know two things about him: 1) He is born of God; 2) He knows God. But notice carefully that verse eight does not say that someone who does *not* love: 1) Is not born of God; 2) Does not know God. No, not at all. It does not say the one who does not love is not born of God. The previous verse says the one who has this kind of love must be born of God because this kind of love is sourced in God. The unbeliever cannot manufacture this kind of love. But it does not say if a person is not loving in this way he is not born of God. It claims he does not know God.

In our introductory section on right loving (1 John 2:3-11) John used the word "know" in the sense of intimacy with God. Here he comes back to the same thought. A person can be born of God but quenching the Spirit.

He could be walking in darkness. If so, he is quenching the Spirit, not walking with the Spirit, and therefore not enjoying the fruit of the Spirit like love and joy. If this is true of him, we can certainly say he is not close/intimate with God. He does not know God in this intimate sense, as we have discussed previously. So, the person who exercises *agapē* love has a relationship with and fellowship with God. The person who does not exercise *agapē* love might be a person who has a relationship with God but no fellowship with Him. It's true that a person who lacks this kind of love might be an unbeliever, since unbelievers cannot produce this kind of love, but just to observe that a person is not exercising this kind of love does not prove he is an unbeliever. He could be a believer out of fellowship.

But let's get back to something positive. This is such a beautiful passage it is a shame to spend time on subtleties that probably never entered John's mind, or his readers, for that matter. We do it only because we feel compelled to expound this book from a dispensational point of view so we can show how it elucidates Luther's wonderful statement that we can be justified and sinful at the same time (*simul iustus et peccator*). Ironically, this is something Dortian Calvinism cannot do and stay consistent within its own system.

John gave us a mandate to love (4:7-8). But what does that look like? A picture is worth more than a thousand words. Now he gives us a picture, a manifestation of love (4:9-10).

MANIFESTATION OF LOVE

In this the love of God was manifested toward us, that God has sent His only begotten Son into the world, that we might live through Him. In this is love, not that we loved God, but that He loved us and sent His Son *to be* the propitiation for our sins (4:9-10).

Here, then, is a visible picture of this kind of love in action. We observe four things:

All Giving

Which of the three loves from our chart is this? Ah, yes, this is the third type, *agapē*, all giving. That's the first way to tell if my love is a spiritual love. Is it all giving, or am I expecting something in return. Giving can be a manipulative tool. We give to get. That kind of love is *philē*, not *agapē*.

Notice how much the word *philē* sounds like our word "feeling." C. S. Lewis pointed that out when he wrote:

> Being in love is a good thing, but it is not the best thing. It is a noble feeling, but still a feeling …. Who could bear to live in this excitement for even five years? But of course, ceasing to "be in love" need not mean ceasing to love. Love in a second sense, love as distinct from being in love, is not merely a feeling. It is a deep unity, maintained by the will and deliberately strengthened by habit; reinforced by the grace which both partners ask and receive from God. They can have this love for each other even at those moments when they do not like each other; as you love yourself even when you do not like yourself. They can retain this love even when each would easily, if they allowed themselves, "be in love" with someone else. "Being in love" first moved you to promise fidelity; this quieter love enables you to keep the promise.[1]

And Shakespeare said, "Love sought is good, but given unsought, is better."[2] Both Lewis and he are trying to underscore the giving aspect of perfect love. And the really good news for the Christian is that this kind of love is a fruit of the Holy Spirit. Our responsibility, as Watchman Nee has written, is to release the Spirit.[3]

Ultimate Sacrifice

Do you see where it says Jesus became the *propitiation* for our sins (v. 10)? Earlier John pointed out that an example of genuine love would be to meet the physical needs of a brother (1 John 3:17). Here he takes it to another level: our spiritual needs. Ephesians 2 says we were once dead in our trespasses and sins, children of wrath, enemies of God. But through His sacrifice Jesus broke down the wall, bridged the gap, reconciled us to our Creator, and satisfied God's demand for justice.

Let's go back to that picture of the tabernacle we saw when we began this study (see Diagram 1 on page 16).

We have spoken of John 17 as our great High Priest interceding for His people, just as the high priest of Israel would enter the Holiest Place, the Holy of Holies, on behalf of the people of Israel. But in the case of Jesus, He laid down His own life; He sprinkled His own blood on the Mercy Seat inside the Holy of Holies. When we discussed 1 John 2:2, we mentioned that the word for propitiation (*hilasmos*) and mercy seat (*hilastērion*—Rom 3:25) have the same root and, in this case,[4] the same root meaning. Just as he had this concept in his mind in his gospel, so John still has this picture in his mind of perfect love, Jesus laying His life down on the mercy seat for us, the sacrifice necessary to meet our deepest spiritual need. That is divine love, perfect love.

Now there are all sorts of expressions of *agapē* love which do not require the ultimate sacrifice of one's life. John seems to imply that even our *agapē* love can grow and mature. That is precisely what the word *perfect* (*teleios*) means in this context—complete, mature. John will go on to say that as we allow His perfect love to operate through us, His love in us can also be perfected, completed, matured. It's a growth process. As we allow the Spirit to live through us more and more consistently in our lives, we experience more and more of His love operating through us. And this love is not just giving, but it is sacrificial giving. You see, I can give without sacrificing. There is nothing wrong with that as long as I am not giving to get. But my love is more complete, more mature, more perfect(ed) when my giving involves sacrifice.

I remember the story of the little girl who had just memorized John 3:16. She asked her father, "If God loved the world so much, why didn't He offer Himself? Why did He send His Son?" For a moment the father was stumped. Then it dawned on him. "Well, honey, think how much more love it took for God to send His Son than to offer Himself. It would be much easier for me to sacrifice my own life for a good cause than to sacrifice you, my only daughter."

It has been my privilege through the years to see many, many young people offer their lives for full time Christian ministry. On occasion I have found it necessary to sit down with some angry parents who thought I was responsible for keeping their kids from becoming millionaires. Like me, I guess they were counting on their children being there to support them in their old age. I've always told my four kids that my life goal is to live long enough to be a burden to them. And I am well on my way toward that goal. But what a privilege it would be if one of my children chose to lay down his/her life for the kingdom cause. Would you be excited if one of your children chose that path?

But in this picture John paints of perfect love, there is more involved than just going into full time Christian service. Christ's sacrifice involved going to a foreign country.

Underprivileged Foreigners

Jesus was seated at the right hand of His Father in the third heaven. When the Lord went into service, His father didn't give His blessing and send Him to another nook of heaven to minister to the angels. He sent Him to a bunch of foreigners. More than foreigners, it was a third world country, a bunch of underprivileged foreigners.

Right now I am sitting in the home of a missionary from the United States to Germany. I'm not sacrificing anything. I just finished a glorious walk through a German forest. I cooked a steak for supper and am working in a well-furnished office. Just took a sip of carbonated German tea. I'm a long way from a third world country. I've seen Haiti, several times. I'll never forget crossing a river in a dugout canoe with Walt Baker, who spent the first ten years of his mission work in Haiti living with his family in a corrugated tin shack contiguous with two hundred other tin shacks, dirt floor, no running water. They had to boil water from the river and use a lot of coolaid in order to get a decent drink. The conditions in Israel were not that bad, but by today's standards, it was certainly a third world country.

I heard Robert McQuilken, former president of what was Columbia Bible College, give a commencement address for Dallas Seminary a few years ago. He retired from his ministry at the college to care for his diseased wife. He had had the chance to cross the country a few times as he spoke in different churches. He would listen to the pastors talk. His text for the commencement was that great passage in Philippians 2 where Christ gives up the riches of heaven to become poor for our sakes. McQuilken said all he heard from pastors these days in America was about "filling" instead of "emptying." He didn't mean "filling" of the Holy Spirit. He meant "filling" up the pews—making the church larger and larger (the mega church trend). He wondered why he didn't hear more about "emptying." Then he told about his own son, Kent, who left the privileges of American ministry to follow in the steps of Mother Theresa in Calcutta. Kent's famous father came for a visit, and they went down on the streets. After looking at a number of down-and-outers lying on the streets, Kent said, "Dad, the only way you can tell the ones who are alive from those who are dead is by the number of flies."

There is certainly nothing wrong with full-time ministry here in the States. Hopefully not. That's what I do. But like McQuilken I worry a bit when a pastor feels like a failure if his church isn't at least five thousand. The size of the average church in America is less than three hundred. I don't think McQuilken was against big churches; I think he was against big heads. As our love grows more and more like Christ's, perhaps we will hear more about "emptying" than "filling."

First Blood

Jesus loved us first. We love Him because He first loved us (4:19). He shed His blood for us before any of us would think of striving against sin until the shedding of our blood for Him (Heb 12:2). He loved us even if and when we did not love Him. God proved His love for us in that while we were yet sinners, Christ died for us (Rom 5:8). He gave His life for us when we were diseased and dying, spiritually.

I recently heard John Patrick, M.D., speak to a gathering of physicians about morality in medicine. Dr. Patrick is a professor of medicine in Canada. His specialty for years has been in the area of malnutrition. His studies have taken him to the starving children of Africa for many successive summers. Not wanting to spend the whole summer away from his wife and three daughters, he takes them along. Now all of his daughters have reached college age. Each of them had the experience of holding a starving child when the child died of malnutrition. It has stamped them for life. Now all three of his daughters have chosen to return to Africa to give their lives to minister to these underprivileged children. As a side note, Dr. Patrick said that none of his children wound up a materialist. There was just something about living among and ministering to a group of people who had so little in terms of material possessions that inoculated these young women against the cancer of accumulation. Interesting, isn't it, not only the impact loving the underprivileged first has on them, but also on those who are doing the loving?

Well, I'd say John can paint with the masters. What a portrait of His love. But now John wants to give us some motivation to love others in this way. We've heard the mandate (4:7-8); we've seen the manifestation (4:9-10); finally, he offers some motivation for love (4:11-12).

MOTIVATION FOR LOVE

> Beloved, if God so loved us, we also ought to love one another.
> No one has seen God at any time. If we love one another, God
> abides in us, and His love has been perfected in us (4:11-12).

The word *so* (*houtōs*) implies a comparison. In other words, if God loved us in this sacrificial, giving, initiating kind of way when we were underprivileged foreigners, then we ought to love each other in the same way. Maybe our love cannot be as perfect as Christ's love, but it can grow in that direction. That is the goal. Just as Jesus said on the Sermon on the Mount, "Therefore, be perfect as your Father in heaven is perfect"

(Matt 5:48). Or as God exhorts through Peter, "Be holy as I am holy" (1 Pet 1:14). These are the lofty goals of the Christian life. Can we do it? No way. Can Christ? He lives in us, and He is the only one who can measure up.

John makes the statement that no one has ever *seen God*. He is thinking of the unveiled glory of God. The shekinah glory must have veiled God even from Adam and Eve before they sinned. Moses (Ex 33:18-23) and Isaiah (Isaiah 6) came close, but to look directly upon Him would cause death (Ex 33:20). Yet there is a way to see God. When we observe His love at work among us, then, in a way, we are looking at God, for He is love, and when we love as He loved, it is He who lives in us who is the very source of this love. When we are loving each other in this way, God *abides in us*. Since *abides* is fellowship lingo, this could be a reference to individual fellowship with God, but it might also include a group experience of special intimacy with Him. It's *perfect love*.

This kind of giving, sacrificial love among us makes the world sit up and take notice (John 13:34-35). Will Durant, the historian who has often been cynical toward Christianity, noticed:

> All in all, no more attractive religion has ever been presented to mankind. It offered itself without restrictions to all individuals, classes, and nations; it was not limited to one people, like Judaism, nor to the free-men of one state, like the official cults of Greece and Rome. By making all men heirs of Christ's victory over death, Christianity announced the basic equality of men, and made transiently trivial all differences of earthly degree. To the miserable, maimed, bereaved, disheartened, and humiliated it brought the new virtue of compassion, and an ennobling dignity.
>
> Into the moral vacuum of a dying paganism, into the coldness of Stoicism and the corruption of Epicureanism, into a world sick of brutality, cruelty, oppression, and sexual chaos, into a pacified empire that seemed no longer to need the masculine virtues of the gods of war, it brought a new morality of brotherhood, kindliness, decency, and peace. So molded to men's wants, the new faith spread with fluid readiness. Nearly every convert, with the ardor of a revolutionary, made himself an office of propaganda.[5]

What more can we say on behalf of *perfect love* in community?

CONCLUSION

We are riding the crest of John's third wave, a part of which is right loving—perfect love. In his mandate to love, manifestation of love, and motivation for love he has painted a portrait of God's love that far transcends the imperfections of human love. Through the humility of Christ he has given us a picture of love that sacrificially gives to underprivileged people in a foreign world. And Christ drew first blood—His own.

This leads us to a rather stunning conclusion. It may well be that my most intimate fellowship with God may *not* occur *when I am alone.* "Oh, boy. Now you've done it. After all the sermons I've heard about the importance of a quiet time alone with God, you're telling me that the most intimate moments occur when I'm around other people? Get real." Could be. John certainly says God's love is perfected when I am reaching out on a horizontal plane. That's also what makes the world stop in its tracks for a closer look. After all, believers with the love of God in them do many things the world would consider odd:

1. We give our money away.
2. We forgive deep and cruel injustices.
3. We see people as more important than possessions.
4. We ignore barriers of race, class, and culture as we embrace the worth of others who are not like us.
5. We turn down promotions and transfers when they upend our priorities with God, family, or ministry.
6. We are willing to give up comfort and security to go to the remote and difficult places on the globe.
7. We are willing to die rather than give up our faith.

---

[1] C. S. Lewis, *The Problem of Pain* (New York: Touchstone Books, 1996).

[2] William Shakespeare, *The Twelfth Night*, III, i, 170.

[3] Watchman Nee, *Release of the Spirit* (Cloverdate, IN: Ministry of Life, 1965).

[4] The author is well aware of the "root fallacy," which he thinks does not apply here.

[5] Will Durant, *Caesar and Christ* (New York: Simon & Schuster, 1944), 602.

LESSON 17 "Perfect Love: Part I" I John 4:7-12

1. Do you remember your "first puppy love"? How would you describe "perfect love" in the human context?

2. Note the divisions, the book sets forth for dealing with this scripture.

   a. _____ to Love

   b. _____ of Love

   c. _____ for Love

3. On page 210, Dave says "this kind of love is not something a non-Christian can understand or produce" and "I don't think a Christian can produce this kind of love either." What is his point?

4. In what ways is "agape" love different from "phile" and "eros" love? Which of the three "loves" is John talking about?

5. Drawing on the discussion on pages 212 and 213, explain verses 7 and 8.

6. How does 4:10 explain "agape" love?

7. As we mature as Christians, how might our demonstration of agape love change? How does "emptying" and "filling" (page 216) relate to our maturing?

8. Why do you think John inserted "No one has seen God at any time" into verses 11 and 12? How does that statement fit within the context of the remainder of these verses?

9. While the world may think Christians are "odd" when they see us demonstrate agape love, they are also attracted to Christ by that demonstration. Let's do a little self-assessment to see how well we are doing with the seven ways we may show God's love on the "horizontal plane" (page 219). Using a ten-point scale (10 = perfect) grade yourself on the seven characteristics.

   _____ 1. We give our money away.

   _____ 2. We forgive deep and cruel injustices.

   _____ 3. We see people as more important than possessions.

   _____ 4. We ignore barriers of race, class, and culture as we embrace the worth of others who are not like us.

_____ 5. We turn down promotions and transfers when they upend our priorities with God, family, or ministry.

_____ 6. We are willing to give up comfort and security to go to the remote and difficult places on the globe (maybe even places near where we live).

_____ 7. We are willing to die rather than give up our faith.

– 18 –

PERFECT LOVE: PART 2

1 JOHN 4:13-19

It was Dion Warwick who sang that beautiful song, "What the world needs now, is love, sweet love, it's the only thing there is just too little of." And thirty years later I don't think anything has changed. In this war torn world of terrorism and fear a little love would go a long way. And it is not just the world and the nations that need love. We individuals need love as well. Children need love. Parents need love. Teenagers need love. Even old people need love. Don't laugh.

That reminds me of the old man who was rowing a boat on a lake when a frog swam up to him and yelled, "Mister! Mister! I'm really a beautiful princess. Kiss me and we'll live happily ever after!" The man put the frog in his pocket and rowed to shore. The frog called out again, "Hey, Mister! I'm really a gorgeous princess. Kiss me and we'll live happily ever after!" Still the old man said nothing and walked down the road toward town. The frog was getting angry at being ignored. "Mister, why don't you kiss me? I told you I'm really a beautiful princess." "Listen, lady," the man replied. "I'm 90 years old. At this point in my life I'd rather have a talking frog."

Ya, ya, I know it's a stupid joke, but it illustrates a point. He was just lonely. There are times when just having someone to talk to can mean more to a love relationship than anything else. But that is precisely where most love relationships break down. How many people can you open up to and not risk rejection? Can you open up to your wife or husband? According to Dr. Larry Crabb:

> Every person alive has experienced sometime the profound hurt of finding rejection when he or she longed for acceptance. We came into marriage hoping for something different, but inevitably we soon encounter some form of criticism or rejection. The pain that results is so intense that it *demands* relief. So we retreat behind protective walls of emotional distance, angry with our partners for letting us down so badly, unwilling to meet again at the level of deep needs for fear of experiencing more pain.[1]

It is these walls of self-protection which keep us from talking to each other, sharing on an intimate level. Crabb lists the following as typical layers of self-protection:

1. Unwillingness to share deep feelings;
2. Responding with anger when real feelings are hurt;
3. Changing the subject when the conversation begins to be threatening;
4. Turning off, claming up, or other maneuvers designed to avoid rejection or criticism;
5. Keeping oneself so busy with work, social engagements, entertainment, church activities, or endless chatter that no deep sharing is possible.[2]

Crabb goes on to say, "I am persuaded that most couples today live behind thick protective walls of emotional distance that block any hope for developing substantial oneness at the level of our deepest personal needs."[3] Wow. That sounds a little bleak.

Is there a way to break through these walls? Can that be done? Can the Bible help? I think so, and that's what 1 John 4:13-19 is all about. We are talking about perfect love. All of 1 John 4:7-19 revolves around this subject. So far we have looked at 1 John 4:7-12, but now we want to move into 1 John 4:13-19. These verses break down into love perceived (4:13-16) and love perfected (4:17-19).

LOVE PERCEIVED

> By this we know that we abide in Him, and He in us, because He has given us of His Spirit. And we have seen and testify that the Father has sent the Son *as* Savior of the world. Whoever confesses that Jesus is the Son of God, God abides in him, and he in God. And we have known and believed the love that God has for us. God is love, and he who abides in love abides in God, and God in him (4:13-16).

John introduced the subject of perfect love back in 1 John 2:5. But he did not tell us how to get there. Then he built on this introduction to perfect love in chapter two with another section on love in chapter three. He told us not to love in word and in tongue, but in deed and in truth (1 John 3:16). As an example of love which goes beyond mere words, he encourages us to meet each other's material needs. But in his climactic section on love, which began in 1 John 4:7, John says God's love can be perfected in our very midst when we love one another in the community of believers.

We learned in the previous verses that *agapē* love is a divine love which is produced by the Holy Spirit. On their own, humans cannot produce this kind of love. It is a spiritual love which is completely selfless. On our own we are not capable of complete selflessness. But because this love is a fruit of the Holy Spirit (Gal 5:21), a brand new Christian can enjoy and share this kind of love. But *agapē* love can also "grow up." It can mature. It can be perfected. Do you remember our chart on the three kinds of love?[4] Here it is again:

LOVE

eros	*philē*	*agapē*
Body	Soul	Spirit
Physical	Emotional	Spiritual
Selfish	Half & half	Selfless
Getting	Getting & giving	Giving

How do you perceive love? I find it interesting to listen to little children as they ponder the T-Rex questions of life. Some four to eight year old children were asked about their perception of love. As we read some of their answers, which of the three types of love from our chart is being described by the child:

1. Love is the feeling you feel before all the bad stuff gets in the way.
2. Love is when a girl puts on perfume and a boy puts on shaving cologne, and then they go out and smell each other.
3. Love is when your eyelashes go up and down and little stars come out of you.
4. Love is when mommy sees daddy smelly and sweaty and still says he's handsomer than Robert Redford.
5. Love's when you kiss all the time. Then when you get tired of kissing, you still want to be together and you talk more. My mommy and daddy are like that. They look gross when they kiss.
6. Love is when your puppy licks your face even after you left him alone all day.
7. Love is when you tell something bad about yourself and you're scared they won't love you anymore. But then you get surprised,

because not only do they still love you, they love you even more. (How's that for perception in a four to eight year old? Hmmm. This is the kind of love we want to talk about.)

When we left love in 1 John 4:12, it had been perfected. It had grown up. We suggested that this kind of mature love needs community (other people). We might parallel this to what James tells us about sin in Jas 1:14-15. He says sin begins as a temptation in the mind. Then when our own lust of our heart merges with the temptation in our mind, Sin is conceived in the womb of our soul. After a gestation period, baby Sin is born into the world of our actions. With exercise and food, baby Sin grows up. When Sin becomes a full-grown adult (mature), she produces death. The point is that for Sin to mature, it must be born into the world of action. With repetition it grows up to maturity.

Divine love is the same way. It may begin with a good intention in the womb of our spirit, but at this point it is only an embryo of love. For this love to be fully developed, it must be born into the world of our deeds, our actions. Properly nurtured and exercised, love becomes a full-grown, mature, and attractive young woman. And the world takes a look.

So this kind of love needs external expression to become mature. That's why Jesus said He gives his disciples a new commandment to "love one another as I have loved you." That commandment is like a golden parrot hopping from branch to branch in this book, repeating itself over and over. Jesus says when we learn to love each other this way, then the whole world will know that we are His disciples (His fully-devoted followers). This is mature, perfect love.

Someone may say, "Well, that's just my trouble. I'm not even sure that God has that kind of love for me." If I am in the midst of a severe trial, how can this be God's perfect love? I feel abandoned by God. Yes, I can understand that. There may not be a more lonely island on this planet than an island in the Sea of Misery called "Abandoned—By God." The people who live on this island are good people. Most of them have spent their lives loving God and serving Him. But somewhere on life's journey they have been blind-sided by a debilitating disease, a financial wipe-out, children who have dishonored the name of God and lack natural affection, ... you name it.

This sink hole of life has not been something uncommon to man. Believers and unbelievers alike face devastating trials in this world which is passing away. The trials, if this makes any sense, are really not the problem.

The problem is that these trials have hit such good, faithful believers in Christ. This is when they feel exiled to the island called abandonment. Yes, "Abandoned—by God." It's the combination of their faithfulness to God and the devastation of their trials that leaves them feeling abandoned by Him. If He really loved them as He claims, how could He let this happen to them? If this is perfect love, let me have some of the imperfect stuff, OK?

When a believer wakes up in the morning to the sunshine of God's love, he can face most any trial. After all, Paul claimed that "neither death, nor life, nor things past … can separate us from the love of God in Christ Jesus." But when someone begins to doubt whether God really does love him after all, then a devastating trial can reduce even the strongest and bravest of believers to feeling like a splattered bug on the windshield of life.

But in the context of a community of believers, where one believer sacrifices to meet the needs of another (whether material or psychological or spiritual) we can *know that we abide in Him and He in us.* That is, we can know we are having close, intimate fellowship with Him. It is this believer in this kind of community who can experience a fresh wave of confidence (*know*) in God's love. It is in this kind of community that the cross is openly confessed and the blood of Christ is preached. In this place of open confession of the cross, once again the fundamental proof of God's perfect love for us is displayed, confirmed, and emphasized.

When the text says *of His Spirit*, it does not say God gave us His Spirit; it says He gave us *of* His Spirit. And it really *does not say Holy Spirit*; it just says *pneuma*, spirit. It could be either Spirit or spirit. In this context of community we might paraphrase it like this: "By this we know that we abide in Him and He in us [deep, mutual fellowship], because He has allowed us to share in His S/spirit of love."

Of course, it is only the Holy Spirit who can produce such perfect love in us; remember, *agapē* is the first fruit of the Holy Spirit. When we see this kind of love demonstrated in our midst, we can know with certainty that God abides in us. That's when we sense His love. The word *seen* goes back to 1 John 1:1 and 1 John 4:12. He says no one has seen God at any time. But in 1 John 1:1 it says the apostles had seen and handled the "Word of Life." And John said he wanted his readers to have the same fellowship with the Father and the Son that the apostles had experienced (1:3). Well, his readers couldn't see and touch the physical Jesus, but they could *see and testify* concerning the *life* that comes from fellowship with the Father and the Son.

When we observe sacrificial love in the community of believers, John seems to be saying that we have a reincarnation of the Father's love which was a perfect love, a love that sent His only begotten Son into the world to save the world through His own sacrificial love on the cross.

Let me flesh this out. One of the "spiritual gifts" God has sent to our church is an ex-Englishman named Paul. His father was a physician in England, but Paul's tender heart tilted his prodigious mental gifts in the direction of veterinary medicine. He came to one of our best schools of veterinary medicine in the U.S., the veterinary school at Texas A&M. He came to our church after he had been a Christian about a year, but long after he had established a very successful private practice near The Woodlands. With a mind like a steel trap, he lapped up all the exegetical training I could give him without actually matriculating in seminary. He had never taught a Sunday school class, but when given a chance he treated it like beginning a new medical practice. He wrote notes to everyone who visited his class. It grew from six to sixty.

About to guide a tour in Israel, I needed a substitute for the pulpit. I saw Paul eating with his staff at The Black-Eyed Pea and asked him if he would consider preaching for me. It's a little sadistic of me, but I sort of enjoy watching the blood drain out of a guy's face when I ask him that relatively harmless question. He said he would pray about it. A week later he called to say he was going to turn me down because he had never given a standing-up speech before and thought he would die of stage fright, but then he reconsidered and thought if that's how God wanted him to leave this world, he would lay down his life. We got together for some coaching and to work out the exegesis of a passage, and I said, "Look, Paul, your exegesis is great. Don't get up there and apologize for anything. Just share your gift."

Well, off I went to Israel, wondering the whole time how it would go for Paul. When I returned, one of the first things I did was to get the tape of his sermon and listen. (I had been told by others that he was so nervous he had to sit on a stool to keep his knees from shaking.) He started off without apology (a tough thing for first timers). He said, haltingly, "Well, Dave told me to just get up here and share my gift, ... so I'm going to spay a cat." Well, that brought the house down. He went on to tell a couple of jokes about the Queen so the audience could get used to his slight English accent and then said, "You know, in the old country we never said 'Amen' if we liked something a speaker said. We just said, 'Heahr, heahr.' So if I say anything at all that you like or encourages you during this message, would you please say,

'Heahr, heahr'?" Well, there were "heahr, heahrs" sprinkled all through the tape. I haven't gotten that much audience participation since I preached at an African-American church in Galveston. When he finished, the entire audience rose up and said, "Heahr, heahr."

In relatively short order (three years) Paul became the most beloved (*phileō*) person in our congregation. But he seemed to have an increasing difficulty speaking. What began as a rather halting delivery became labored. At age thirty-eight Paul was diagnosed with Lou Gehrig's disease, what Scott Turrow describes in his novel *Personal Injuries*,[5] the "cruelest disease." ALS, its usual cognomen, slowly eats away at the nerves which control our muscles. The mind never deteriorates. When the lungs no longer operate, the afflicted can opt for a lung machine. Most do not. When the eyelids no longer operate, a nurse can be hired to stand-by to keep the open eyes from drying out with drops of water.

I don't think I can describe the sadness that came over our church body when the news rolled in like a tsunami. Of course, the wave was followed by all sorts of debris like, "Why him? Of all people, Lord, he is one of your most gifted and beloved. Is this your perfect love?" The daggers of doubt assaulted us like hail stones. We, more than he, stood with mouths agapē at the mysterious ways of God with men. The outpouring of divine love for this man has been one of the great blessings in my life to witness, though I can't say I wish it were so. We all want to hold onto him as his muscles slowly twitch away as though we could prolong his time with us.

Of course, we have all prayed for a miracle from God to heal him. But while we wait for that possibility, the love pours in—financial gifts, transportation, on site help for his wife, and on it goes. Someone working for the *Houston Chronicle* heard about the special relationship between Paul and our church and did a feature article on him. The world is watching. On a recent trip to Israel, Paul and his wife went along. By that time he was in a wheel chair. At every stop he needed assistance getting from the bus to his wheel chair and back again. In many places his wheel chair would not roll smoothly or at all, so a group of our men would carry him. When we had our farewell dinner near Tel Aviv, our Jewish guide, whom I have used on many tours, leaned over to me and said, "I have been guiding for many, many years and have seen hundreds of people come here with one physical disability or another, but I have never seen so much love poured out by a group for a handicapped person."

Paul is still with us. He's rolled into church on his reclining wheel chair. He's the only one who both gets and appreciates some of my corny humor. He can't say "Heahr, heahr" or "Amen" anymore, but I know he's travelin' with me when he groans quite audibly after one of my daft comments. Of course, I don't know if he's groaning out of the misery caused by my bad humor or if he's overcome with his desire to laugh (I choose the latter), but it just endears him to me more. Barring a miracle, he will never teach again. Does he understand God's sovereign purpose in his life? Doubtful. None of us does. But does He doubt God's love for him? Not on your life. He has experienced more love in the last two years than in all the other years of his life combined—in community.

John says this kind of divine, sacrificial love shared within the Christian community is the love of the cross demonstrated all over again. This is a little like John 2:11 where Jesus' disciples, who had already believed in Him (John 1), see His first miracle and believe all over again. It's not their initial faith. But it brings a fresh wave of confidence in Him as Messiah. This is what pours over us when we hear the preaching of the cross in open confession of Jesus as the Son of God, the Savior of the world.

> And can it be that I should gain
> An interest in the Savior's blood?
> Died He for me, who caused such pain?
> For me, who Him to death pursued?
> Amazing love! How can it be
> That thou, my God, shouldst die for me?

And now with this fresh vision of Christ on the cross and God's perfect love for me, I am able to enter into sacrificial love for my brothers. As we pour out from our hearts the tangible needs of a brother like Paul, he is able to have God's love for him reaffirmed as well. Abandoned by God? No way. The outpouring of Christian love for him from his brothers and sisters convinces him that God really does love him after all. That's why John goes on to combine the words *known and believed*, both in the perfect tense. These verbs speak of the state of intimate knowledge and total trust in the fact that God loves us. Again, since these are "stative" verbs (see the discussion on 1 John 2:3) I would prefer to understand them with an emphasis on the present results, the *intensive* perfect, and translate them with the English present tense: "And we *know* and *believe* the love God has for us."

Nothing can separate us from His love:

> Who shall separate us from the love of Christ? Shall tribulation, or distress, or persecution, or famine, or nakedness, or peril, or sword? As it is written,
> "For Your sake we are killed all day long;
> We are accounted as sheep for the slaughter."
> Yet in all these things we are more than conquerors through Him who loved us. For I am persuaded that neither death, nor life, nor angels, nor principalities, nor powers, nor things present nor things to come, nor height nor depth, nor any other created things, shall be able to separate us from the love of God which is in Christ Jesus our Lord (Rom 8:35ff).

And we perceive His great love for us best in community. But there is still a problem. In a conference at our church, Larry Crabb said a survey was taken in which he asked people to write on a piece of paper their response to this one question: "What is the single thing in your life you are most ashamed of and would be most embarrassed for others to know?" It was an anonymous survey. Dr. Crabb said he thought the response would be something sexual. It was not. The most common response was: "I am afraid for people to find out how far I am from being able to love people as God wants me to love them."

Remember, God wants us to have *agapē* love, selfless love, unconditional love. But there is something which holds us back. What can open the doors to perfect love?

LOVE PERFECTED

> Love has been perfected among us in this: that we may have boldness in the day of judgment; because as He is, so are we in this world. There is no fear in love; but perfect love casts out fear, because fear involves torment. But he who fears has not been made perfect in love. We love Him because He first loved us (4:17-19).

Purpose of Perfect Love

The word *that* is a signal for the purpose of mature, divine love. As this love is born of the Spirit into our lives, it grows up and matures. That can only happen in community, as we express it toward others. When we do this, we don't have to fear God. We don't fear His coming. Our hand is not in the cookie jar. We anticipate His coming. We can't wait for His glory to be displayed throughout the universe, the open, public display of all His character attributes: His love, His justice, His truth, His holiness—all these and more for every creature to see.

We can actually have *boldness in the day of judgment*. We have seen the word for *boldness* before (*parrēsian*), only it was translated "confidence" (1 John 2:28) in the day of judgment. For those who believe that Jesus will come back to the earth to reign for a thousand years (the Millennium) the judgment John talks about here is the Judgment Seat of Christ (2 Cor 5:10) when all believers will be judged for the lives they have lived since becoming believers.

The believers who are experiencing intimate fellowship with the Word of Life can be confident at the Judgment Seat of Christ. That was a primary benefit of abiding in Him back in 1 John 2:28. And we know we are abiding in Him when we observe perfect love demonstrated in our community of believers, for at the end of verse sixteen John says, "God is love, and he who abides in love abides in God, and God in him." The word *abides* (our clue to fellowship, not relationship) occurs twice here. Notice the reciprocal "he … in God, and God in him." Deep fellowship/intimacy. But there is something that can keep us from enjoying this reciprocal love, and that's fear.

Prevention of Perfect Love

Fear and *agapē* love are mutually exclusive. *Agapē* love has no fear. In fact, this kind of love casts out fear because fear has *kolasin*. This is the word translated as *torment* in the NKJV and "punishment" in the NIV and NAS. Because of the proximity of the thought of confidence at the Judgment Seat of Christ, it was assumed that the fear of this judgment bore its own punishment or torment. But this word *kolasin* is a word occurring only twice in the NT (here and in Matt 25:46 where it does mean punishment). And it wasn't until the twentieth century that writings were discovered in Egypt which help us understand more possibilities for the meaning of this word. The statement that "perfect love casts our fear because fear has torment" just never made much sense to me. But *kolasin* is also used of pruning a fruit tree to *stunt its growth*. So, fear keeps our love from growing up. Fear of what? That which we all fear in relationships, whether it's with God or men— rejection. Most of us are afraid of rejection from other people. Those who aren't have felt the sting of rejection so much they have lost their ability to consciously feel at all. This fear of rejection *stunts* the growth of perfect love.

We get a real clue from the statement that *we love God because He first loved us*. He was the initiator. We were His sinful enemies. Time and time again He had felt the sting of rejection from us. Even after He came to earth and began to display His wonderful acts of mercy, compassion, and healing, Jesus was rejected by men. We built a high wall of rejection between us and Him. But because "God is love," perfect love, He is not afraid of rejection. It hurts. It grieves Him deeply. But He is not afraid. So He set His cross down next to that wall of rejection built by our sins ... and He climbed that wall, for you and me. We love Him because He *first* loved us. Fear of rejection is what keeps us from making the first move, especially if we have already been hurt a number of times by someone who means a lot to us.

So I agree with three of my favorite dictionaries of NT Greek, which suggest "restraint" as the best English translation of *kolasin*.[6] In other words, fear holds us back; it *restrains* us. It keeps or *prevents* us from reaching out in sacrificial, selfless, unconditional love. But when we release the Spirit, He can and will produce the fruit of *agapē* love in our lives. He will cast out the fear which retrains us.

What we are saying here is that only God's love (mature *agapē*) can bust through the sinful layers of self-protection which keep us from experiencing oneness with Him and other believers (intimacy/fellowship). We all enjoy the feelings of *philē* love in marriage, friendships, families, even church. But without growing *agapē* we will lose those feelings and never get them back. The mistakes we make in relationships because of our sinfulness can create enough pain to destroy all positive feelings of one toward another. But growing *agapē* can cast out fear. We can reach out again.

But how can we be sure our *agapē* will keep growing? How can I get this perfect love?

CONCLUSION

There is a connection between "Love Perceived" (4:13-16) and "Love Perfected" (4:17-19). If you were to drive around Houston in the mid-60s, you might have caught up with a rather slow, thirty-six horse power VW Beetle. If you came up slowly behind this car, you might have noticed it was being driven by a person with two heads. Actually, it was bride-to-be and I, cheek-to-cheek. I had taught Betty how to shift the gears, so she sat strad-dled across the two bucket seats and operated the stick shift while I manip-ulated the pedals. This is what people do when they are "in love."

We even had our own song—"My Cup Runneth Over With Love"—sung by Ed Ames. That's the way we were. Each of us had a cup that needed love. She would hold out her cup to me, so I would pour some from my cup into her cup. Then I'd hold out my cup to her, and she would reciprocate by pouring from her cup to mine. It was wonderful. Then we got married.

No, that did not end this glorious relationship. We had plenty of love to go around, so we kept each other's cup full. The books said the first year would be the toughest, so at the end of a year I asked, "Was that tough for you?" She said, "No, was it for you." I said, "No way. It was wonderful." Then we got pregnant. Things began to change. We had to establish a new system to accommodate three instead of two. Then we got pregnant again. Another new system. We began to notice that our cups had cracks in them. I had a leaky cup, and she had a leaky cup.

I'd hand out my leaky cup and say, "Fill …. Fill, please." Being a loving wife, she would pour some from her cup into mine, but then stop. I would say, "Fill more, please." She would say, "Hey, there's not much left for me. Couldn't you share some of yours with me?" Ever so graciously (of course), I'd come back, "Well, you can have a little bit, but don't take too much." But the cracks in our cups got larger. After years of pouring back and forth from one cracked cup to another, we woke up to discover both cups empty. Now what?

That's when the Lord did an amazing work in our individual lives and in our marriage. He taught us the truth of 1 John 4. He taught us that until I *perceive* God's perfect love for me, I am not able to dispense love to another on any kind of sustained basis. As long as I go to another human being with my cracked cup, it will never stay full. I will never have enough to share with others around me. Sooner or later, I won't be able to stand any more rejection, so I will pull my cup away and put it on the shelf somewhere.

But if I will hold out my cracked cup to God, He is more than capable of using His infinite supply of perfect love to fill my cup and keep it filled. He has enough love, for God is love, to fill my cracked cup and my wife's and yours and the cracked cups of the whole world, if we will just go to Him first. Then with my cup full of His love, but still cracked and leaky, I can share some of His perfect love with my wife, and my children, and you, and you, and you. You see, Ed Ames had the right idea: "My Cup Runneth Over With Love." He just had the wrong source. Any human being is a limited source. Only His infinite love can keep my cup running over, overflowing, with love.

If I extend my cup of love to you, and you reject my love so that I spill a bunch on the floor, I can still go back to the Lord and say, "Fill …. Fill, please." It's as though the Lord leads us to the edge of a cliff and says, "It's My will for your life that you jump." I respond with a stupid smile on my face and say, "Excuse me?" "You heard me," says the Lord. "This is my will for you, so jump. Right over here. I want you to go to that person who hurt you and reach out to them. I don't want you to build a protective layer. If you've got one, I want you to cut right through it." "But, Lord, I don't want to jump. That's the pit of rejection down there, full of sharp rocks. I might get hurt. I can't stand rejection."

The Lord comes back, "Have you forgotten something? Have you forgotten about my infinite love for you? I have a bunji cord of love tied around you. You know what my will for your life is? Jump for Jesus, and you'll find that you might get near the bottom and might even bounce off the wall of this cliff a couple of times on the way down, you can be hurt by people, but you can't be destroyed. My bunji cord of love is there, even though you don't feel it while you are in free fall. It will bring you up before you are destroyed. And you can love again."

When I was learning this truth, I was taking a shower and heard a knock on the door. We had only two children at the time, a boy about seven and a girl about five. It was my daughter Christie knocking. I stopped the shower, but the knocking had also stopped. She had shoved some wadded up sheets of writing paper under the door and left. She was just learning to read and write a little bit in kindergarten. I dried off and unfolded the papers, three of them.

On the top piece of paper she had scratched out "My Sinnes" at the top and next to that wrote "Anderson, Christie." Then she listed her "sinnes": "I hid from my mother, I argude with my brother, I played chase in the house, I didin't pratise my peano, I realy sinned." Man, I thought, we are raising a kid with an overly sensitive conscience. She had two other sheets of paper, so I looked at the next one. It was a little more positive. It said, "I love my mommy, I love my daddy, I love Jimmmy, I love me, and I love you too." Hmgh, I thought, how could she love her older brother who picks on her, and her parents, and you too (people outside the family)? Where did she get that?

Then I read the third piece of paper and had my answer. It read, "Jesus loves me, this sine (precocious, she was into trig early on) O, for the bible tels me so. Letose oones to him be laling, they are weeek, but he is sraling. Yes, Jesus loves me; yes, Jesus love me; yes, Jesus loves me, the bible tels me so."

I looked at these three little sheets of paper in order and realized, "My gosh. This is 1 John. She first of all confessed her sins. That's chapter one. And underlying (third sheet) the fact that she loves mommy, daddy, Jimmy, and you is the fact that she knows that Jesus loves her. That's chapter four.

How is it that kids get it so much more easily than we do? Could it be that they haven't felt enough rejection yet to obscure their perception of God's love for them? I don't know. But I do know this. The key to perfect love (4:17-19) is perceived love (4:13-16). A full perception of His perfect love for me can help my own love "grow up" by removing the fear of rejection, which prevents me from loving others as He has asked me to do.

Yes, Dion was right when she sang, "What the world needs now is love, sweet love." But she was wrong when she sang, "It's the only thing there's just too little of." There's an infinite supply of love—enough for the whole world and more—but people are looking for love in all the wrong places.

---

[1] Larry Crabb, *Marriage Builder* (Grand Rapids: Zondervan Publishing House, 1982), 32.

[2] Ibid., 33.

[3] Ibid.

[4] The NT also speaks of a fourth kind of love, *storge*, which speaks of family love and loyalty but is only used once in the NT, and that is in a compound form.

[5] Scott Turrow, *Personal Injuries* (New York: Farrar, Straus and Giroux, 1999).

[6] See Henry Liddell, *A Greek-English Lexicon* (New York: Oxford University Press, 1996); James Moulton & George Milligan, *The Vocabulary of the Greek Testament* (Grand Rapids: W.B. Eerdmans, 1952); and Gerhard Kittel, *Theological Dictionary of the New Testament* (Grand Rapids: W.B. Eerdmans, 1985).

LESSON 18 "Perfect Love: Part 2" I John 4:13-19

1. What are your thoughts about the five typical layers of self-protection cited by Larry Crabb (page 224)? How might these barriers impact our fellowship with God?

2. Explain this quote on page 226, ". . . mature love needs community."

3. What is the significance of John saying " . . . he has given us of his Spirit" (verse 13)?

4. How does Paul's story as a victim of ALS have anything to do with God's perfect love (pages 228-230)?

5. What is your understanding of this quote on page 230,

   ". . . sacrificial love shared within the Christian community is the love of the cross demonstrated all over again"?

6. What fear(s) may operate in our life that keeps us from enjoying intimate fellowship with God and experiencing His deep reciprocal love?

7. How is understanding the Greek, kolasin, critical to making sense of verse 18?

8. Conclusion: "A full perception of _____ for me can help my own love "_____" by removing the _____, which prevents me from loving others as He has asked me to do. How can I fill in the "blanks" in my living this week?

– 19 –

THE SOURCE

1 JOHN 4:20–5:5

Most of you have probably seen the movie version of the life of Mohatma Ghandi. Ghandi studied Christianity in England but never became a Christian, according to him, because Christianity didn't seem to work for Christians. Although he was not impressed by the Christians he met, he was very impressed with Jesus, especially His teaching in the Sermon on the Mount, and Ghandi himself tried to incorporate this wisdom into his own life.

At one point in the movie version of his life, civil war has broken out between what is now Pakistan and India, primarily over religious division between the Muslims of Pakistan and the Hindu people of India. Ghandi lies on a cot after weeks of fasting in protest of the war. A distraught Hindu man approaches him. His only son, still a little boy, has been shot and killed in the conflict. His heart is full of sadness, bitterness, and revenge. Ghandi can barely speak, but tells the man how to heal his own heart. "Find a little Muslim boy whose father has been killed. Take that boy as your son, and raise him as a Muslim." The distraught man walked away completely confused and disappointed. Apparently he thought the weeks of fasting had weakened Ghandi's ability to reason. It made no sense to him whatsoever.

Just as Jesus' words in the Sermon on the Mount make no apparent sense: "Love your enemies, bless those who curse you, do good to those who hate you, and pray for those who spitefully use you and persecute you" (Matt 5:44). It doesn't seem to make any sense, especially in a world where vengeance seems to be the energy source which drives the entire culture. I was in Kenya after the Rwanda tribalcides. I asked my host, a missionary friend, if something like that could happen in Kenya, one of the more advanced countries in central Africa. "Oh yes," he said, "Tribal hatred and vengeance goes back for centuries."

Into the midst of this kind of world Jesus brings what seems like an impossible message: "Blessed are you when they revile and persecute you, and say all kinds of evil against you falsely for My sake" (Matt 5:11). And when He finishes the first big section of His sermon, He concludes by saying, "Be perfect, as your Father in heaven is perfect" (Matt 5:48). We say, "Ah, well, no problem." Peter got the message, so in his first letter he quotes God from the OT when He says, "Be holy, as I am holy." And John got the idea. In his first letter he says we should have perfect love. Perfect love casts out fear.

This, after all, is the goal of Christianity—perfectionism. We are called to live a perfect life. Let's put it another way. We are called to be like Jesus, the only one, as far as we know and believe, who lived a perfect life. The burden of trying to be perfect is so heavy, someone has observed, "The Christian life has not been tried and found difficult; it has been tried and found impossible." So how can we deal with this? How can we put together the demands of Scripture with the realities of life?

One solution to this tension between holy expectation and unholy performance is to change the standard. They make the demands relative. "No one can be perfect, you know, so there must be some sort of sliding scale here." The result of this kind of thinking is comparison. We compare our righteousness with the righteousness of those around us, either in the church or out in the world. We point our search light on people we think are less righteous than we. This makes us feel pretty good about ourselves. This kind of comparison in the church leads to judgmentalism and legalism. This leads to a loss of joy. The pressure of performance, even if the standard has been changed to relative righteousness, plucks the fruit of the Spirit right off the tree of victorious Christian living.

There is another solution to the tension between the standard of perfection and our imperfect performance. The solution is not to change the standard. God spelled out the standard in Scripture very clearly. Be perfect. Be like Jesus. There is nothing wrong with that standard. We shouldn't try to change it. As we move from the OT through the NT, the writers of Scripture did not change the standard. There is no compromise, no relative righteousness, no sliding scale. The problem isn't the standard. The problem is the source.

John calls for perfect love. He does not call for a change in the standard. He calls for a change in the source. In 1 John 4:20–5:5 we are coming down the mountain of perfect love.

John is giving us his finishing thoughts on right loving—dealing with our brothers—before he moves on to his climactic section of right learning. Someone will surely say, "I can love God without loving my brother." It's an old objection. John will say, "No, we are not changing the standard." So he reaffirms the mandate to love (4:20–5:1) and the measure of love (5:2-3). But when he explains the means to love (5:4-5), John points to a new source to enable us to meet God's perfect standard. He doesn't change the standard; he changes the source.

MANDATE TO LOVE

> If someone says, "I love God," and hates his brother, he is a liar; for he who does not love his brother whom he has seen, how can he love God whom he has not seen? And this commandment we have from Him: that he who loves God *must* love his brother also. Whoever believes that Jesus is the Christ is born of God, and everyone who loves Him who begot also loves him who is begotten of Him (4:20–5:1).

Most Christians will shrink back at the prospect of loving our brothers/sisters with perfect love. When the knife of guilt stabs us, we can sidestep the issue by saying, "Well, at least I love God." Not so, argues John. How can you love someone you have never seen if you can't love someone you have seen? (Easy, we might say. Our problem is that we have seen other Christians up close, and we don't like what we see. We don't see faults in God, so it's easy to love Him compared to our Christian brother.)

Here we must remind ourselves of the kind of love John talks about. The emphasis here is not on feelings or emotions, but rather actions and deeds (3:16-18). The word for love throughout John is *agapē*, a word found only once in all of secular Greek, that is, Greek outside the Bible. And the amount of non-biblical Greek literature we have must be a thousand times more than the amount of Greek we have in the Bible, but this word *agapē* occurs in that literature only once. That should be a clue to us that this kind of love is only from God. And the issue here is not whether we feel warm and fuzzy toward God, but cold and callous toward our Christian brother/sister. The issue is action.

Remember his example of love in 1 John 3:17? If we *see* our brother in need and don't *do* something about it, how does the love of God abide in us? If I can see a physical being and am not willing to meet his physical needs, how can I possibly love a spiritual being whose needs I cannot see? That's his reasoning. God's commands draw our love for God and our brothers together. If we don't keep His commands, we don't love Him. And He commands us to love other believers. So, if we don't love other believers, we don't love

God. Thus, to claim to love God when I don't love my brother/sister makes me a liar.

You will notice that the word *must* is in italics in the NKJV. That means it was not actually in the Greek, but the translators put it in here because they thought it expressed John's intention. But it might be better to put "*should*," as we find in the NASB. "OK, Lord, I give up; I should love my brother. But who is my brother?"—a very likely question. The answer? *Whoever* (no exceptions) believes Jesus is the Christ. John never defines a Christian any other way. A Christian is not defined by life-style, good works, or obedience. So, one who believes in Jesus is "born of God." He does not tell me to open a fruit inspection table offering so much love in exchange for good fruit. I don't spot my Christian brother by his good fruit. Non-Christians can have what looks to us like good fruit. Many Jewish homes have better family values than Christian homes. No, we identify a brother by his confession, not by his fruit.

Someone will surely say, "Oh, yes, a person must certainly profess Christ in order to be a Christian. But his profession/confession might be false. A good root will produce good fruit." Oh, boy. Here we go again. In my front yard is a humongous oak tree. It's branches are so long they go from the house to the street. But if you were to drive by my house during the winter, you couldn't tell if that tree was alive or dead just by looking at the external appearance of the tree. No one can tell if it's alive or dead during the winter … no one but God. With God's supernatural knowledge He knows if the tree is alive or dead. He can see the root. All we can see is the fruit. The fact that there is no fruit for a period of time does not prove there is not root. Since I am not omniscient, when a person confesses Christ as His Savior, I take him at his word. That's what John does.

"But, how can I love some Christians? They are such hypocrites. They don't deserve to be loved." My own mother used that as an excuse to stop going to church for a few years. My brother-in-law was riding along in the car with her one day and asked her why she had stopped going to church. She said, "Oh, there are just so many hypocrites in church. I just can't stand to worship with them." My brother-in-law thought a moment and then said, "Well, where would you expect to find hypocrites? You have to go to church to be a hypocrite." Good point. Not everyone in church is a hypocrite, but church is the main gathering ground for Christian hypocrites. And we should love hypocrites. Why? Because God is the only one who can separate the wheat from the tares. If they profess Christ, we should love them.

Our love for people who confess Christ is not based on their performance. If everything about you were known by others, do you deserve to be loved? No, our love for the child of God is based on our love for the Father of that child. If we love the "Begetter," we should love the "begotten." If we love the Father, we should love His children. No love for the children? Then, no love for the Father.

I have a friend who calls me every three or four months from Nebraska. He's read some of my journal articles and heard me speak a couple of times at conferences. So he makes a list of doctrinal questions, calls me on the phone, and we discuss these problems long distance. When we are finished, he asks me about each of my children. He calls them by name, though he has never met any of them. He's been doing this for years. He prays for them. I know he does because he keeps a little list of the requests made the last time he called and specifically asks me about them. He loves my children. You know why? Probably because he's never met them, you say. Now that wasn't nice. No, he loves them because, for some reason we have yet to ascertain, he loves their father. To love the father is to love his children.

My children are an extension of me. It doesn't matter about their performance when it comes to loving them. My friend probably prays harder for the children who are doing as well as the others. But he has a love for them, all of them. It's a supernatural thing. He has it because he loves their father. And that's precisely what John is saying. The reason we are to love each other is because we love the Father. When we love the Father, we love those who are "begotten" of the Father, those in His forever family. Whoever believes Jesus is the Christ is born of God, and everyone who loves the Begetter also loves His begotten.

OK, John, I concede that if I do love God, then I must love His children. But how do I know if I am loving His children? I certainly can't say I *feel good* about all of them.

MEASURE OF LOVE

> By this we know that we love the children of God, when we love
> God and keep His commandments. For this is the love of God,
> that we keep His commandments. And His commandments are
> not burdensome (5:2-3).

So, how do I know if I am loving my Christian brother or sister? No problem. Just keep His commandments. Even if we think of the ten commandments, the last six deal with loving other people. You've heard it said to fathers, "The best way to love a child is to love his/her mother." It is loving other believers when we model the Christian life for them. This is even more important than meeting their physical needs; it points them toward the kind of life that can meet their spiritual needs.

So, my love for other believers can be measured by the degree to which I keep the commandments of God. But doesn't this put me right back into performance, legalism, and relativism (my obedience compared to those around me)? No, because *the commandments of God are not burdensome.* Wow. Is that some kind of statement? John just sort of slipped that one under the door on us.

Why aren't the commandments of God burdensome? According to the Pharisees, there were at least 613 commandments the Jews were responsible to keep. And in the Sermon on the Mount, which Ghandi liked so much, Jesus raised the bar. Unless your righteousness exceeds the righteousness of the scribes and the Pharisees, you have no chance of entering the kingdom of heaven, says Jesus (Matt 5:20). These people had been taught it was wrong to commit adultery, but Jesus went one further: it was sinful just to dwell on adultery in your heart. These people were taught it was wrong to murder someone, but Jesus went further: it was sinful to be angry at your brother without any cause. Whatever interpretation the Pharisees had given of the Law, Jesus took it to another level. The point is that the responsibility of the Christian, if anything, was greater than that of the OT believer. They had heard they were to love their neighbor as themselves. Now Jesus gives them a new commandment: love each other as I have loved you.

Talk about a heavy yoke. But, again, ... there is nothing wrong with God's *standard.* It's a question of *source.* In the fourth book of *The Chronicles of Narnia* C. S. Lewis tells the story of "The Silver Chair." A little girl named Jill is lost in a dense forest. She's scared, crying, and has a tremendous thirst. If she doesn't find water, she'll die. Suddenly, as she follows a turn in the path, she sees a beautiful, gurgling stream. She breaks into a run, but just as she gets to the stream she sees a huge Lion right on the edge of the stream. She pulls up short, scared to death. She looks at the lion, and he beckons her to come and drink. "If you are thirsty, come and drink."

Jill is skeptical. "May I—could I—would you mind going away while I do?" asked Jill. The Lion answered this only by a look and a very low growl. And as Jill gazed at its motionless bulk, she realized that she might as well have asked the whole mountain to move aside for her convenience. The delicious rippling noise of the stream was driving her nearly frantic. "Will you promise not to—do anything to me, if I do come?" asked Jill. "I make no promise," said the Lion.

Jill was so thirsty now that, without noticing it, she had come a step nearer. "*Do* you eat girls?" she asked. "I have swallowed up girls and boys, women and men, kings and emperors, cities and realms," said the Lion. It didn't say this as if it were boasting, nor as if it were sorry, nor as if it were angry. It just said it.

"I daren't come and drink," said Jill. "Then you will die of thirst," said the Lion. "Oh dear!" said Jill, coming another step nearer. "I suppose I must go and look for another stream then." "There is no other stream," said the Lion.[1]

Lewis puts these words in the mouth of Aslan, the Christ figure, as he talks to a scared little girl. Christ says, "Come unto Me all you who labor and are heavy laden, and I will give you rest." Christ said, "Come unto Me and drink, and I will give you rivers of water to quench your thirst." There is only one stream with the water of life to take away your thirst. And there is only one Source of the water of life. And of this Jesus spoke of the Spirit He would send.

The problem isn't with the standard; the problem is with the source. As long as I think I am obligated to keep the law of Christ, I will always live a joyless and to some degree a hypocritical life. Until I go to the right Source, there is no hope. So in 1 John 5:4-5 John brings us to the right Source. If the mandate to love was in 1 John 4:20–5:1 and the measure of love was in 1 John 5:2-3, then the means to love is in 1 John 5:4-5. We finally get to this question of where we can get that perfect love.

MEANS TO LOVE

> For whatever is born of God overcomes the world. And this is the victory that has overcome the world—our faith. Who is he who overcomes the world, but he who believes that Jesus is the Son of God (5:4-5)?

Here is something really interesting. Both the NKJV and the NASB say *whatever* (*pan*) is born of God overcomes the world. The Greek does not say "whoever." Since we are talking about people, I would expect John to say "whoever" is born of God. But the NASB and the NKJV are absolutely correct. The text says *whatever*. This is important because the emphasis here is on our *source*. Victory comes not through a created being (whoever), but through the Creator. The new birth itself is victory over the world system.

And the new birth, this victory over the world, comes *by faith* in God, the Creator. We got our first victory (new birth) *by faith*; all subsequent victories are *by faith* as well. Jesus was our substitute in death; He must also be our substitute in life. This is what Paul was trying to say: "I am crucified with Christ; nevertheless, I live; yet not I, but *Christ lives in me*; and the life, which I now live in the flesh, *I live by the faith* in the Son of God who loved me and gave Himself for me."

It has been said that the hardest thing in the world for a non-Christian to believe is in the substitutionary death of Christ, but the hardest thing in the world for a Christian to believe is in the subsitutionary life of Christ. We got victory over death by His death; we shall have victory in life by His life. This is what it means when it says, "Christ lives in me."

One day a woman came to a tennis pro to ask if he would give her two sons lessons, ages five and six. That's how he made his living, so he said he'd be glad to. Well, the next day she showed up with her boys, and they showed up with their rackets—adult size. He immediately knew they were in trouble. They could hardly grip the rackets, let alone swing them properly. It looked more like someone turning in a circle to throw the discus.

But the tennis pro was being paid to teach, so he got on the other side of the net and began to throw balls at the boys so the ball would be in just the right position and easy to hit. No way. The balls went past the boys before they could even get the rackets back, let alone through. So he got someone else to throw the balls while he went around on the same side of the net as the boys. He got behind one of the boys, put his hand over one of the boy's hands, told him to relax, and did the stroke for him. Stroke after stroke. Through his strength the little boy was learning the right motion. Then he did the same with the other little boy.

Then the first little boy said, "I think I've got it. Let me try it myself." So he tried it alone. No way. He was simply too young to have the strength to handle an adult size racket. So the pro went back around to help the boy again. But this kid still thought he could do it. So instead of relaxing, he tried to add his strength to the pro's strength. But the strength of the little boy, what little there was, was just enough to get in the way of the pro's strength, so even he couldn't hit the ball over the net. So once again he had to convince the boy to relax, to rest in his strength. Then the ball started going over the net again.

Abide in Him. That's what John is trying to teach us. It's the same lesson Jesus taught in the Upper Room. Like most of the truth in 1 John the lessons come straight from Jesus in the Upper Room. Like a good disciple John is passing on what the Master taught him: "I am the vine, you *are* the branches. He who abides in Me, and I in him, bears much fruit; for without Me you can do nothing" (John 15:5). The problem is not the standard; it's the source. We must relax and rest in His power. "I can do all things through Christ who strengthens me" (Phil 4:13). "For with God nothing will be impossible" (Luke 1:37). He hasn't set an impossible standard. It's only impossible for us, but not for Him. "The things that are impossible for men are possible for God" (Luke 18:27).

CONCLUSION

What John is trying to teach us here is expressed elsewhere in the NT in many different ways. Perhaps the most referenced passage in textbooks on progressive sanctification, or the victorious Christian life, or what we are calling growth in *agapē* is 2 Cor 3:18, which says, "But we all, with unveiled face, beholding as in a mirror the glory of the Lord, are being transformed into the same image from glory to glory, just as by the Spirit of the Lord."

Most of this verse is pretty clear. Certainly the product is clear—we are going to be made like the Lord, into His image. And the Source is clear— this molding or sculpting or transformation will not be done through our power, but through the work of the Spirit of the Lord. But when I ask people about the responsibility of the Christian in this verse, they often just stare at me with a blank look. And then I say, "You've got it!" because that is really what the verse teaches "beholding as in a mirror the glory of the Lord."

Our responsibility is to turn our eyes upon Jesus; look full in His wonderful face. When we do this, we are beholding the glory (the open public manifestation of the character qualities) of the Lord. We see His love; we see His mercy; we see His truth; we see His peace. As we simply behold Him, His Spirit, like a divine Michaelangelo, molds us into the same image as the Lord. It's what Earl Nightengale calls the strangest secret in the world. And that secret is this: you become what you think about. As you think about your sins, you will become more sinful. As you think about the Lord, you will become more like Him.

This is why the epistles start with our position and move to our condition. It's because there is a dynamic link between the two. As we focus on our position it affects our condition. When we focus on our position in Christ, our condition becomes more like Christ. He is our source. When I try, I fail; when I trust, He succeeds.

Nathaniel Hawthorne seemed to understand this truth in his short story called "The Great Stone Face." The setting is a lush valley in a small town in the Northeast. The town had a legend about a certain rock configuration on the side of a steep bluff. This configuration looked to the town folk like the face of an old man, a man full of grace, full of kindness, full of wisdom. And there was a prophecy which went along with the Great Stone Face. According to the prophecy, one day a man would come to their valley who had the very likeness of the Great Stone Face. He would come to do wonderful things and great good to those who lived in the valley.

The key figure in this story is a little boy named Earnest. His mother had told him about the prophecy of the Great Stone Face. So he would go out after school to look at the Great Stone Face. He wanted to be sure to recognize the wise man who would come to their valley, so he spent hour upon hour just staring at the Great Stone Face. One day as he was looking at the face in the rocks it appeared to him that the man in the face smiled at him and gave him a wink of approval.

But Earnest kept looking for someone who would come to the valley with the likeness of the Great Stone Face. A great millionaire came to the valley who passed out gold coins to the people. His name was Mr. Gather Gold. Earnest went to look at him in his limousine, but as he got close, Earnest thought, "That's not the likeness of the Great Stone Face. It's the face of greed."

Another man came years later. His name was Mr. Blood and Thunder. He was a great war hero, a general. But as Earnest got close to the general he thought, "This is not the likeness of the Great Stone Face, for there is no compassion." A great politician came to the valley—Mr. Stoney Fizz, but he had the face of manipulation.

Years went by, but no one came to the valley with the likeness of the Great Stone Face. By this time Earnest had become a minister in the small valley. He ministered year after year in a small church, yet his fame grew beyond the valley. His wisdom was sought out by people far and wide. Politicians, statesmen, wealthy, and poor—all searching for pearls around the feet of Earnest.

Finally a poet came to the valley. Earnest thought perhaps this poet would fulfill the prophecy about the Great Stone Face. His poetry was noble; it was lofty, full of grandeur and glory. But even he fell short. Finally, Earnest was an old man, and the prophecy had not been fulfilled. The poet had remained in the valley, for he had learned so much just listening to Earnest.

One evening Earnest was preaching in an open air cathedral right next to the mountains, directly under the Great Stone Face. From Earnest's lips wisdom poured like water over a waterfall, encouraging people to love, peace, and good works.

Just as Earnest was striking a pose, reflecting on a thought he was about to express, some clouds settled in around the brow of the Great Stone Face. The poet looked at the Great Stone Face. Then he looked at Earnest with his white shock of hair. Irresistibly he cried out, "Behold, behold, Earnest is the Great Stone Face." And all the people looked, and it was true. Earnest had fulfilled the prophecy. But when the message was over, Earnest took the poet by his arm and walked back home with him, still hoping that one more noble, more humble, and more wise than he would come to the valley and reflect the visage of the Great Stone Face.

We become what we think about. As we think about Jesus, we become like Jesus. We have trusted in His substitutionary death; now we must trust in His substitutionary life.

-----

[1] C. S. Lewis, *The Chronicles of Narnia* "The Silver Chair" (New York: HarperCollins Publishers, 1953), 21-23.

LESSON 19 "THE SOURCE" I JOHN 4:20-5:5

1. What are some types of fellow believers that you find particularly difficult to love? (Please don't name them!!!)

2. On page 245, we find these two statements: "The problem isn't the standard. The problem is the source." What meaning do you attach to those statements?

3. Pages 246-248 reflect John's mandate "to love" our brothers (and sisters) in Christ. How can we do this when some of them are egotistical, hypocritical, and generally difficult?

4. What connection do you see between this scripture and the original ten commandments?

5. Why aren't the commandments of God burdensome?

6. John uses the word "whatever" rather than "whoever" in verse 4. (This is the preferred translation.) Why is this important?

7. How do you relate " . . . he who loves God must love his brother also" to "We must relax and rest in His power" (page 252)?

8. In what ways does the statement, "We become what we think about" pertain to the scripture in this lesson?

9. Is it time to have a "thinking overhaul"? See Romans 12:2 and Ephesians 4:23.

– 20 –

STANDING ON THE PROMISES

1 JOHN 5:6-13

Jody Dillow, in his book *The Reign of the Servant Kings,* tells the fascinating story of John Duncan:

> John Duncan was born in 1796 in Aberdeen, Scotland, the son
> of a shoemaker. Although not well known, his influence upon
> Jewish missions was great. He was affectionately called "Rabbi"
> Duncan because of his immense knowledge of Hebrew literature
> and his espousal of the cause of the Jews. In fact, when he applied
> for the Chair of Oriental Languages in the University of Glasgow,
> there was no one who was qualified to examine him. He read flu-
> ently in Syriac, Arabic, Persian, Sanskrit, Bengali, Hindustani,
> and Mahratti, as well as Latin, German, French, Hebrew, and
> Greek!
>
> While studying in Budapest, he met a brilliant Jewish schol-
> ar, whom he led to Christ. This man was later to become the
> most learned writer on the life of Christ in the nineteenth centu-
> ry, Alfred Edersheim.
>
> Becoming a Christian was not easy for Rabbi Duncan, and
> believing that he was saved was even harder. He struggled so des-
> perately with doubt concerning his salvation that on one occa-
> sion, at a prayer meeting of professors and students, Duncan,
> who was presiding, broke down and wept, saying that God had
> forsaken him.
>
> In his quest to find subjective assurance that he was truly
> born again, Duncan turned repeatedly to Caesar Malan, through
> whom he was converted. Malan was ordained to the ministry in
> Geneva and apparently preached with great power and evangeli-
> cal zeal. Malan's pastoral method of helping Duncan find assur-
> ance was through the use of a practical syllogism. He asked
> Duncan the following logic:

Major Premise: He that believeth that Jesus is the Christ is born of God.
Minor Premise: But I believe that Jesus is the Christ.
Conclusion: Therefore, I am born of God.[1]

This is just another way of saying if A (a believer in Jesus as the Christ) = B (a person born of God), and A (a believer in Jesus as the Christ) = C (Me), then B (a person born of God) = C (Me). Through this logic Duncan found rest for his troubled soul—for two years. Then the doubts returned. Now he wondered if he really believed sufficiently. A dark depression entered his life. He was afraid he was not elect (reprobate). He asked that these words be published after his death:

> I can't put a negative upon my regeneration. I don't say I can put a positive. Sometimes hope abounds, and at the worst I have never been able dogmatically to pronounce myself unregenerate …. Sometimes I have strongly thought that what is formed between Christ and me shall last forever. At other times I fear I may be in hell yet. But if I can't affirm my regeneration, I can't deny it; my self-examination can go no further.[2]

In time Duncan turned from trying to have faith in his faith to having faith in his fruit. The Geneva Academy, which trained so many pastors for the Continent and Great Britain, began the industry of Christian fruit inspecting. Theodore Beza, who succeeded John Calvin in Geneva, decided that Christ only died for the elect. Therefore, He would not be a good source of assurance, for if one looked to Christ for his assurance of salvation, he might be looking at a Savior who did not die for him (if he's one of the non-elect or reprobate, which is the very issue at stake). But if we can't look to Christ for the assurance of our salvation, where shall we look? Ah, ha, I must look at the fruit in my own life. Good fruit will mean a good root. So, Duncan pursued another syllogism:

> **Major Premise:** Those who are born again will necessarily produce the fruits of regeneration in their lives.
> **Minor Premise:** I have the fruits of regeneration.
> **Conclusion:** I am born again.[3]

But, alas! Just as Duncan developed problems believing he had sufficient faith to be saved, so now he developed problems believing he had sufficient fruit to be saved. At one point in his struggle he wrote in his journal, "I was in a terrible agony last night at the thought of a Christless state, and that I might be in it. The fear of it exhausted my faculties."[3]

What a tragedy, to go through one's Christian life believing Christ is the Savior, but not having the assurance that if you died, you would wake up in His presence. That is the approach taken by most of the people in Christendom today. After all, the great Augustine said a person could never know for sure that he was among the elect in this life. Yet this seems to go directly counter to 1 John 5:13, which says, "These things I have written to you who believe in the name of the Son of God, that you may *know* that you have eternal life." We want to look closely at this particular verse. It is the verse used in many gospel tracts to give a person the assurance of his salvation. I use it.

When someone has trusted Christ after I present the gospel, I ask them to read this verse to me aloud. I look away while they are reading, so they know I am not looking directly at the text. When they come to the word *believe*, I interrupt them and ask, "Bob, do you believe in Jesus?" They will usually say they do. Then I have them continue reading. This time, when they come to the word *know*, I rather abruptly interrupt them and ask, "Doesn't that say 'guess'?" They usually look a little puzzled and then say, "No, it says *know*." I mildly protest by saying, "Well, doesn't it say 'hope'?" Now, with a little more conviction, they usually say, "*No*, it says *know*." Then I very quickly say, "That's right. It says *know*. So, Bob, if someone comes up to you a couple of weeks from now and asks you if you will go to heaven if you die, you don't have to say, 'Well, I guess I will.' Or you don't have to say, 'Well, I certainly hope so.' You just say, 'Yes, I will,' because you *know* so."

What is ironic to me is that the very verse I and thousands of others have used to give people assurance of their salvation immediately after they trust Christ as their personal Savior, has been turned around by others to say not only do you have to believe, but you have to walk in the light (1 John 1:5), you have to keep the commandments (1 John 2:3), you have to love your Christian brothers and sisters (1 John 4:7-8), you have to hate the world system (1 John 2:15), you have to practice righteousness (1 John 2:29), and on and on the list goes.

Because 1 John 5:13 begins with the words *these things*, they believe that all the things written from the beginning of the letter to 1 John 5:13 are included in *these things*. Thus, all *these things* become the criteria by which you can test whether or not you are among the elect. In this study we will try to demonstrate that *these things* in 1 John 5:13 does not refer to everything from the beginning of the letter up to this wonderful promise, and indeed, that this is one of the most assuring of all texts when it comes to knowing we will be with the Lord when we die. You can know this very moment, right where you sit, that you are born of God and will spend eternity with Him. You don't need to fear hell, and purgatory is pure fiction.

We are in the third wave of John's principles of fellowship. Each wave has had three dolphins which keep resurfacing in the letter: right living, right loving, and right learning. In 1 John 5:6-13 we look away from one porpoise to another. We look away from right loving to right learning. This third wave is the largest of all because it is the climactic section in the treatment of each of these principles. The section on right loving developed perfect love for us. And now, in this section on right learning, we come to the heart of the gospel itself, a gospel the enemies of Christ would love to dilute or undermine. The MO of the enemies of Christ, the antichrists, is similar throughout the ages. Like lung cancer they go for the air supply, two lungs, if you will, in the Body of Christ: God's Work (5:6-9) and God's Word (5:10-13).

ATTACK AGAINST GOD'S WORK

> This is He who came by water and blood—Jesus Christ; not only by water, but by water and blood. And it is the Spirit who bears witness, because the Spirit is truth. For there are three that bear witness in heaven: the Father, the Word, and the Holy Spirit; and these three are one. And there are three that bear witness on earth: the Spirit, the water, and the blood; and these three agree as one. If we receive the witness of men, the witness of God is greater; for this is the witness of God which He has testified of His Son (5:6-9).

One of the heresies floating around in the early church was the teaching that Jesus was just a man, that the divine Christ came upon Him at His baptism and left Him on the cross. In other words, just a man died for us. Sounds like the anti-Christian play "Jesus Christ, Superstar," in which the theme song said, "He's just a man, just a man, and I've had so many men before, in so many ways, he's just one more"—sung by a converted prostitute.

Water was a reference to His baptism; *blood*—a reference to His cross. At His baptism the Father said He was well-pleased, and the Spirit came upon Him. The Holy Spirit was not the *divine Christ* coming upon Jesus, the man. The Spirit was distinct from Christ and came upon the God-man, Jesus Christ.

In a court of law the Holy Spirit would be put on the stand as a character witness; the water and the blood would be entered as Exhibit A and Exhibit B. All three gave credibility to the Person and work of our Lord and Savior Jesus Christ. If a case among men is established by the word of two or three witnesses (Matt 18:16), then two or three divine witnesses should be even more reliable: the Spirit, the water, and the blood.

Today the enemies of Christ in the world attack God's work in two primary ways: His work of creation and His work of redemption. In creation we are told that we arrived by chance into this world and only the evolutionary forces of the natural world worked together to come up with *homo sapiens*. It's interesting, but the Ph.D.s in biology on our university campuses won't even come to the debates on evolution any more because they realize their theory is more religion than science.[4]

It always amused me that they call evolution a theory and treat it like a fact. According to the scientific method, it doesn't even qualify as a good hypothesis. Why? Because in the scientific method we must begin with an observation. And the most important observation for evolutionary theory has never been made—a positive mutation from a lower species to a higher. Of course, for evolution from the primordial mess to human mass we need tentontrillion positive mutations going from lower to higher. We have never observed even one. For Newton to come up with his law of gravity, he first observed the apple falling from the tree. Positive mutations, which are very rare, *within* a species do not count.

Well, you can be sure that the Apostle Peter believed in the creation story (2 Peter 3). And we know that Jesus believed in the Genesis creation account (Matt 19:4-6). Malachi believed in it (Mal 2:15). And I just bet Adam and Eve believed in the creation event. (Permit me a moment of humor.) It reminds me of the night that Adam stayed out until four in the morning. When he got back, Eve wanted an accounting. "Are you sure you aren't seeing someone else?" she railed. "Oh, no, honey," replied Adam defensively, "You know when God made you, He made one of a kind. You're the only one in the world for me." That seemed to satisfy Eve until she heard Adam snoring. Then, before she could go to sleep, she carefully counted each of his ribs to make sure they were all there. She obviously believed in creationism.

One day there will be a judgment of the world like there has never been before. It will be so horrible it will make WWII look like a fireworks display.

Men and angels alike will wonder how a loving God could bring such a judgment. I am talking about the Great Tribulation period described in Revelation 6–19. So there is a big time out in heaven in Revelation 4–5 to justify the ways of God with men. And in Rev 4:11 we find out that God's judgment is just because everyone belongs to God by virtue of creation: "You are worthy, O Lord, to receive glory and honor and power; for You created all things, and by your will they were created and exist." He created us, it says. And the Creator has the right to do with the creation as He wishes, especially when they reject Him.

But a second work of God that has consistently been attacked by Satan through the ages is His work of redemption. And in Rev 5:9, "You are worthy to take the scroll, and to open its seals; for You were slain, and have redeemed us to God by Your blood out of every tribe and tongue and people and nation." We belong to Him by virtue of Redemption. He has paid the price for the sins of the whole world. In 2 Pet 2:1 it even says that false teachers have been redeemed by God. That does not mean they will go to heaven. It means the price for their sins has been paid. But unless they accept the redemption on their behalf, Christ's work of redemption will be wasted on their behalf. Yes, wasted, except for the fact that it does justify the incredible judgment on the world in Revelation 6–19, because in Revelation 5 we read that we have been redeemed by the Lamb.

So the enemies of Christ attack His work (5:6-9); but they also attack His Word (5:10-13).

ATTACK AGAINST GOD'S WORD

> He who believes in the Son of God has the witness in himself; he who does not believe God has made Him a liar, because he has not believed the testimony that God has given of His Son. And this is the testimony: that God has given us eternal life, and this life is in His Son. He who has the Son has life; he who does not have the Son of God does not have life. These things I have written to you who believe in the name of the Son of God, that you may know that you have eternal life, and that you may *continue to* believe in the name of the Son of God (5:10-13).

If a person does not believe the testimony that God has marshaled on behalf of the Person and work of Jesus Christ, he is calling God a liar. In other words, he is saying God's Word in not reliable. It's a direct attack against the Word of God. If the "Wicked One" (5:18) cannot get us to doubt

God's work (sending His Son to die in our place), then he tries to get us to doubt God's Word (or both, since the two are connected in this passage).

What, specifically, does God's Word say about Jesus? "That God has given us eternal life this life is *in* His Son." Since this eternal life is in His Son, it follows that if a person has the Son, he also has life (eternal life); and if a person does not have the Son, he does not have life. What must I do to have the Son? The only requirement mentioned in 1 John (or anywhere in the Bible, for that matter) is to believe. There is absolutely no mention of one's performance, one's fruit, or one's obedience as a requirement for having the Son or for having assurance. John says we can *know* (not guess or hope) that we have eternal life if we believe in the name of the Son of God.

But what about *these things*? Isn't this a reference to the entire letter, that is, a thematic statement for the book? In other words, we don't just need to have faith in order to *know* that we have eternal life, but also: keeping God's commandments, loving one's brother, resisting the world and the devil, etc. Right?

No, the statement "these things we/I write (or have written) to you" occurs several times in the letter (1:4; 2:1; 2:26). In each case, it refers to the material just written in the previous section. It does not pick up all the material from the beginning of the letter (see especially 2:26 to make this clear). In 1 John 5:13 the "these things" points to the testimony/witness (*martyria*, the noun, or *martyreō*, the verb) which has been mentioned seven times in 1 John 5:9-12:

> If we receive the *witness* of men, the *witness* of God is greater; for this is the *witness* of God which He has *testified* of His Son. He who believes in the Son of God has the *witness* in himself; he who does not believe God has made Him a liar, because he has not believed the *testimony* that God has given of His Son. And this is the *testimony*: that God has given us eternal life, and this life is in His Son. He who has the Son has life; he who does not have the Son of God does not have life. These things I have written to you who believe in the name of the Son of God, that you may know that you have eternal life.

What John is arguing for in this passage is the credibility of God's testimony (witness). It is greater than that of men. And this witness or testimony is that God has given us eternal life, and this life is in His Son. We can either accept or reject this testimony.

Notice that we are not called upon to search our faith to see if it is real. We do not have to have "faith in our faith." We are called upon to have faith in what God says about His Son. Our assurance is at stake here, yes, but more important than that is the credibility of God. It is His witness that is at stake. We either believe it or reject it. In fact, in 1 John 5:13 we find echoes of John 5:24 where it says, "Most assuredly, I say to you, he who hears My word and believes in Him who sent Me has everlasting life, and shall not come into judgment, but has passed from death into life.

CONCLUSION

So poor "Rabbi" Duncan was caught between two poles. He either was trying to gain assurance by putting his faith in his faith, or by putting his faith in his fruit. He wound up doubting if he had enough faith and if he had enough fruit.

> Don't put your faith in your fruit;
> Don't put your faith in your feelings;
> Don't put your faith in your faith.
> Your faith is only as good as its object.
> Put your faith in Jesus Christ, Son of the living God.

Martin Luther once wrote:

> ... the sort of faith that does not look at its own works nor at its own strength and worthiness, noting what sort of quality or new created or infused virtue it may be .... But faith goes out of itself, clings to Christ, and embraces Him as it own possession; and *faith is certain that it is loved by God for His sake.*"[5]

And John Calvin in his early writings said of saving faith:

> We shall now have a full definition of faith if we say that it is a firm and sure knowledge of the divine favor toward us, founded on the truth of a free promise in Christ, and revealed to our minds, and sealed on our hearts, by the Holy Spirit.[6]

Several years ago Samuel Beckett wrote a play called "Waiting for Godot." In this particular play the curtain opens with two guys standing around with their hands in their pockets, waiting at a train station. They don't seem to have much purpose. They aren't doing anything. They don't have a plan. Just sort of staring at each other.

When someone comes along to ask what they are doing, they explain that they are just waiting … waiting for Godot. When asked who Godot might be, they don't know. When asked what Godot will do when he gets here, they don't know that either. Someone just said that when he comes, things will get better. So, here are two strangers standing around waiting for a stranger they don't know to do something they know not what.

As the play goes on, Godot never comes. They finally give up and are ready to leave, but they can't leave. They stay at the train station with their hands in their pockets, glued to the floor, doing nothing, waiting for nothing, their lives meaning nothing.

Decades later there was an anniversary celebration of the play in honor of Samuel Beckett. Someone asked him, "Mr. Beckett, now that fifty years have passed since you wrote this play, will you tell us who Godot is?" He replied, "How should I know?"

Now there were a couple of people in this play putting their faith in someone they'd never met to do something they'd never heard of, and they never went anywhere in their lives. That seems to be Beckett's way of saying, Godot represents all our pipe dreams out there, dreams that will help us escape a meaningless life, but at the same time will prevent you from doing anything with your life that will count.[7]

Aren't you glad we aren't waiting for Godot? We are waiting for God, Someone we know, Someone with whom we have a personal relationship, Someone who can make our lives count forever, Someone who has gifted us for a purpose, Someone who has enabled us to have an eternal impact.

I've never had the chance to visit Lithuania, but I read about a hill over there called the "Hill of Crosses." It is a mound of earth about thirty feet high, covered with homemade crosses that villagers had planted upright in the ground. A forest of crosses—high iron crosses, towering like lodge pole pines over an underbrush of stubby, wooden and cement crosses. You could hardly see the ground for the crosses.

Each cross represented a promise and a loved one who had died as a stranger in exile or in prison, usually in a Russian prison. The Hill of Crosses had been sacred to the villagers for a hundred years. It was a mystic place to them, a holy place where the pious gathered almost every day to pray and remember. They clung to the promises that one day Jesus, who died on the cross for their sins, would return to reunite them with those they loved who had gone before them.

Then in 1940 the Russians came to this hill nine miles east of the village of Siauliai. The Russians viewed the crosses as a superstitious insult to their religion of atheism. So they made a law against planting crosses on the hill. But it didn't do any good. Villagers sneaked in under the cover of night and planted their crosses anyway. The Russians rolled in their bulldozers. They burned the wooden crosses, buried the cement crosses, and melted the iron crosses. But still the people came, one or two at a time, and planted their crosses at night. And still they came to pray during the day. At last, in 1988, the Russians gave up and left the Hill of Crosses in peace.

Now the crosses have taken on a new meaning for the people of Siauliai. People cluster around the hill now and remember how the mighty Russians mustered their machines against their crosses and how the crosses beat them back. Each cross planted during the time of occupation when it was forbidden to plant them has become a reminder that the forces of atheism could not keep down the Lord Jesus Christ and the promise of hope He brings to all who believe in Him, the personal God who loved us and gave Himself for us.[8]

Satan has tried to bull doze God's promises, but they won't go away. These promises are the sure foundation of our faith, for the Word of God abides forever.

> Standing on the promises of Christ my King,
> Through eternal ages let His praises ring!
> Glory in the highest I will shout and sing,
> Standing on the promises of God.
> Standing on the promises that cannot fail
> When the howling storms of doubt and fear assail;
> By the living Word of God I shall prevail,
> Standing on the promises of God.

---

[1] Joseph C. Dillow, *The Reign of the Servant Kings: A Study of Eternal Security and the Final Significance of Man* (Hayesville, NC: Schoettle Publishing Co., 1992), 245. He is quoting from John E. Marshall, "Rabbi Duncan and the Problem of Assurance (I)," *The Banner of Truth* 201 (June 1980): 16-27.

[2] Ibid., 27.

[3] Ibid., 28.

[4] Kirby Anderson, personal interview, Trinity Pines, TX, November 17, 2001.

[5] Martin Luther, *What Luther Says: An Anthology*, comp. Ewald M. Plass, 3 vols. (St. Louis: Concordia Publishing House, 1959), 1:496, italics mine.

[6] John Calvin, *Institutes,* 3.2.7.

[7] Lewis Smedes, *Standing on the Promises* (Nashville: Thomas Nelson Publishers, 1998), 143.

[8] Ibid., 183-84.

LESSON 20 "STANDING ON THE PROMISES" I JOHN 5:6-13

1. Many people struggle with "assurance of salvation." What are some of the factors that seem to undermine "assurance"?

2. How does 5:13 address this matter of assurance?

3. The scripture for this lesson tells of "three that bear witness in heaven" and "three that bear witness on earth." What do you understand about these witnesses?

4. Today the enemies of Christ in the world attack God's work in two primary ways: His work of _____ and His work of _____ (page 255). What evidence could you offer to support this statement?

5. The enemies of Christ attack His work but they also attack His Word. Can you think of examples from current events/widespread practice?

6. In what sense does an unbeliever make "Him (God) a liar" (verse 10)?

7. What is John referring to when he says "these things"? Why is it important to understand his reference?

8. How can we avoid having "faith in our faith" as a basis for our assurance of salvation?

9. Explain how the words "Standing on the Promises" (page 260) seem to capture the essence of this lesson.

21

THE FOUNTAIN OF LIFE

1 JOHN 5:14-17

He was born in San Tervas de Campos, Spain, in 1474. There is no record of his birth, parents' names, or of his preteen years. In his younger years he served as a squire and earned the nickname "poor knight." From that day on he trained himself in the arts of war and survival to prepare himself for a future of daring and unimaginable adventures to the unknown.

In 1493 he joined Columbus on his second voyage to the Americas. After that he settled on a Caribbean island named Hispaniola to improve his fortunes and start a warlike life. At that time on Hispaniola he became a military commander and a deputy governor. In 1506, he discovered a nearby island named Borinquin, which was later renamed Puerto Rico. He became that island's governor two years later. Still, he wanted more wealth, power, and glory, Ponce de Leon begged and persuaded the king to grant him men and ships to search for the infamous "Fountain of Youth."

In his quixotic quest, he became the European discoverer of Florida, which he named "Pascua de Florida" (feast of flowers) after a Spanish Easter holiday, for he landed there on Easter Sunday. Unfortunately, he missed God's subtle message that Easter Sunday. Ponce de Leon lost his life in Florida when he was killed by the poison from an arrow. He was looking for life in all the wrong places. Jesus is the one who promised the woman at the well a fountain of water springing up into everlasting life. Of course, He was not speaking of a physical fountain of water, but a spiritual fountain of living water which would give everlasting spiritual life.

What is this "Fountain of Life" Jesus talks about? Is it something we only discover after we die? I don't think so. John has been talking about it with different terms in his first letter, 1 John. In the "Introduction" to his letter John mentions that his purpose (1 John 1:3-4) in writing is that his readers might have "full joy." There it is. "Full joy." If one is full of joy, he has discovered the "Fountain of Life" right here and now. He does not have to wait for it in the next life.

At the end of his letter John words it a little differently, but it is the same song, second verse. He says, "He who has the Son has life; he who does not have the Son of God has not life." Life ... life. What life? He calls it eternal life in the following verse. But this eternal life is not something we get in the next world. It is something we get right now. It can best be described now as a higher quality of life than we experienced before we had the Son. And one of the aspects of this new life in Christ which makes it a better quality of life right here and now is joy. As one of the fruits of the Holy Spirit, the joy of the Lord or the joy of the Holy Spirit is a joy the world does not know. And it is our present possession when we practice the principles of fellowship outlined in this book: right living, right loving, and right learning.

Now as John begins to bring us to the end of the letter, he gives us another lesson on joy. He comes back to the beginning of his letter. Our passage is 1 John 5:14-17. When we read these verses, we do not see anything about joy. But, as we have seen so many times before, these verses in 1 John are based on previous verses John has written, specifically in John 13–16. In John 16:22-24 Jesus speaks of this perpetual joy that can be ours. He talks about the perpetual joy that will be ours when He returns to the earth. But He also talks about a "full joy" that can be ours even now when we pray in His name. And that is precisely what He is getting at in 1 John 5:14-17. In these verses we see the promise of prayer in Jesus' name (1 John 5:14-15) and the practice of prayer in Jesus' name (1 John 5:16-17).

THE PROMISE OF PRAYER IN JESUS' NAME

> Now this is the confidence that we have in Him, that if we ask anything according to His will, He hears us. And if we know that He hears us, whatever we ask, we know that we have the petitions that we have asked of Him (5:14-15).

These verses don't mention joy. But when we look back at the seed bed for these verses in John 16:22-24, we can see that Jesus connects present joy with answered prayer:

> Therefore you now have sorrow; but I will see you again and your heart will rejoice, and your joy no one will take from you. And in that day you will ask Me nothing. Most assuredly, I say to you, whatever you ask the Father in My name He will give you. Until now you have asked nothing in My name. Ask, and you will receive, *that your joy may be full* (John 16:22-24).

He tells us to ask the Father in His (Jesus') name. When we receive what we ask, our "joy will be full," which is exactly the same expression in Greek in John 16:24 that we have in 1 John 1:4. So, when John speaks of praying in 1 John 5:14, he most certainly has the joy in mind that he mentioned in John 16 and 1 John 1.

The entire prayer discussion comes out of the "life" discussion in 1 John 5:11-13. There he indicates that our initial experience of faith ("who believe" = believers; the Greek construction here does not refer to present, on-going faith, but rather the initial, one time faith that gave us eternal life) can be followed by subsequent experiences of faith "in the name of the Son of God" (it is this phrase that reminds him of Christ's prayer promises in the Upper Room).

Another way of saying it would be this. After our initial faith in the name of Jesus, which gave us our first experience of eternal life, our subsequent expressions of faith in His name (when we pray) will bring new experiences of eternal life (joy). We need to keep before us the understanding that the primary emphasis in "eternal life" is quality, not quantity. Remember, unbelievers exist forever. It's their quality of existence which differs so from the believer who dwells in the presence of the Lord.

There is a qualifier here, however, when it comes to answered prayer and the joy that comes with these answered prayers. We must ask *according to His will.* Here are some reasons for negative answers to our prayers:

1. Domestic Strife—1 Pet 3:7
2. Committing Evil—1 Pet 3:12
3. Contemplating Evil—Ps 66:17
4. Lustful Prayers—Jas 4:3
5. Lacking Faith—Jas 1:5-7
6. Contrary to His will—1 John 5:14

But what does it mean to pray "according to His will"? Is this His providential will which arches over human history and includes man's sin (the cross) to accomplish His ultimate glory? Or is this His actual desired will, which excludes sin, for God never desires sin? Jesus' struggle in the Garden of Gethsemane may be helpful. There He prays, "Father, if it is Your will, take this cup away from Me; nevertheless not My will, but Yours, be done." We can see that the word "will" occurs in this prayer twice, but what we cannot see in English, is it is two different Greek words. One speaks of God's predetermined decree for human history (*boulēma*), while the other speaks of Jesus' personal desire (*thelēma*). It was not Jesus' personal desire to be separated from His Father for the first time ever. Nevertheless, He was willing to submit to His Father's overall plan for human history, which included a provision for man's sins (the cross) and incorporated the evil choices of men (the cross) to accomplish this plan.

Thus, we get a distinction here in the meaning of "will." The word used by John here in 1 John 5:14 speaks of His personal desire (*thelēma*). If our understanding of the word is correct, then John is not telling us to throw our requests up to heaven to see which ones happen to fit into His overarching "will" for human history, which includes both His directive will and His permissive will (our sins). We don't know what His providential will is, so this kind of prayer is something of a shot in the dark.

What we have here is a prayer promise designed to build our prayer confidence. If we understand "His will" here to mean His providential will, then this does nothing for our confidence. John connects our confidence with God's hearing. There seems to be a direct connect between God's hearing and answered prayer. John openly states that if God hears our requests, we can be confident He will grant those requests. We don't get the picture here of God's hearing a bunch of our requests and throwing out the one's which don't coincide with His providential will. Rather, if He hears it, He answers in accordance with the prayer. This throws us back to the question of His will. How can we know whether we are praying according to His will or not?

Instead of using "according to His will" as sort of a divine filter to keep the prayers from reaching His throne room which are contrary to divine providence, the better sense might be to pray according to what we know the desires of God are. In other words, pray according to His revealed will, something we already know to be His will. If we do this, then we know He hears us, and we can be confident He will answer.

Now "His will" has been identified for us in 1 John. It is to keep His commandments. And 1 John 3:23 gets specific: one of His commandments is that we believe in the name of His Son Jesus Christ and love one another, as He gave us commandment. In other words, I already know that He wants me to love my brother. If I am having trouble doing this, I can come to Him in prayer. I say, "Father, I know it is your revealed will that I love so and so. However, it's not within me. The pain they have caused is too great for me to overcome. But I know you live in me. And I know it is your will for me to love this person. Therefore, I pray that you would love them through me. I know you hear this prayer, and I am confident that you will answer."

Here is another example. Someone has asked me if the commandments John wishes us to keep are the ten commandments. The answer is yes and no. First of all, the ten commandments were never brought into the NT. They are part of the Old Covenant. We now have a better covenant, a New Covenant. In this covenant we are responsible for the Law of Christ, not the Law of Moses. It is a more demanding covenant, as already explained. However, within the Law of Christ nine of the ten commandments from the Old Covenant has been included. One of those is to honor one's father and mother. I have met a lot of Christians who have difficulty understanding how to do this or finding the wherewithal to do it. But it is God's clearly revealed will for us. Therefore, if we pray that God would show us how to honor our parents and would actually live out His will through us, we can be confident He will hear this prayer and answer it positively.

This kind of praying is a lot different from praying, "Lord, I'd like to have three million in my retirement account when I retire. Now, I don't know if this is your will or not, but this is what I am praying for, and, if it is your will, then I am confident it will happen." I am not saying such a prayer is an illegitimate prayer. I'm just saying I do not think that is the prayer promise John has given us in 1 John 5:14-15.

But what about *in Jesus' name?* John told us to pray in Jesus' name (John 16:22-24) and we would get what we asked for. Does this sound like formula Christianity? Just tack "in Jesus' name" on the end of a prayer, and God promises to answer. Well, we have that old problem of the spirit of the law and the letter of the law, don't we? As we know, Christianity is not magic. In magic the practitioners manipulate the supernatural powers to accomplish their own will. We cannot manipulate a sovereign God. I'm sure any attempt to do so would cause Him to recoil at the attempt. That is why He was not impressed with ritualistic worship in the OT if the hearts of the people were not in the worship.

During the Civil War two friends found themselves under heavy fire. One of them was wounded. When his friend came to his aid, the wounded soldier pulled a small card out of his pocket and painstakingly wrote a note on the back of it. Then he looked at this friend and said, "If I don't make it out alive, and you ever have a need, please go to my father. He's a wealthy man, and I'm sure he would be willing to help you."

Unfortunately, the wounded soldier did die. His friend survived, and years later lost everything he had. In desperate straits, he remembered the card his friend had given him. He pulled it out of wallet, and saw that it was the business card of his dead friend's father. He looked him up and gave his name to the secretary. She went into the busy man's office and came out with bad news, "I'm afraid Mr. Billings will be tied up in meetings most of the day." That's OK, said the desperate man, I'll just wait here. The day wore on. This former soldier was desperate, so he gave the secretary his card again and asked to see her boss for only five minutes. She took the request into her employer, but came out with the same bad news. "Mr. Billings will be tied up all day. He simply doesn't have time to see you."

Completely defeated and discouraged, the young man got up to leave, and then he remembered the card in his wallet from his friend. He pulled it out and read the back of the card to see what his friend had written. There in faded script was a note to Mr. Billings: "Dad, if this card ever gets to you, please help the bearer. He's my best friend and stayed with me until I died. Signed, Your son, Charlie." With new hope, he handed the card to the secretary and asked her if she would give this to her boss. Within seconds, Mr. Billings bounced out of his office and said, "Why didn't you send this card in hours ago. I would do anything, for Charlie's sake."

The Father's infinite love for His Son has been transferred over to us. He is especially touched by those who are His Son's best friends because they keep His commandments. And He wants to manifest His love for them for the sake of His Son. That's the spirit of the promise to answer prayer requests in Jesus' name. Our heavenly Father is willing to do most anything for Jesus' sake.

John wants to give his own example of prayer in Jesus' name, so that's what he does in the next two verses. If we had the promise of prayer in Jesus' name in 1 John 5:14-15, then we have the practice of prayer in Jesus' name in 1 John 5:16-17. But before we look at the practice of prayer in Jesus' name, we need to say a word about our outline of 1 John (see pages 78-79).

Since the section appears to be primarily about prayer, why would we call this right living—dealing with our sins (5:14-17). It's because of the example John is about to use. He comes to the brother who is not able to deal with his own sins, or at least has failed to practice the principles of fellowship explained by John in this letter. John even mentions the most destructive type of sins a believer can commit, at least as they concern his own life. That is, sins which lead directly to premature, physical death. John says there is one more principle which can lead to victory over sin when a person cannot find his way out or chooses not to try. It's the prayer of brothers who love and care about their brother captured by sin.

In this third wave of principles for fellowship, the barriers are at their height. Our biggest problem in right loving is our own fear of rejection; our biggest problem in right learning is to not believe the testimony of God regarding His Son; and our biggest problem in right living is sin which can lead directly to death. But when we observe our Christian brothers sinning, whether it's a sin leading directly to death or not, we have an opportunity to love him by praying for his deliverance from sin in the name of Jesus. That's what John explains in 1 John 5:16-17.

THE PRACTICE OF PRAYER IN JESUS' NAME

If anyone sees his brother sinning a sin *which does* not *lead* to death, he will ask, and He will give him life for those who commit sin not *leading* to death. There is sin *leading* to death. I do not say that he should pray about that. All unrighteousness is sin, and there is sin not *leading* to death (5:16-17).

One area where we can be confident that God will answer our prayers positively is if we ask Him to help us love one another, as already mentioned. Of course, we don't need prayer for help in loving those who love us. It is the brother/sister who we think has sinned against us that we have trouble loving. We need God's help. We need to ask for that help in prayer. In fact, to just be able to pray for our brother who has sinned against us is an act of love (Matt 5:44).

Now when we pray for the sinning brother we can be confident that God will answer our prayer positively. In fact, God will give the one who prays for his brother "life" to pass on to his brother ("*he* will ask, and He will give *him* life—the first "he" in the text is the antecedent to the "him" because the second "He" refers to God who answers the prayer, and "life" is given to *those* plural, who are committing sin.). Thus, the name of Jesus becomes a "Fountain of Life" for the sinning believer who gets a longer life plus joy when he repents and for the praying brother when he receives a positive answer for his prayer. We get joy from answered prayer, and the sinning brother gets restored joy when he returns to fellowship (and potentially a longer life).

This promise does not extend to those brothers/sisters who are committing sins which lead *directly* to death. All sin leads to death (Prov 11:19; Rom 6:23; Jas 5:20). But not all sins lead *directly* to death (envy, lying, slander, gossip, pride, manipulation, anger, deception, lust, hypocrisy, for example). Some sins are so serious, it may be God's will to take a brother/sister home

(1 Corinthians 5; 11:27-32). Or an early death may be the natural consequence of serious and repeated sin (Jas 1:15). It does not say we cannot pray for such, but there is no guarantee of deliverance.

CONCLUSION

What is the "Fountain of Life"? It's not:

1. Unbelief—It was Voltaire, that great infidel, who wrote, "I wish I had never been born."
2. Money—Jay Gould, that great American millionaire, who had plenty of money, said when he was dying, "I suppose I am the most miserable devil who ever lived."
3. Position or Fame—Princess Di died prematurely because she could not escape the clutches of her own fame.
4. Infidelity—Thomas Payne in his last moments said, "Oh, Lord, help me. Oh, Jesus Christ, help me." This was perhaps the first time he'd ever used the name of Jesus Christ in a reverent way.
5. Pleasure—Lord Byron spent the entirety of his life reveling in pleasure, but he said at the end of his days, "My days are in the yellow of leaf; the flower and the fruits of life are gone; the worm, the canker, and the grief are left for me."
6. Power—Napoleon said at the end of his life, "Alexander, Caesar, Charlemaigne, and I founded empires. But on what did we found them? On force. Jesus Christ alone founded His on love, and today there are millions who would die for Him."

What is the "Fountain of Life"? Prayer for our brothers opens the door to the fountain of life. And it does not have to be prayer for a brother who is in sin. He may have other needs. Recently, a man in our church named Tom and I decided to take a couple of hours on a Saturday to ride our motorcycles up to Richards, Texas, have lunch and come back. Tom lives life to its fullest. He's a dedicated Christian, a dedicated engineer, a dedicated Aggie—but he also has a brain tumor and four lung tumors (though he has never smoked and played football for Texas A&M). He has been using some alternative medicine from Brazil to treat his cancer and has seen good success of far.

Now I need to explain that my motorcycle is an old 1987 Harley "Wannabe," which is what die-hard Harley fans call a Honda. Tom had a beautiful, in-perfect-shape Harley. So we headed out. At the mid-way point he stopped and asked me if I'd like to ride a real bike for awhile. I said, "Sure," so off I went on his Harley while he trailed behind. We drove through the national forest on some nice curves and came to a straight away. Tom was about a hundred yards behind me, but as I went around a corner, I looked back, and no Tom. I waited awhile, but when he didn't show, I went back to discover he had fallen. A dog had come out, Tom hit the breaks, but the front tire hit a break in the asphalt, and the bike went down.

Tom skidded along with the bike for about thirty yards. Without a helmet he would have left his brains all over the road, because there were chinks in several places in his helmet where his head bounced along the road. Except for a collapsed lung, several broken ribs, and a lot of "road rash" he was OK. The following Saturday we drove back to get my bike, which we had to leave because it was "totaled." Tom said he'd like to see where he fell. So we went over and looked at the beginning of the skid marks. Tom was an experienced rider and knew how to do high speed stops, so he was still amazed that he had fallen. But when he saw the break in the asphalt where his front tire twisted, he understood why he went down. It turns out another man went down in the same spot a year before and died.

Well, Tom went to the point where the bike hit the road and began pacing along the skid path until he came to the point where he stopped rolling. Then he said, "This is where I stopped, isn't it." I said, "Yep." "Well, I lost about $2.25 in change. Did you pick it up?" he asked. A little incredulous, I replied, "Not that I remember."

Well, you got to get the picture here. This is a guy with bandages wrapped all over his arms, legs, and chest. He could have starred in "Return of the Mummy." And he goes back to where the bike fell and starts pacing off from that point to where he stopped rolling. Then he bends down and actually starts picking up a few coins. I'm thinking, he could have lost his life and he's worried about his lost coins. He looks up and says, "Got most of it," but I could tell he still had a searching look in his eyes. So I bent over to try to help.

I looked down and saw something shiny, but it was too thick to be a quarter, nickel, or dime, but I picked it up. Turned out it was a silver coin with an angel on the front and "Strength" stamped on the back. I said, "Hey, look at this. It's a coin with an angel on it." He whirled around and grabbed that coin with a big smile on his face. "That's what I was looking for. Someone at work gave that to me when I announced I had been diagnosed with cancer. I've had it with me ever since. I always carry it. It reminds me that my hope is in Him. Wow! Jesus really does love me." You could see the joy he had in his face at finding this coin. I said, "You know, Tom, that's what a *personal* relationship with Jesus Christ is all about, isn't it?"

God's up there ... He knows all about us ... He knows our need ... He knows His promises ... and the joy that comes with answered prayer.

Obviously, this piece of silver was much more significant to Tom than its monetary value. To him it symbolized God's love and care for him as he battled this deadly disease. And as he has made his cancer public, it has been our privilege as his brothers and sisters in Christ to pray for him. Recently he sent me an email update:

> Howdy!
>
> I had my three months follow-up tests for my metastatic melanoma last week and my results continue to be good. My brain tumor is still 2mm overall, but there is now a visible "cavity" in the center, so the overall mass is less. This is an indicator that the brain tumor is continuing to die. I also continue to experience either minor reduction or a stable condition regarding four measurable tumors in my lungs.
>
> I want to thank everyone again for their continued prayers and support. Prayer works, and I ask that you continue to pray for my complete healing. God has been truly amazing in my life so far as I have dealt with this difficult disease. Although these have been difficult times, I have experienced so many blessings through this ordeal.
>
> One of my blessings is reinforcement of the many wonderful friends like you that I have. I recently received a note from one of these friends titled "Friends in my Life." The thoughts conveyed in these words were appropriate for how I feel about each of you in my life. I would like to share with you as an expression of my sincere appreciation for your love, support and earnest prayer for my renewed health ... from one friend to another:
>
> > *I have a list of folks I know ... all written in a book, And every now and then ... I go and take a look. That is when I realize these names ... they are a part, not of the book they're written in ... but taken from the heart. For each name stands for someone ... who has crossed my path sometime, And in that meeting they have become ... the reason and the rhyme. Although it sounds fantastic ... for me to make this claim, I really am composed ... of each remembered name. Although you're not aware ... of any special link, Just knowing you,*

has shaped my life … more than you could think. So please don't think my greeting … as just a mere routine, Your name was not … forgotten in between. For when I send a greeting … that is addressed to you, It is because you're on the list … of folks I'm indebted to. So whether I have known you … for many days or few, In some ways you have a part … in shaping things I do. I am but a total … of many folks I've met, You are a friend I would prefer … never to forget. Thank you for being my friend!! From Proverbs 17:17—"A friend loves at all times, and a brother is born for adversity." Each of you has become a "brother" during my adversity to which I am truly indebted.

– God bless, Tom

If Ponce de Leon had paused long enough to worship the risen Lord on that Easter Sunday when he discovered Florida, he might also have discovered that the "Fountain of Life" is in the heart of every person who believes that Jesus is the Christ, Son of the living God.

LESSON 21 "THE FOUNTAIN OF LIFE" I JOHN 5:14-17

1. Does the account of Ponce de Leon searching for the "Fountain of Youth" remind you of any values that seem to dominate our culture?

2. What is the connection between I John 5:4-5 and John 16:22-24? How do these scriptures relate to "Maximum Joy"?

3. What does it mean to pray "according to His will"?

    What does it mean to "pray in Jesus' name"?

4. Six reasons for negative answers to our prayers are listed on page 265. Can you think of an example of each of the six that would help you understand why some prayers are not answered?

    Domestic Strife (1 Peter 3:7) _____

    Committing Evil (1 Peter 3:12) _____

    Contemplating Evil (Psalm 66:17) _____

    Lustful Prayers (James 4:3) _____

    Lacking Faith (James 1:57) _____

    Contrary to His will (1 John 5:14) _____

5. On page 253, three "biggest problems" are identified. List them.

    "Our biggest problem in right loving is _____ "

    "Our biggest problem in right learning is _____ "

    "Our biggest problem in right living is _____ "

    Select one of the areas that you will focus on in the weeks ahead.

6. What is your understanding of John's directions regarding prayer in verses 16 and 17? What is "sin leading to death" and "sin not leading to death"?

7. Why do you think this lesson is titled "The Fountain of Life"?

22

PRAYER FOR A PRODIGAL

1 John 5:18-21

Recently I ran across some verse written by Ruth Bell Graham in her book *Prodigals and Those Who Love Them* entitled "Had I Been Joseph's Mother." It goes like this:

> Had I been Joseph's mother
> I'd have prayed
> protection from his brothers
> "God, keep him safe.
> He is so young,
> so different from the others."
> Mercifully,
> she never knew
> there would be slavery
> and prison, too.
> Had I been Moses' mother
> I'd have wept to keep my little son
> praying she might forget
> the babe drawn from the water
> of the Nile.
> Had I not kept
> him for her
> nursing him the while,
> was he not mine?
> —and she but Pharaoh's daughter?
> Had I been Daniel's mother
> I should have pled
> "Give victory!
> —this Babylonian horde
> godless and cruel—
> Don't let him be a captive
> —better dead,
> Almighty Lord!"
> Had I been Mary,

Oh, had I been she,
I would have cried
as never mother cried,
"Anything, O God,
Anything …
—but
crucified."
With such prayers importunate
my finite wisdom would assail
Infinite Wisdom.
God, how fortunate
Infinite Wisdom
should prevail.[1]

As I read that, I thought to myself, I must not understand the word "prodigal." I never thought Jesus was a prodigal son; nor Daniel. We don't even have a record of any sin on the part of Jesus or Daniel. So I looked up prodigal in Webster's Dictionary. It said "prodigal" meant "wasted." A prodigal child is one who wastes his or her life. Well, Joseph wasn't a prodigal. Nor was Moses or any of those mentioned in the poem.

There are very few experiences in life more heart-wrenching for a parent than having a prodigal child. To have a mentally or physically challenged child would test the patience and love of any parent. But to see a child waste his life . . . One woman wrote James Dobson about her feelings:[2]

> Dear Dr. Dobson:
>
> Your radio interview with Dr. John White was so helpful. I had already read his book, *Parents in Pain*, but it ministered to me again.
>
> We have three daughters, ages 20, 23, and 24, raised as well as we could do it. I read Kesler and I read Trobisch. I did the best I could to be a good example and to follow Christian standards. I spent hours trying to show them that each one was valued and loved immensely. I tried to give them room to be individuals and we both enjoyed watching them develop into adults. In our zeal we never even bought a TV set!!!
>
> Results: we have two daughters who couldn't have turned out better and one who couldn't have turned out worse. Our oldest daughter is a college graduate, has a productive job, is loving her Christian walk and is a joy to have around.

Daughter #3 caused us untold grief and worry and finally at age 18 ran off with a 29-year-old thrice-married ex-convict (who was still married to wife #3). For 3 weeks I sat at the kitchen table all day in shock.

I didn't know that anyone could endure that much pain and still live. At first I thought I would commit suicide. Then I thought I would go around forever with FAILURE branded on my forehead. My husband and I had long discussions about whether we should drop out of the church and not attempt to minister to others because of our failure. It shook our marriage to the roots. We felt like 26 years went down the drain. It was so embarrassing to see people who knew what had happened. It was worse to run into people who didn't know, because they might ask how our girls were. I would cut people absolutely dead so they wouldn't have a chance to ask …

I tell you, Dr. Dobson, that it would be easier to bury children than it would be to see them using their bodies for such shameful purposes—those bodies that we've lovingly washed, bandaged, dressed, stuffed good food and vitamins into, kept out of the lake and off of the roads—using their lives to advance the cause of Satan. I sincerely hope that you never hear your kid say, "I hate you. You've ruined my life and I never want to see you again," and walk out coolly.

I want to tell you something else about the effect this has had on our family that we didn't expect. Our oldest daughter says: "I will never have any children. Parents spend years doing their best for the children, and suddenly at age 14 the parents become despised enemies. I refuse to put up with that for myself."

I could go on for several more paragraphs, but I think you get the idea, as much as you could, not having gone through it yourself.

God bless you. Keep up the good work,

Sincerely,

Mary Alice

Truly, Mary Alice is a parent in pain. But she is not alone. In our present culture, if a child makes it through the teenage years and is still walking with Jesus, I'd say it's the grace of God. Oh, you may beg to differ. But as a pastor, I have seen families just like that of Mary Alice, where in the same environment with the same parents with the same Christian values, three kids go this way and one just the opposite. Truly, if a child grows up in a home where the parents love the Lord and live their lives for Him, the chances are far greater that the child will also become a believer and live for Christ than if he grew up in the home of unbelievers who live for this world, but there are no guarantees.

As John finishes up his book on the "Fruit of Fellowship," his mind was on praying for Christian brothers or sisters who may have wandered a great distance down the path of sin. Some may even be close to falling off a cliff into premature physical death. He encouraged us, as an act of love, to pray for them. But is there any hope that these prodigals might come home?

Yes, there is. As John finishes out his book, he may have had these prodigals in mind. In our outline I have labeled this conclusion to the letter "Encouragement for Little Children" because that's how verse twenty-one begins. But as I have studied these verses, all I could think about was how they could apply to the parents of the prodigal children John may have in mind who have wandered far into darkness, far from fellowship road. I might as well have called this conclusion "Encouragement for Parents in Pain."

But I want to extend this encouragement to more than just parents in pain. I also want to extend it to prospective parents who may be afraid to bring children into a culture so rampant with drugs, pornography, gangs, and oppressive pressure from their peers to compromise their Christian values. What encouragement can we give to parents who have already brought children into this world and have dedicated them to the Lord—what encouragement is there for them that their children won't be torn apart by the meat-grinder of our worldly society? And what encouragement can we give to parents who have children on the thresh hold of the teenage years, children about to experience the mad rush of hormones and the oppressive pressure of their peers? I think we can find this encouragement at the end of 1 John, this little letter about the "Fruit of Fellowship," about the joy we can find in this life when we are walking closely with God.

It shouldn't surprise us to discover that John continues his fondness for threes (triads) as he closes out his letter. We remember not only the three waves and the three "porpoises" in the overall organization of the letter, but the three "If we say that we ..." statements in chapter one and the three "He who says ..." statements in chapter two. Here in his conclusion John plays three notes in staccato fashion to alert us to his final points: "We know that ..." (v. 18); "We know that ..." (v. 19); and "we know that ..." (v. 20). The encouragement he gives to parents and all believers, for that matter, concerns something about *knowing that* every believer, including a prodigal, has "God's Seed" within him (v. 18), and *knowing that* every believer, including a prodigal, is really on "God's Side" whether he knows it or not (v. 19), and *knowing that* every believer, including a prodigal, has "God's Searchlight" in his possession in case he ever gets lost and wants to find the way home (v. 20). Let's look at these points of encouragement one at a time.

GOD'S SEED

> We know that whoever is born of God does not sin; but he who has been born of God keeps himself, and the wicked one does not touch him (5:18).

We saw the expression *whoever is born of God* in 3:9; it is a reference to the divine nature birthed within us by God's seed. Whatever comes directly from God cannot sin because there is no sin in His seed. Sin is against God's nature. This divine nature is portrayed as a person (a figure of speech known as personification, that is, to treat something which is not a person as though it were, like calling a ship "she"). That's why this nature is called "whoever," "he," "himself," and "him."

There is precedent for doing this in Pauline literature. For example, Paul refers to the new nature in the born again person as the "inner man" (Eph 3:16) who is strengthened by the Spirit of God and is capable of resisting the pollution of this world. Here John says the wicked one (Satan) does not *touch* this inner man, or that which is born of God. Though the devil may work through the lust of the flesh, the lust of the eyes, and the pride of life, he cannot touch our inner man, which is born of God.

Our core self is sinless and cannot be touched by Satan. So, parents, if your child is a believer, he/she cannot be touched in his/her inner self, which houses the divine seed of God and is completely sinless. This is his/her true nature. Whatever your child has gotten into, it does not affect who he/she is at the core. Zane Hodges has expressed it well:

> At the very moment we are most humbled by our sinful failures, and when we confess them, it is helpful to be confident that those failures have not really changed what we are as children of God. The enemy, try as he might, cannot really touch us. He can only attempt to persuade us that he can, or has. But if we know the truth stated in this verse, he will not be able to deceive us. For if we let him, Satan will use our failures to lead us to further failure. So, after every sin, deeply though we may and should regret it, we

ought to rise from our confession to God *knowing* that we are the same inwardly holy persons we were before we failed![3]

Parents, some of you have children who have gone after this world. Some of these prodigals have been damaged by drugs. Others have been twisted by the perverted values of this world system. Do not give up. Do not lose hope. For if your child is a believer, at the core of his being he can neither be tempted nor touched. The seed of God within him remains inviolate. As long as that seed remains, it can be watered by your prayers. As long as that seed remains, it can still grow. As long as that seed remains, it can blossom and eternal fruit can be born. Do not give up.

One minister friend of mine used to say his greatest fear in life was that his four children would not grow up to glorify Christ. All went well with children one, two, and three. But in the first year of college, his fourth child had to be brought home from out of state. The problem? Kleptomania. They had to put their precious youngest daughter, their baby, into a psychiatric ward for observation in order to find out what would cause a child from a home like hers to become an incurable thief. As the months wore on with their child still in a hospital, promises like the one we are reading about right now became a primary hope. There was no question that this child had trusted Christ while still living at home. Therefore, God's seed was in her. A fundamental change had taken place in her make-up. A new nature was born within that could not sin, could not be touched by evil or the evil one, could not even be tempted. That new nature born of God is a beach head, a base from which the Holy Spirit can work within that child to bring healing to her soul, and to bring her home.

So God's seed resides in every child of God, even a prodigal. It is important to know that. But there is more encouragement here. Not only does the believer have God's seed within, he is also on God's side.

GOD'S SIDE

We know that we are of God, and the whole world lies *under the sway of* the wicked one (5:19).

The second fact from which we can draw encouragement is to know who is on God's side. John says we know that we are *of God.* To be "of" something in 1 John is to be on the side of the something. We saw this in 1 John 3:10b, 19 and 4:4. In reference to believers it means to have a dynamic, spiritual link to God, who is obviously capable of giving us victory over the world. To be "of God" means we are on His side, and He is on our side. The world lies like a limp puppet in the lap of the evil one, ready to be filled with his power. On the other side, we lie in the lap of the Lord, ready to be filled with His power.

Parents, if your child is a believer, he/she does not belong to Satan's world, and he/she will always feel like a foreigner in this world system. Your child will never feel completely comfortable in this sin-sick world. This world is not our home, we're just passing through; our home is way out there, somewhere beyond the blue. The child of God who wanders about aimlessly in darkness will always have a basic discomfort. They will always know something is wrong, something just isn't right. This is not the real me.

Parents, God can turn discomfort into disgust. When your child's discomfort turns to disgust, he will turn towards home. Regardless of what this child tells you, if he gets sucked into the cesspool of this world, he is acting out of character, and he will never be completely comfortable. Don't listen to his lies. Keep praying that his discomfort will turn to disgust, and God will bring him home. When he finally realizes that he is wasting his life eating slop with the pigs in the pig sty, he will turn his eyes toward home.

Because of God's seed within your believing child, he is on God's side whether he consciously senses that or not, and he will feel like a foreigner in this world. God can turn this discomfort into disgust so that he will want to come home. But how will he get there?

GOD'S SEARCH LIGHT

> And we know that the Son of God has come and has given us an understanding, that we may know Him who is true; and we are in Him who is true, in His Son Jesus Christ. This is the true God and eternal life. Little children, keep yourselves from idols. Amen (5:20-21).

This is the only time John uses the word *understanding* (*dianoian*) in this letter. It speaks of a spiritual radar system or search light the Holy Spirit uses to direct us to the true God. There are many false gods in the world (as the next verse warns), which can lead us far from the path of God. This internal guidance system can help bring us home. It's what Paul would call the "mind of Christ" (1 Cor 2:15-16).

When John says we are *in Him* or *in His Son Jesus Christ*, it refers to our condition instead of our position, as it usually does in Paul. In 1 John 2:5-6 John equates being "in Him" with abiding in Him, just as the branch is to abide in the vine in John 15. Although to abide in the vine is taken by some to be a statement of our position in John 15, we have already seen how "abiding" in John 15 is connected with fruit bearing, joy, and answered prayer—our condition, not our position. In other words, these are statements about our fellowship with God, the thematic subject of this letter. And this fellowship is eternal life, where the emphasis is on the quality of our life, not the quantity. These are the very thoughts with which John began his letter (1 John 1:1-4)—"eternal life" (1:2) ... "fellowship" (1:3) ... and "joy" (1:4). Thus John has come full circle.

Parents, the mind of Christ will always be there as a base for the Holy Spirit to whisper what is right in the ear of your child. And this inner, spiritual intelligence or search light can be used by the Holy Spirit to guide your child back home.

John concludes with a strange finish to a letter. In some ways verse twenty-one seems disconnected from everything he has been talking about. But John has used the word *true* three times to describe our God. Our God is the one who is true. Our spiritual radar system helps us recognize the true God in contrast to the false gods in the world. And what is a false god, other than an idol? And idols can destroy our fellowship with God.

We don't have to study the OT long to see that while kings ruled in Israel, idolatry reigned in the temple more years than Yahweh. God used the Assyrians and the Babylonians to purify His people from their idols. And since it was King Solomon who introduced idolatry into Israel through his intermarriage with foreign wives, we see how easily idolatry can creep into the life of a wise man who was even used by God to write inspired revelation.

Idols are usually good things. The bronze serpent (Num 21:4-9) was initially used by God to heal the Israelites from snake bites. But eight centuries later (2 Kgs 18:4) Hezekiah had to destroy the bronze serpent, for it had become an idol called Nehushtan (piece of bronze) to which they burned incense. Our idols are usually not evil things, but rather good things: our possessions (cars, houses, even yards), our retirement accounts, our bodies, our success—you name it.

Here's a couple of hints on how to spot an idol. Is it becoming more important to me than people (my family, my friends, my ministry)? Is it blocking my view of the Lord? They say an idol is like an eclipse of the sun—the moon gets in the way. When something gets between us and God's light, then darkness creeps in and whatever is blocking that light is an idol.

Beware! Solomon was no dummy. He thought he was doing something good by expanding the land of Israel out to the borders promised by God to Abraham. But he had to compromise the guidelines laid down by God for a king (Deut 17:17) in order to do it.

CONCLUSION

Hopefully, these closing verses have brought some encouragement to parents. If your child has chased after the idols of this world, John assures our hearts with three promises from God: 1) God's seed is in that child if he/she has trusted Christ somewhere along the way; 2) If he/she is born again, then he/she is on God's side and will never be completely comfortable living for this world; and 3) God's search light within that child can guide him/her back home to his/her Christian roots.

Here's a prayer (taken from a secular play) of a father for the physical return of a boy from war whom his daughter hoped to marry. Maybe it could be applied spiritually to one of your children, or the child of a friend of yours. Perhaps we can use it as a "Prayer for a Prodigal."

God on high, hear my prayer
In my need you have always been there.
He is young, he's afraid
Let him rest, heaven blessed.
Bring him home, bring him home, bring him home.
He's like a son I might have known,
If God had granted me a son.
The summers die, one by one,
How soon they fly, on and on,
And I am old, and will be gone.
Bring him peace, bring him joy
He is young, he is only a boy.
You can take, you can give.
Let him be, let him live.
If I die, let me die;
Let him live, bring him home, bring him home, bring him home.

And here are three specific prayers from parents in pain whom I know. In each case one of their children chased after an idol which has sent their ship of faith to the bottom of the sea. Maybe one of them fits the need of one of your children or the need of a child you know:

> I pray, dear Lord, that, as you turn the hearts of kings, you would turn my son's heart from the idol of intellectualism, which has made shipwreck of his faith.

> I pray, dear Lord, that you would turn the sweet smell of success into an odor more repulsive than a clogged sewer. Bring my boy back to his roots. Bring him back to the faith of his fathers.

> I pray, dear Lord, that you would smash the idol of sexual freedom and the pursuit of pleasure that has turned my precious daughter down a path of family turmoil and dysfunction. May she discover her true identity in you, my Sovereign Lord.

> AMEN

---

[1] Ruth Bell Graham, *Prodigals and those Who Love them* (Colorado Springs: Focus on the Family Publishing, 1991), 69.

[2] James C. Dobson, *Parenting Isn't for Cowards* (Waco, TX: Word Books, 1987), 71-73.

[3] Zane C. Hodges, *The Epistles of John: Walking in the Light of God's Love* (Irving, TX: Grace Evangelical Society, 1999), 242-43.

LESSON 22 "PRAYER FOR A PRODIGAL" I JOHN 5:18-21

1. How does the poem by Ruth Bell Graham speak to you?

2. How does the definition of "prodigal" alter your understanding of that word?

3. What examples of "prodigal" can you draw from your own life experiences?

4. How would you explain 5:18? How is it that "whoever is born of God does not sin"?

5. What does it mean to be "of God" (v. 19)?

6. How are we encouraged to pray for a prodigal (page 281)?

7. John's conclusion to this letter may seem somewhat strange. Why would he make reference to "idols"?

8. Discuss "Idols are usually good things."

9. How can you spot an idol?

10. What "idols" are referenced in the three prayers on page 284?

11. Review the Conclusion on page 285-86. What are the three principles of fellowship? Why does JOY increase as nonconformity between a believer's condition and position decreases? So, how may I experience MAXIMUM JOY?

CONCLUSION

John wrote this short epistle about *maximum joy*. He says as much in 1 John 1:3-4. And John knows the source of maximum joy. It comes from *fellowship* with the Father and His Son Jesus Christ. And this *fellowship* can vary in its quality and depth. The deeper the *fellowship*, the greater the joy. In order to have *maximum joy* there must be intimate fellowship. So John writes about the principles of *fellowship* in the body of this letter in order that his readers might grow in their intimacy with the Father and His Son. The greater the intimacy, the greater the *fellowship*; the greater the *fellowship*, the greater the joy.

The principles of *fellowship* surface in the body of this letter like porpoises in the sea: three principles arising successively and repeatedly—right living, right loving, and right learning. These principles are not requirements for an eternal *relationship* with the Father and His Son Jesus Christ. No NT writer has made that more clear than John, who repeatedly claims that the requirement for eternal life is to believe in Jesus, the very source of eternal life. Faith alone—the cry of the Reformers. No, these principles (right living, right loving, and right learning) are not requirements for an enduring *relationship* with God, but they are requirements for joyous *fellowship* with Him.

This brings us back to the apparent contradiction experienced by Martin Luther—*simul iustus et peccator* (simultaneously justified and a sinner). This expression defined Luther's experience after he had been justified but still found himself dealing with daily sin in his life. Yes, this is the normal Christian plight—*declared righteous* (justified), but still wrestling with *sin* as he travels this sod. Righteous in his *position* (his standing before God in Christ), but sinful in his *condition* (his walk with God on planet earth).

This sinful *condition* does not mean the person was never justified in his *position* before God. It merely means that his *condition* on earth is in need of progressive purification (sanctification) to conform it to his *position* in heaven. One day (1 John 3:1-3) his *condition* will be completely conformed to his *position*. Until then there are varying degrees of nonconformity of his *condition* to his *position*. The greater the conformity, the greater the joy.

In order for the believer to experience *maximum joy*, he must understand that failure to understand and practice the *principles of fellowship* set forth in 1 John do not indicate that he never had a *relationship* with God. If these principles set forth in 1 John are tests of whether we have a *relationship* with

God or not, our joy will be minimal at best. There will always be lingering doubts about whether our faith in Christ was "saving faith" or sufficient faith. Doubt does not produce joy.

John understood that it is *fellowship* with God that produces joy. So he wrote one book (the Gospel of John) with a primary theme of *relationship* and a sub theme of *fellowship*. Then as a follow-up to his Gospel, John wrote a letter (1 John) with a primary theme of *fellowship* and a sub theme of *relationship*.

Understanding the difference between *position* and *condition*, or *relationship* and *fellowship* is fundamental to a Christian life of joy. And understanding the primary principles of *fellowship* (right living, right loving, and right learning) is imperative in order to experience *maximum joy*.

GRACE THEOLOGY PRESS

Timely **Resources**.
Timeless **Grace**.

Birthed from a desire to provide engaging and relevant theological resources,
Grace Theology Press is the academic imprint of Grace School of Theology.
In a world where many say "truth is relative," Grace Theology Press holds fast to the
absolute truth of God's Word. We are passionate about engaging the next generation of
ministry leaders with books and resources that are grounded in the principles of free grace,
which offers a gift you cannot earn and a gift you can never lose.

gracetheology.org